COMING OF AGE

COMING

OF AGE

by ESTHER LLOYD-JONES, Ph.D.
Professor of Education
Teachers College, Columbia University

and RUTH FEDDER, Ed.D.
Assistant Superintendent and Supervisor of Special Education
Lehigh and Bucks Counties, Pa.

WILDSIDE PRESS

COMING OF AGE

PREFACE

Every period of life has its special assets, its immunities, and its problems. The period from sixteen to twenty-five is no exception. While one is in this period of his life he has special advantages. He usually possesses, for instance, a great deal of physical vitality. He thinks very little about how he feels because he almost always feels "tops." Among the immunities that he usually enjoys is the immunity from heavy financial responsibility for others than himself. When he lies awake at night listening to the well-known wolf howling at his door, he is usually primarily concerned about one victim—himself—and not about a wife or a child besides.

To the older person, weighed down by family responsibilities, perhaps, and harassed by the idea that he must find a better job if he is ever to be able to save anything for his old age, the late teens and early twenties appear in retrospect surrounded by a rosy glow. To him, those years seem synonymous with superb health, personal freedom, and exquisite romance. The advantages and immunities of his own maturity, on the other hand, are often too vaguely appreciated.

On the whole the rosy features of adolescence and young adulthood have been somewhat overdone. To the young man or woman, life currently presents many problems that are to the one who must solve them very real indeed. Some of these problems are related to economic cycles and national crises. These, of course, operate differently on different age groups. Other problems are more permanent features of adolescence and young adulthood itself, with less relation to the state of world affairs that may prevail at the time. It is necessary for young people to solve courageously and

v

with some success all the various problems that confront them if they are to move on into their late twenties and thirties with fair assurance of being able to meet successfully the problems typical of those later years.

During the past ten years young people have had to face such serious problems arising out of economic recession and unemployment that various national agencies have turned a good deal of attention to this age group. Among the most valuable of the studies of youth made during the past few years are those of the American Youth Commission under the sponsorship of the American Council on Education. These studies have served admirably to reveal and call the attention of the general public to the special problems confronting youth because of weaknesses in our economic and social structure. These studies have also intelligently analyzed and made clear to the young people themselves the vague but vast social and economic problems with which they have had to struggle. The authors, with the generous permission of the American Council on Education, have drawn heavily on the results of these American Youth Commission Studies.

In their personal and professional associations with young people, the authors have also been impressed with other problems of young people which are even more fundamental and persistent than the problems arising from faulty economic and social organization. The very process of growing up, of gaining independence from one's primary family group, of establishing a successful home of one's own, of turning from self-concern to concern for others, of discovering a set of values by which one can live—all this at times thrills and at other times completely discourages a young person as he is swept chronologically on through his late teens into early adulthood.

Because the authors have been close to the whole complex situation within which young people today must try to create successful and satisfying lives, they have been stimulated to write this book. It is addressed primarily to young people themselves. It is written in a spirit of considerable humility. It by no means provides easy formulas for success or even for easy evasion of difficulties.

We have tried to keep the discussions "down to earth," so that a person reading it by himself would not lose his way in a theoretical consideration of the problems. We hope, also, that it may be useful for discussion groups and as a text for college classes. The authors have experimented with the book, with some success, as a basis for a more fundamental kind of counseling than could otherwise be offered an individual within an allotted period of time.

Throughout the book there are many direct quotations from young people themselves. A large number of these are taken directly from a study that one of the authors made under the auspices of the American Council on Education. The study occupied a year's time and included personal interviews with several hundred men and women students in a number of colleges. This material is used here with the kind permission of the American Council on Education.

In addition to quotations from the experience of college students, material has been drawn from the files of the Guidance Laboratory of Teachers College, Columbia University, and from contacts that the authors have had through various community agencies with young men and young women who have not gone to college.

We are grateful to the many young people and to the several adults who have read the book and given most helpful criticism at every stage of its development.

To the publishers who have given us permission to quote copyrighted material we wish to express our appreciation.

ESTHER LLOYD-JONES,
RUTH FEDDER.

CONTENTS

CHAPTER I

PERSONALITY IN THE MAKING

Most of us entered this world as some seven pounds of possibilities, loudly protesting. As the first cry was uttered, the doctor probably sighed, "Thank God, he's normal."

Fortunately, most of us have learned since our youngest days that protests and rebellion alone cannot get us very far; that, if we would develop reasonably well-adjusted, mature personalities, we must learn to behave more constructively, to meet positively—even to shape—the circumstances of life. And, fortunately, we all gradually discover that we have inherited an infinite capacity to react to various stimuli.

FORCES THAT DIRECT OUR BEHAVIOR

Behind this complex resourcefulness which makes individuals of all of us when we are still very young, there are some basic ways of behaving. Adler, a well-known pyschologist, suggests that people can be divided into two main groups. The extroverts say "yes" first and then try to get out of it. The introverts say "no" and then try to get in. In other words, Adler believes that, in general, some people face life eagerly and take their problems in their stride, whereas others shrink from life and from other people, becoming solitary souls to whom life is rather complicated.

Within these basic behavior patterns, there are, of course, many variations. Each of us at any given moment is striving in his own way to get out of life what he wants most. Pragmatism (does it work?) and practicality (will it get me what I want?) are usually the factors that determine in each case what we will do. A certain way of behaving has value for an individual because it either gets him what

1

he wants or helps him to escape what he wishes to avoid. This behavior pattern has usually evolved over a long period of years. It may have had its origins in childhood or as early in life as the individual could size up a situation, decide what he wanted from it, plan out ways of getting what he wanted, then try out the methods that he had evolved. The methods that worked he repeated. Gradually his attitude toward himself, toward other people, and toward life became interwoven with his way of behaving. Thus what Adler calls "a style of life" evolves.

Most of the circumstances to which we must react involve contacts with other human beings. We respond in one way or another to these contacts. We may, for example, react by remaining primarily interested in ourselves, possibly scornful of others, possibly resentful of the claims of others upon us, adopting the idea that "everyone is queer but thee and me, and thee is a little queer." Or we may gradually become concerned more about others than about ourselves; we may grow eager to find a place among other people and to make a contribution to the world. We all need to learn how to work and live together more harmoniously. Today's problems call for socially sensitive and mature, honest, yet sincere and critically minded individuals who use their influence toward smooth and effective cooperation in work that must be done wherever they find it to do.

How can we bring ourselves to become that kind of person? That is the challenging and persistent problem which each of us faces. All that some of us see of ourselves and of the personalities of people whom we feel that we know is a kind of personality silhouette, namely, this habitual style of behaving. We have no difficulty in recognizing people by these silhouettes because no two people are alike. No two, furthermore, deal in exactly the same way with what looks on the surface like the same experience. Some people shun new experiences; others fairly jump out to meet them. Some individuals take all experiences so casually that they seem not to profit by them in the sense of learning from them, still others take each experience so seriously that life seems overcomplicated to them.

It would be fascinating to try to fill in details, to give color or life to a black-and-white silhouette in a picture frame. It is equally fascinating, although much more difficult, to attempt to interpret personality silhouettes, to see why an individual has adopted a certain pattern of behaving, to understand why he thinks, feels, and acts as he does. Fully as important as analyzing others is the necessity of examining our own behavior honestly while we are attempting to develop a keener understanding of others. Understanding others helps us to gain insight into ourselves; understanding ourselves helps us to an appreciation of the directing forces behind the behavior of others. We may, in fact, become more generous in our estimate of others as we realize that we can often see our own struggles reflected in their experiences.

However, if behavior is to be understood, it must be interpreted as well as described. Should we desire to know why an individual behaves as he does, we must understand what he wants most out of life. To gain insight into mechanisms of behavior, we must continually ask ourselves, "What am I or what is this other person really seeking to accomplish by this behavior?" Experts on behavior problems have proved that every individual's behavior in any situation is rooted in and caused by factors far deeper and more vital to him than the immediate situation would imply. Therefore, if we would explain why a person has evolved a given style of behavior, we must know what experiences he has had and what interpretations he has given to those experiences.

STYLES IN BEHAVIOR

Examples of the far-reaching effects that experiences have on individuals are not hard to find. As we meet one person after another, we realize that in each one the mainspring of

his behavior is the accumulation of influences that have
profoundly affected the course of his life.   These influences
an observer can clearly understand because an individual
consistently acts in accordance with them.   Psychologists
have even given labels to some of these influences.   If a
person seems to be so completely under the influence of one
of his parents that he has lost his ability to think for himself,
he is said to have a mother or a father fixation.   If he seems
to be striving constantly for excellence, he is said to be a
perfectionist, to have a drive for power, or to be overcom-
pensating for a hidden sense of inferiority.

Let us examine some specific cases.

A young woman reported that throughout her college
experience her mother had been the controlling influence in
her life.   She had lived at home during all four years of her
college life.   Every night she told her mother the details of
the day.   The mother then evaluated the daughter's reactions and advised her about what she should do the following
day.   To some extent, this young woman thought her
sorority had been taking her mother's place, because her
sorority sisters had helped her to make decisions and to live
up to her ideals.

This sort of external influence is probably the simplest
kind of guide to action that any of us ever has.   This young
woman was largely the product of habits established in the
process of acting unquestioningly in accordance with her
mother's advice.

Rather similar to the case of the young woman is that of
the young man who described his relation to his father thus:

My father is the biggest thing I have gotten out of college.   I
went to his prep school; I joined his fraternity here at college; I've
come to know him better and better since I entered college.   We
are very close to each other.   He takes the place of all the friends
of my own age.   I always spend Saturday night at home with my
father.   He takes me to his club and I know most of his associates
well.   I don't know what I would have done without my dad to
talk things over with during college years.

An individual's response to this kind of direct powerful influence may be as simple and as easily observable as the foregoing examples illustrate. Some people seem to act rather consistently with a good deal of docility in direct accordance with the wishes of people whom they respect a great deal. They seem to reserve to themselves little right to modify in terms of their own thinking the wishes of these people. They become, in the simplest sense, direct products of their environment.

On the other hand, an individual may be only outwardly docile. His genuine response to a situation may eventually manifest itself in a way very surprising to the person who thought that the other individual was docilely accepting control over his life. An example of a type of influence seeming to retard development is a young man who said his home life had certainly influenced him.

He had been brought up by his father's sister since his fifth year, when his mother died. He lived with his aunt, his father, and his brother. His aunt had had to contribute some financial support for the boys and had "run them to a fare-thee-well." The boy had lived at home during four years of college, never having been allowed by his aunt to live in a dormitory, although he had to commute long distances every day. His aunt never allowed him to participate in parties or extracurricular activities. He guessed she "just wanted him at home nights." He had never been allowed to have any dates. His aunt wanted him to go through medical school, and he planned to go. If he lives "through four more years without blowing up entirely and doing something very ungrateful," he said he expected to be ready for sainthood.

Another type of person can be understood best when one realizes that everything he does and thinks and feels has some relation to a general feeling of superiority or inferiority which colors all his life. Although this feeling may originally have had an external source, by the time an individual has reached the age of eighteen the feeling usually seems to emanate from the depths of the person himself. Such a feeling can and does act as a powerful force in shaping the behavior of some individuals.

Young people who have always felt inferior with regard to physical appearance, for example, may be controlled more powerfully by this feeling than by any other influence. Take the case of Molly, who represents many girls of eighteen. She became very red of face as she gave the following explanation.

Well, probably the thing that has made more difference to me than anything else in college is the fact that I've been called "Tubby." In high school it didn't matter because there was only a small group of girls, and they didn't, somehow, make me very conscious of myself. But when I came to college and there were a lot of boys as well as a lot of strange girls, it just killed me to have them call me "Tubby." I've been elected president of my sorority, but I don't much care about it. I've dieted and dieted, but dieting doesn't seem to make me look any different. I'm kind of disgusted with college and everybody in it and I don't find much right now that is worth bothering about. I've started a few times to tell friends about the way I feel and I always get laughed at. Everybody thinks I'm kind of amusing.

In trying to understand people, we cannot count on an individual's acting in a way that can be explained simply. Some people, *because* they have an underlying sense of inferiority, actually strive all the harder to give an external impression of feeling very sure of themselves. Underneath, however, their lack of assurance about themselves persists steadily and powerfully, even though it is often as difficult for such persons to admit this even to themselves as it is for us to discover it, since they act in just the opposite way. They give the impression of feeling superior. The following examples show how such feelings work.

A pretended feeling of superiority with regard to mental ability has had its influence on my development. Someone told me in my freshman year that my intelligence test score had been exceptionally good, but I soon discovered that the test score didn't do me any practical good unless I worked hard too. I've had to get over my feeling of pride at having made such a good score. Really I had a feeling of inferiority with regard to my previous deficient scholastic training, but I've just about gotten over that, too, because I found out that if I worked I didn't need to worry much about previous deficient training.

Feelings of inferiority have almost gotten me down, I'd say. With regard to sophistication, I feel inferior. So I try to appear more assured than most of the fellows I go with. I had to, because I've always been a sleepy-looking kind of kid and every once in a while someone tells me about it. I'm younger than most of my friends; I think I've felt that, too. All of these things have made me drive myself to try to make up for them. I know that I've done big things in activities largely because I felt these inferiorities so keenly.

Adler, White, and other psychologists have pointed out that a sense of inferiority may ultimately be a powerful source of strength to an individual. Of course, a sense of inferiority sometimes encourages an individual to conform to an undesirable type of group conduct because he does not feel capable of standing out against the group. On the other hand, an inferiority feeling may simply serve to provide him with a goal of superiority. It may make him feel so uncomfortable that he strives mightily to overcome the reason for his discomfort. This kind of reaction is illustrated by a boy who was terribly ashamed of his family —their physical appearance, "the way they yell at each other," the way their house looked, the neighborhood they lived in. He said that he thought probably he had gone to school and worked as hard as he had in chemistry, and won the honors he had, partly in order to compensate for the way he felt about his parents.

Reactions of the same general type were described by other young people.

I came to the city rather unsophisticated, I suppose, but with pretty definite ideas of right and wrong. I've spent most of the

last few years on the defensive trying to justify my own moral
character to the friends I've made. I feel decidedly on the defensive about it, and I don't quite understand why I should, because
I honestly think my own moral character is higher than the
standards of the group. So many of the fellows are awfully self-
indulgent. The conflict I've felt at this point has made me be
constantly self-critical and self-evaluating.

I've felt a definite sense of superiority because of pride in my
racial tradition. I know I have a good mind and I know that no
one here has a better family background than I have. This has
served as a much-needed protection when I might have felt that
I was being looked down on as a foreigner. I am able to use my
pride to steady myself when I might otherwise get thrown off
my course.

Once when my face was all broken out, I became very bitter,
suspicious, and morbid. This really constituted for me a period
of almost enforced reflection because I shut myself off more or less
from the world on account of it. Then I had an appendix operation. After that my face cleared up. Queer as it may seem, this
experience strengthened me greatly. I have come, as a result, to
have lots more self-understanding and lots more wisdom about the
world in general and the way things work. I've always been kind
of shy. I've had a general sort of inferiority. I thought that
forcing myself to leave home to work would cure me. But I found
that just having a job didn't completely solve the matter. I've
had to keep at it constantly to prove myself to myself.

Still other individuals can be understood only if we
believe that there is a strength that comes from attempting
to cope with whatever is difficult in our experiences. We
know, for example, that many fine men and women are
products of good homes. Yet we have all known unusually
fine men and women who have risen out of the most
unfortunate environments. To some degree, life sets up
hurdles for all of us—they may be uncongenial home conditions, health handicaps, poverty, or some kind of persistent temptation or destructive influence. Some of the
strongest, most dependable, and personally secure indi-

viduals are those whose lives would seem to others to be very hard.

People can learn how to meet misfortune successfully by meeting misfortune successfully. Sometimes they can even convert it into good fortune. They can learn how to resist unfortunate influences by refusing to be influenced by them. People develop strength of personality by dealing as successfully as possible with all the situations with which they are confronted, but especially with those that are essentially difficult. Only as we see the significance of difficult experiences can we understand how certain people were able to build up the strength of personality which they possess. The two young men whose lives are sketched here are good examples of making the best of unfavorable situations.

Because of a very unhappy home situation in which the parents despised each other, in which one brother was serving a sentence in a Federal prison and another brother was an advanced homosexual, one young man has been motivated to do much reading and studying. He has—in an indirect way because of all these unfortunate conditions—achieved understanding and freedom and maturity far beyond that possessed by most of his contemporaries.

Another young man, the son of a coal miner, said he had been an enthusiastic participant in the wild life of the young people of the community as well as a passive participant in the slovenly laxness of his own home. Then somehow—through some books a librarian gave him to read, he thought—he became disgusted with it all. At the age of twenty-six, he decided that he wanted an education, that he could work and put himself through college. He was certain that if he had not felt such a thorough revulsion of feeling for his home and his family, for their ways of thinking and acting, that he never could have stood what he had to put up with to get through college creditably while earning every penny of his way.

It cannot be denied that a great many individuals are influenced in their development by the example of leaders in a group as well as by their own active participation in that group. Even nonparticipants are frequently deeply influenced by suggestions made by leaders who are admired and trusted, although those leaders may have no intention of affecting a given individual's behavior. Young people repeatedly testify that they have been greatly stimulated by an individual whose opinion they valued—he may have been a superior on a job, or a respected class leader in a school. Through this leadership, they assert, they have set new goals, refined their sense of values, or been motivated in some direct way to improve themselves.

Sometimes an experience crashes into a person's life with such force that it affects every subsequent experience. There is such a powerful emotional reaction on the part of the individual to that one experience that permanent learning seems to take place. All subsequent development of that individual has been genuinely affected.

For instance, a young woman said that until the preceding year she had considered it the smart sophisticated thing to do to play with the idea of suicide. She had talked glibly concerning it in discussions held in the wee, small hours. She had obtained a good deal of attention through this device; she had held the enthralled interest of younger girls. She fancied herself in the shocking role she pictured for herself. Her whole outlook on life had been drastically changed, however, by one cataclysmic experience. She was driving her father to his place of business. At a busy corner, her automobile was smashed, her father was killed almost instantly, and she herself was seriously hurt. She said that she remembers coming to faint consciousness for just an instant soon after the accident. It seemed to her that she was lying in a truck—as she learned later she had been. She felt herself sinking, and her one driving thought was that she most certainly did not want to die. That one moment has acted as a powerful antidote. In relating the experience, she said that she is now trying to be honest and grip at reality.

For many people, however, there is no fixed point to which they can refer as having determined the direction of their development. There is neither a dominating influence nor a crippling sense of inferiority for which they must compensate. The influences that determine their development emanate from their active, alert, and selective participation in many types of experiences which life has presented to them. Young people who are leaders among their fellows mention as most important in their development the opportunities given them to carry responsibility, to know the thrill of working hard and of achieving success. They say that not only have they learned through these experiences to exercise loyalty, tact, diligence, and intelligence, but also that they have matured as they attempted to shape the positive attitudes and develop the desirable qualities of their fellows. Mary's development, described in the following paragraph, is due to experiences like these.

Mary is an outstanding leader in a school and a very attractive person. She said that her home had been of tremendous influence during her college years. Her mother was a graduate of the college Mary attended and a member of the sorority that Mary joined. Mary said that her mother had always held before her the ideals of this sorority and had urged her, even before college days, to live by them. During Mary's freshman year, her mother had died. Her father had determined to keep the home together for Mary and her brother. Mary had lived at home, a distance of some seven miles from the campus. She had taken charge of the house, had maintained a B average in her schoolwork, had become president of one of the women's organizations, had taken an active part in athletics, and had kept a wonderful sense of balance withal. Her father had cooperated in every way. Mary did all the necessary shopping. Either she or her father prepared dinner, depending upon which one came home first. They cooperated in doing the dishes and in other tasks. Her father had insisted that Mary take an active part in school activities; he felt that experience in group life and in amateur athletics was of tremendous value for character and physical health.

Mary analyzed her experience of strenuous participation in more endeavors than most individuals would dare attempt, and concluded that she had gained from this wide experience strength and wisdom that would have been impossible for her to achieve otherwise. Individuals who must constantly utilize time wisely, who must exert real effort to keep various interests progressing satisfactorily find such experience of inestimable value. They learn in the process to develop their potentialities, to recognize, to appreciate, and even to increase their own strength. They heighten their ability to work well with other people. They develop a technique for making a place for themselves among others and thus for contributing their part to the life of the world.

These examples have illustrated some of the kinds of influences that are determining factors in young people's development. As we observe ourselves and others, we learn that some individuals exhibit a persistent disposition to deal with experiences solely in the light of what they have been taught to do; they are slaves to habits learned in the past. Other individuals allow their overpowering feelings of superiority or inferiority to be their sole guides to action. Some move almost wholly under the guidance of other persons by whom they are influenced. Still other individuals consistently face and grapple with difficulties as they arise; they expect to solve their problems and to triumph over obstacles.

There are an infinite number of other possible influences besides those discussed here. The conclusion to be reached is that an individual seldom deliberately chooses a particular way of behaving; usually the primary influences in his life are largely responsible for his developing a particular behavior pattern. From without and from within, directly and indirectly, quietly and consistently or dramatically and suddenly, people receive spurs to action that are determining factors in their development from that time forward.

RELATIONSHIP OF PERSONAL AND SOCIAL PROBLEMS

We cannot count on growing up in an orderly fashion; we cannot always predict where and how growth is likely to take place. We do know, however, that sound maturing involves for the individual an increased awareness of himself combined with an increased awareness of others.

Young people often struggle between what they want and what society seems to prefer that they should have. Society actually seems to create difficulties for many young people by neglecting to furnish further opportunities for growth. In fact, many young people who are interested in social experimentation aimed at the relief of suffering, at the release from insecurity for others because they themselves know what it is to have unrealizable ambitions, find that comparatively few people are willing to throw their energies wholeheartedly into these causes. The young person may then become resentful because society is not intent on improving the lot of all, discouraged because he does not find understanding, humiliated because he does not seem to be needed.

Most of the time, fortunately, it is not too difficult to reconcile one's own goals and self-interest with the social good. Because social experimentation aimed at increasing the security and happiness of individuals is becoming more widespread and effective in our country, young people can continue to believe that there still remains a place in society for inventive, resourceful, and thoughtful youth, that the best efforts of youth are needed in order that this country can move on to levels hitherto unattained.

It is not difficult to see how closely personal problems and social problems are related. On the other hand, there is wide variation in the way these two sets of problems may

be solved for a given individual, since the solution, to be
satisfactory, must be acceptable both to the individual and
to his social group. Some people with cheerful outlooks
and outgoing personalities seem to conquer difficulties
fairly easily—although they never underestimate them.
They seem to get along well with people. Others have
personality traits that make their adjustments and their
relationships with people difficult and not entirely happy.

Although we sometimes judge another's behavior as
desirable or undesirable, the sensitive individual recognizes
that most behavior and most really effective insight is
developed through a person's real attempts, adequate or
bungling, to meet situations as his life unfolds. The
behavior that we judge as undesirable is inevitably a
reflection of the individual's unsuccessful efforts to adjust
himself to a difficult, unhappy, or even antisocial environment in his home, his school, or his neighborhood.

An individual is born into a home. He develops his own
style of life as he attempts to get along with his parents,
his brothers and sisters. Later, as he is exposed to a world
outside his home—to playmates, teacher, pastor or priest,
policeman or judge, the boss or the foreman, the gang or
the country club—he tries to develop the kind of qualities
and characteristics that will enable him to get along successfully, to gain prestige in those particular social groups.
We become constantly more involved in social relationships
as we grow older, and it is true that any single trait or
characteristic of ours might have developed differently or
been absent entirely if we had been born into a different
type of home, attended a different kind of school, lived in a
different neighborhood, or had a different vocational
experience.

This statement does not imply, however, that an individual is molded by his environment without the interaction
of his own personal behavior patterns. It is true that in
our society many individuals find it impossible to live happy
lives. The struggle for bare existence or for economic

security is so severe for some people that primitive, almost brute characteristics sometimes develop as a defense in those who are forced to live under unfavorable conditions. On the other hand, every individual in every environment constantly faces social problems for the solution of which he feels that he has insufficient insight, knowledge, skill, or experience to make the most intelligent choice or plan. If he can solve his personal problems successfully, he is sometimes saved from a feeling of too great defeat or failure when faced by social problems that he cannot solve because of conditions that he cannot change. And all of us frequently are confronted with such conditions.

Meeting Experiences with Maturity

Since the responses that an individual makes to daily problems have grown out of ways of behaving which that individual has been learning since infancy, each period of our lives must be seen in its relationship to the whole. Every infant begins life in helplessness and complete dependence on others. Gradually he is able to manage himself in such areas as feeding, dressing, talking, and walking. Yet, throughout childhood, the major responsibility for his care and direction rests upon adults, although the child assumes responsibility for an ever-increasing number of details. As the years advance, he leaves the protection of his home and comes under the care and direction of the school and the church. He makes a place for himself in his play group, in his class at school, in his church and community life. He becomes progressively able to solve his own problems, to gain some control over his environment. Others no longer find it necessary to do so much for him.

No individual attains maturity all at once. We strive for it not only during the entire period of time that our physical powers are growing, but even as long as we continue successfully to substitute more and more inner authority

for outer control, as we increasingly assume responsibility
for ourselves.   However, the degree to which we achieve
maturity is affected by external circumstances as well as by
physical and psychological factors.

People vary considerably in the degree of maturity that
they manifest.   Each of us can determine the measure of
our emotional maturity by asking ourselves: In what
manner do I face problems?   To what degree am I competent to assume responsibility for myself in each situation?
How skillful am I in handling relationships with people?
What amount of control over my emotions do I display?   Do I show wisdom in utilizing the resources in my
environment to enhance a security more fundamental even
than an economic one and to build a personality organized
around a purpose that gives me a reason for living?   To
what extent am I equipped to make a constructive contribution to the groups of which I am a member?

An individual must either rely upon past experiences of
success to guide him toward maturity or he must recognize
and face the fact that he lacks those experiences.   Many
individuals have a series of successful past experiences
under the tutelage of a family group from whom they have
received reasonable protection, care, understanding, and
information sympathetically given.   The memory of these
experiences reinforces lagging self-confidence and nullifies a
fear of the unknown.   Other less fortunate individuals must
deliberately search for enough knowledge and skill to give
them the courage to meet situations new to them so that
fear of the unknown cannot force them to regress to an
earlier period of development.

If we are to become mature adults, we must first want to
be; we must also feel fairly sure that we shall have the
necessary skill and information to make us adequate in
adult roles.   With this knowledge comes self-confidence.
We can become mature emotionally if we have had many
of the satisfactions that came with being a child.   However,
if as children we felt unwanted or unloved, then in adoles-

cence we may expend our energy upon and give our allegiance to anyone who will show us the affection that we missed. We may even make ourselves a nuisance to people by our frantic efforts to gain their attention; or we may marry solely to gain the care and affection that we missed as children. Naturally, it is true that no one is always self-sufficient; we all are grateful for sympathy, even for mothering, in our low moments. However, if an individual's main energies are devoted to securing care and affection without reference to other objectives, he is not behaving in a mature way.

We need to be able to believe that we shall be relatively successful as adults. This confidence we can gain most surely from having a sufficient number of experiences of satisfaction or success in meeting failure and difficulty. Such experiences can begin early in life; some psychiatrists state that even an easy or difficult birth experience may affect the security of an individual. Or an individual may have felt threatened when a younger brother or sister was born. Or he may have been subjected to snobbishness, rejections, ridicule, or in some way baffled or hurt in his attempts to achieve status in a group of contemporaries.

For example, he may have been hazed in college or compelled to make a difficult adjustment when his family moved to a new community or when he entered a new school. If an individual lived in a neighborhood where he was the runt or if he was too fat or for some other reason scorned by his playmates and not accepted in games, he might find it necessary to play the "big shot" throughout life, to show off his athletic prowess at middle age, or to be gay and coy at fifty. The person who has been able to move over gracefully when the younger brother or sister came on the scene, who has accepted without too much upset or even very serious attention the early attempts of others to "get under his skin," who has gone on to endure college hazing without undue feelings of panic is progressively earning the freedom to devote himself constructively to experiences in which he can make his efforts count. He will not continue his life as a helpless slave to fear, antagonism, and suffering. Chronological age figures little in emotional maturity of this kind. An adolescent of sixteen may have accepted his own limitations, learned to face failure and to accept disappointment; another individual of fifty may still expect perfection or blame others for his own mistakes.

It is true that some people who have been confronted with serious difficulties may have been so frightened by them that they think of the responsibilities of maturity as something to be dreaded instead of as an adventure to be enjoyed. On the other hand, many individuals have been able to use these same types of experiences as the basis for a realistic confidence in themselves and in life which later difficulties can do little to undermine. Why is this true? Because this deep belief in themselves is based upon an honest estimate of what they can and cannot do, upon a willingness to see themselves as they really are, upon a knowledge that they dare to be different and a faith that they can use their wills to change themselves.

Before we become truly mature, we must know and have faced fear and frustration. Only thus can we come to know our own power to meet whatever situations must be met in life or, as someone has put it, to know our "capacity to suffer." Those elements in life that create difficulty— tensions, frustrations, or conflicts—we must recognize; we must understand their significance. Then we must take some positive action to satisfy those deep personality needs and desires to which they are related and of which they are symptoms. If we would meet the changing conditions of life in a mature way, it is evident that we cannot follow habit and custom unquestioningly. Living on the basis of fixed habits, refusing to accept new viewpoints, following slavishly the dictates of fashion, of parents, schools, or other institutions, betray our lack of ability to think or to act for ourselves. This is a skill that we can learn just as we learn any other skill.

We may have taken the first step in learning to think for ourselves. We may have revolted impatiently against authority in any guise. But we may continue all our lives merely to revolt. We cannot be considered mature adults until we learn to substitute genuine inner control of our behavior for such adolescent rebellion. When we have learned to face squarely situations as they present themselves to us, when we have learned to understand the relationship of an act to all that preceded and to all that will follow it, then we have learned to meet adult life with all its uncertainties since we have learned the technique of meeting change.

Nicholas Murray Butler has expressed this point of view admirably:

The individual is the unit and aim of all education. The individual precedes the social unit, and it is out of individuals and their willing or unwilling cooperation that the social unit is constituted. It is this truth which is the key to an understanding of the fact that all true education is education in freedom, in liberty. It is the mounting through discipline to self-discipline. . . . Liberty is a hard and difficult lesson to learn. It involves the freedom to make mistakes and errors as well as to make successes. It involves meeting temptation to do wrong as well as the opportunity to do right. Liberty has its dangers and its limitations, but so far as human history goes, no form or type of despotism, whether individual or group or social, can for a moment be put in comparison with it.[1]

Ideally, a person should be trained from childhood to make decisions and to accept responsibility for the consequences of the choices that he makes. Thus routine habits are established and his energy is freed for creative work.

[1] "Report of the President of Columbia University for 1930," *Columbia University Bulletin of Information*, pp. 29–30, Columbia University Press, New York, 1930.

In other words, he learns to control his immediate action in the light of future goals. He restrains the immediate expression of a desire in the interest of future achievement or future good. He decides against the joy of absorption in countless details because he is more interested in the sustained application of his efforts toward a distant, but more important goal.

He discovers, for example, that he is free to do only that for which he will pay the price in discipline. He is free to become an excellent swimmer if he will spend hours practicing his strokes. He is free to become a violinist if he will practice playing the violin. He is free to become an engineer if he will so budget his time, even inhibit his desire for social engagements, extracurricular activities, or for the companionship of his best friends sufficiently to ensure that none of these interests interferes with a creditable achievement in his work. A person's "tension capacity"—how much he can and will give up for the sake of some big thing for which he is working—is a measure of the energy that he can put into anything.

Habits of acting intelligently develop as young people connect specific events with their consequences. This is not difficult. Children soon learn the connection of a cause with its consequence; they size up situations in order to see the relationship of means to ends in conduct that they are planning. They understand the source of their difficulty when, for example, they have contracted sore throats because they went out in the rain to play the day that mother was not at home. They can also foresee the consequences of their action—having to go to bed and to take medicine. And because they see how inevitably the consequences follow the action, they are often quite resigned to "taking their medicine," literally and figuratively.

As young people become aware of the sources of their difficulties, as they learn from their own and others' experiences to foresee the results of action that they plan, they learn to criticize, to adapt, even to revise proposed actions in the light of results that they wish to achieve, or of consequences that they wish to avoid. Thus, they gradually develop guides for action which include ideals that they wish to achieve. These are usually expressed in terms of the kind of person they wish to become or of the values that they consider worthwhile in life.

In the light of these ideals they judge their conduct, set up immediate and long-time goals, and make plans for the realization of those goals. Loyalty to an ideal is the perspective in the light of which young people decide that which really matters. To them their daily life seems unimportant and trivial unless they can see how each day's thought and action is contributing, to a degree, toward the fulfillment of some life purpose that they have chosen, some set of values that they consider important enough to work for, live for, even die for.

Maturity must be won. It is not given us, nor can it be absorbed from others or gained by reading books. It can be achieved by each of us only through our own experiences. Even the behavior style develops, we have seen, as each of us tries to adapt to surroundings, to find our way around in the world.

Maturity includes the uniting of unorganized, conflicting, and often unrelated needs and desires into some orderly whole—into some reason for living that actually works, that means something to the individual. The process is not as simple as a choice between the good and the bad. The conflict is usually between two or more "goods" that we must reconcile and build into our lives if we are to know security, achievement, and love. The satisfying of these deep needs is the organizing center of our lives, the incentive for our day-by-day activities, the goal of our efforts. In the light of these needs, an individual determines his immediate choices, weighs the comparative values of his many desires, resolves his conflicts, capitalizes on and directs his energy instead of dissipating it into superficial satisfactions.

Implicit in this definition is the assumption that we have developed a sensitivity to values, that we have acquired a reasonable ability to make our own choices, that we have built habits of intelligent action, that we have displaced external authority by internal control. Only when we have accomplished these things are we truly ready to assume intelligent responsibility for our own lives. We must learn to accept our own limitations, to recognize and to learn from our mistakes and failures, to be honest with ourselves in facing the adjustments that we are making to our frustrations and conflicts. Honesty with ourselves, sincerity in facing and in learning from our mistakes instead of evading responsibility for them or of dissipating our energy in worry concerning them—these are, indeed, marks of maturity.

Chapter II

OUR PERSONALITY NEEDS

If we would further understand the styles of behaving that have been described, we must ask ourselves: what are the reasons, besides heredity, of course, why people take their various experiences as they do, why each individual develops a unique style of behaving? All of us are attempting to get the most out of life. There are some things that everyone needs, that none of us can do without, if we are to live happy, well-adjusted lives. Our behavior pattern is, in part, explained by the fact that all of us are seeking to satisfy basic personality needs.

Basic Personality Needs

In order to understand how we get to be what we are, not only must we be able to interpret various styles of behavior, but we must also discover what each person wants most out of life and to what degree he is able to gain what he most desires. Each of us must be able to satisfy all three of our deepest personality needs. We must all have some security, some love, and some success. These needs exercise an enormous influence upon our behavior, upon the values that we accept, even upon the life purposes that we develop. They affect our attitudes toward ourselves, toward others, and toward the world in general.

Security is not something that we can set out to achieve. An infant could not be said consciously to desire security; yet without adequate care and protection, its welfare, certainly, and even its life might be endangered. Security, however, transcends physical safety. A person must have adequate food, shelter, and clothing to keep alive, but he

23

also needs the confidence that he is a person who will be equal to life's demands, one who can manage his emotional adjustments and social relationships in a mature manner, who will be equal to taking in his stride, without being too seriously retarded, the normal number of frustrations that come to all of us.

Emotional starvation is just as real as physical starvation. In order to grow emotionally, an individual must feel that he is a worth-while person, that he is needed somewhere by someone, that there is a place for him in his family group, in his social group, in a vocation, and in the world. He must have, permeating all that he is and does, the certainty that he can confidently look himself and other people in the face. Then he knows security. Superficial observers describe it as self-confidence or self-respect. An individual with security might describe it as the background against which his life is lived.

Such security an individual first gains, or fails to gain, from his family group. He can be said to have security in his home if he feels accepted there, if he knows that due consideration is given to his welfare and to his desires, if he can talk over with his parents his actions, his interests, his hopes, and his points of view. Even though his parents may disapprove of his actions and disagree with his opinions, he knows that he will be understood, respected, and loved. Ideally, a person should be able to count on similar treatment from his school, his social group, and later from his employers.

Closely related to the need for security is the need for achievement, or for success. Individuals feel useless, develop a sense of not being needed, unless they have opportunities for achievement. Because no one can survive too much failure or defeat, every person must sometimes have the satisfaction of personal achievement; he must know the feeling of usefulness that is gained from the knowledge that there is something which he does well and for which he is appreciated. However, success must not come too easily.

If genuine satisfaction is to be gained by its achievement, failure must be present as a possibility. A satisfactory life seems to be compounded of both success and failure, with the success requiring real efforts for its attainment and the failure not so frequent an experinece as to cause despair.

Finally, there is the need for love, which is to be interpreted in its broadest sense as applying to the general tone of the environment in which a person lives and works. Everyone wants to feel that someone is interested in and concerned about him, that he matters to someone. This kind of experience can spur any of us to greater achievement. It is never too late for those who have missed it to learn their own worth by having someone believe in and appreciate them.

Everyone has these personality needs or drives, but they exist in varying strengths in each of us. Especially is this true by the time that we have passed adolescence. A number of psychologists have classified these drives and given them labels. Thomas,[1] for instance, calls them drives for security, love, and success. Prescott[2] describes in more detail what is meant by fundamental needs. He divides our needs into (1) physiological needs, for such essentials as food, clothing, shelter, activity, and rest; (2) social or status needs, which have to do with our relationships with others —a need for affection, for belonging, for sufficient likeness to others to be accepted by them—and (3) ego needs, needs for experience and for the organization of that experience in such a way that we can find our role in life and fill it in a sufficiently effective manner to develop a sense of worthy selfhood. Examples of ego needs are: rich experiences organized in harmony with reality and with values that the individual grows to accept, increasing self-direction, a balance between success and failure. In the process of

[1] THOMAS, WILLIAM I., *The Unadjusted Girl*, Chap. I, Little, Brown & Company, Boston, 1923.

[2] PRESCOTT, DANIEL A., *Emotion and the Educative Process*, Chap. VI, American Council on Education, Washington, D. C., 1938.

fulfilling ego needs the individual comes to self-realization in both a personal and a social sense.

Each of us is attempting to satisfy these needs in his own way.   We are all different in that for each of us the keystone of our action is determined in some manner or style characteristic of us as individuals.   For some individuals recognized success is more important than anything else in life; therefore the struggle to be superior, the fear of being second-rate, is the clue to an understanding of their life plan.   Of this group, some people may feel that a large amount of success compensates for having less love than other people.   When a person's drive for success is much stronger than his drive for security, he may be willing to adventure into new experiences, to take big risks on the chance of achieving success.   Such individuals are valuable for social progress.

Persons to whom security is most important may plod along without much drive toward brilliant successes.   They may not need or want them.   Nor are they particularly interested in new experiences.   A seemingly permanent security is more important to them than what seems like a transient success or an uncertain adventure.   They desire lives in which they can know a maximum of such security.

In still other individuals, the desire to love and to be loved overshadows all other drives.   Security, adventure, and success are less important to them than the knowledge that somewhere and by someone they are wanted, needed, and loved.   They have achieved what is of most value to them in life if they can feel that they belong somewhere.

The behavior of each individual can, to some degree, be interpreted in terms of the relative importance of these personality needs in his life.   It is comparatively seldom that one need completely dominates an individual's actions; it is because of this fact that certain actions are sometimes hard to explain.   However, a great many puzzling behavior manifestations can be interpreted through an individual's attempts to satisfy the needs that are most important to him.

When Basic Personality Needs Are Not Met

All of us can point out individuals who seem to lack experiences of success, love, or security. Many people do not have sufficient numbers of satisfying experiences, and often the reasons for this lack are outside the control of the person. Inevitably a direct relationship exists between the environment of an individual and the personality that he develops. This does not mean, however, that a person who has grown up in a meager environment, one superficially judged as unfavorable, will inevitably develop undesirable personality traits, whereas an individual who is surrounded with culture and the good things of life will—equally surely—become mature and adjusted. Some individuals from favored homes may develop undesirable, even anti-social traits, while others may emerge out of straitened circumstances and an unfavorable environment as strong, courageous, and mature persons.

The persons who are not getting the most out of life are often those for whom life has been either too easy or too difficult. An individual for whom life seems easy may prove to be irresponsible, fearful, self-centered, and easily hurt. We may discover that he has actually missed basic experiences in love and success, that he does not know security. How can this be possible? In his home, over-protection may have compensated for the real indifference of the adults. He may have become so pampered, having every whim fulfilled, that he has not learned his own strength by fighting his own battles, by making his own decisions, or by working for and achieving something he considered worth while. Intellectually gifted, he may have attended a school where his work did not challenge him; therefore he has never discovered his own capacities or known the exhilaration of conquering a genuinely difficult task. Beautiful to behold, he may as a result have had so much attention that he has missed learning the most elementary lessons in how to earn and deserve on some more reliable

basis the confidence and regard of others.   He feels insecure
and uncomfortable because his most important needs are
really still unsatisfied.   For that reason, the undesirable
personality traits have developed.

If life is too easy, a person may never learn to depend
upon himself; he may never know security or experience
success.   He may merely make unreasonable demands upon
other people, expect the world to fall in his lap.   He may
be incapable of disciplining himself to get what he most
wants.   If life becomes difficult, this person may become
paralyzed with fear, give up trying, retreat into a nervous
breakdown, into drinking, crime, suicide, or insanity.
Much of the latter is known to be functional, to result from
conditions in an environment too difficult for a given individual to cope with.

A person born into a family that already has many
children and little money may experience an environment
in striking contrast to the above.   Parents may have no
time or inclination to show interest, much less affection.
The necessities of life are scarce; there are no luxuries.
With his companions, perhaps force has to be met by force
if he is to be accepted or to achieve prestige among them.
If he is intellectually gifted, he may use his intelligence to
gain attention in school by the number of problems that
he can create.   He may leave school as early as possible.
He may be unable to find work on which he can exercise
his talents.   The person from this environment may also
feel insecure and uncomfortable.   It is not surprising if
such a person becomes hard, aggressive, cruel, sarcastic, and
antisocial, since his deepest personality needs have also
been disregarded.

On the other hand, for some individuals a difficult
environment acts as a spur to achievement.   This was
illustrated by several case studies described in the preceding
chapter.   By facing their problems, these young people
learned their own strength; they gained a fundamental
security.   Some people infer, therefore, that anyone can

conquer any circumstance if he sets himself the task of doing so. They even wonder whether it is not true that, the more difficult the obstacles that an individual must overcome, the stronger he will be. The tradition of the frontier and of the self-made man is still with us. It should not, however, persist independently of a consideration of the particular individual or society involved.

It is true that a mature, well-adjusted personality can develop out of either a favorable or an unfavorable environment. Whether a given person manages, in either case, to conquer his difficulties and to satisfy his fundamental personality needs is determined by the degree to which his capacities are adjusted to the circumstances of his life as these unfold. If an individual overcomes his difficulties, he must have health and intelligence sufficient to the demands of the circumstances he is called upon to meet. He must have courage to face his problems, persistence and stamina sufficient to conquer them. Life must be neither too easy nor too difficult for the capacity of a particular individual if he is to meet it successfully.

What is to be done with people for whom life has been so difficult that their deepest personality needs have not been met? Obviously, they need to "make up" the experiences that they have missed. They must be given opportunities to achieve real successes, to experience relationships in which they know that their worth is recognized and appreciated. On the other hand, they must also be helped to understand and to accept the fact that life, inevitably, will bring the unexpected and the unpredictable, that nowhere are they completely safe from uncertainty. There is no escaping the possibility of risk in the process of living. One must be prepared to meet life as it comes, to handle each situation as it arises with whatever resources of wisdom and endurance one can command.

It is true that we live in a social order where, even under the most favorable conditions, we have not yet learned to create enough jobs to supply everyone. Too often the rewards go to the strong, to the aggressive, or to those with influence. Many individuals, especially young people, are left without the security, stability, and experience of success that a job could give. Because of insufficient incomes, many young people are forced to delay marriage. Many of them live a humdrum existence because neither they nor their parents have the money nor the facilities to develop recreational and avocational skills. It is not surprising that family ties become strained, that many young people lack a feeling of security.

Again, young people may find themselves insecure because they are facing the prejudices of major groups of society against their nationality or their religion, for example. Others may feel rejected or unhappy in homes where children are unwelcome or where insensitive parents attempt to gain conformity to their own desires by threatening to disown a child who will not or cannot conform. Still other young persons may find jobs or be in schools in which they feel like dehumanized automatons rather than like persons making a genuine contribution to society. Again, some may be forced into the position of being "merely a drain on the family" because they can find no place for themselves in the economic order. Our society is truly said to be wasteful of human resources and enamored of mechanical devices. Until nations have learned how to live together in peace, no one anywhere can ever be confident of personal safety or social stability. The young people of any generation may find themselves compelled at any time to abandon every personal plan and cherished hope in order to help meet some great common crisis. Often they may feel that they have done nothing to create the crisis and would prefer no share in what seems to them a totally unholy mess.

The problem of satisfying personality needs is most grave for people who are thus caught somewhere in the stupidities, inequalities, and discriminations of society. Some of them, in spite of help given them, may never survive the shock their personalities suffered when society failed to provide for their deepest needs. Yet everyone of us can do something for ourselves and for people caught in these ways. We all can work in our homes, schools, churches, and communities for a greater degree of national security, for greater international understanding, for an equalization of educational opportunity, for a breaking down of prejudice. Only by this means can society be developed so that it will be able ever more adequately to meet the basic physical and personality needs of more people.

At the same time, we must recognize that social readjustment alone will not solve personal problems. Some young people may be exposed in their homes, schools, and communities to an atmosphere in which consideration, affection, and love are unknown, to an environment that contributes to their lack of security and success. Inevitably, life contains for everyone both success and failure, both achievement and disappointment. But is true that, for some people, the failures and disappointments overbalance the positive experiences.

One person can help another to achieve some success and security if he will share his knowledge, skill, and experience. Often fear can be displaced by self-confidence if a person feels that someone will coach him, will stand by as he undertakes new experiences, will encourage him, will give him the feeling that someone cares whether he comes through and is confident that he will. New forms of behavior, new ways of responding to situations will develop as fundamental personality needs are being more adequately met. The person for whom life has been difficult faces a struggle, but he can conquer his problems.

On the other hand, the people for whom life has been too easy are in a more difficult situation. Too often they have dissipated their energies in devising methods by which they can evade the facing of problems. They yearn to experience a more genuine love, security, and success, but they are often not willing to work to achieve their ends. They have grown so accustomed to having things their own way, to gaining their ends without working, or to having life fairly comfortable and satisfactory without exerting themselves to earn even as much as they possess, that they continue to use their negative or passive techniques without realizing that, by that very process, they fail to gain what they are seeking.

People who have great potential capacities to achieve need to discover that as a result of actual achievement it is possible to earn the approval of others and a pleasant feeling of satisfaction and self-confidence. Approval cannot be counted upon as a natural right. Lasting satisfaction will come from real success; but in order to learn to achieve success in any field, all of us must be willing to yield to discipline. People for whom life has been too easy may, at first, resent discipline. However, when they have once known the feeling of security, respect, and approval accorded them as the result of a genuine accomplishment, they see how transient was the satisfaction gained by their former play acting, how futile the success of getting their own way by alienating others and robbing themselves of opportunities to achieve.

The difficult stage for this sort of person is the transition from temper tantrums, sulking, gossiping, crying, blaming of others, whining, simulating illness, and even threatening of suicide to new ways of behaving. Criticism of such unsatisfactory behavior usually brings no response other than irritation, resentment, and additional insecurity—further unfruitful behavior. If such an individual can find that at least with the one person with whom he is dealing at the moment he is not gaining his ends, he may begin to question the effectiveness of his methods.

Unfortunately, it is too often possible for this type of person to gain his ends by wearing people down and by making a nuisance of himself. People, in exasperation, yield to his demands, no matter how unreasonable those demands may be. Usually the demands are most unreasonable—since the individual who makes them has not learned to consider the needs or desires of anyone except himself. However, if such a person repeatedly finds his accustomed ways of achieving his ends blocked; if, in addition, he can come to believe that the whole experience of success is more conducive to his happiness than forcing other people to give him his way at the expense of those others, then he may be willing to attempt the development of a new life pattern.

When a person has failed over a long period of time to get out of life what he wants most, his behavior patterns may betray this lack of adjustment. Let us observe people who are thwarted in their desires to achieve sufficient security, success, or love—and all of us are thwarted at some points— people who are unable to satisfy one or more of the fundamental personality needs. Some people, when they fail to get what they want, act like infants who failed to grow up. Others might be called the fighters. Still others become the timid souls. Some might be listed as the frozen people, icebound in their past and in their prejudices.

The Infants

Let us consider first the individuals who fail to grow up. In their behavior an observer may find hysterics or temper tantrums; indecisiveness in actions, speech, and even in thinking; demands for their own way; impulsiveness in following new fads, in clothes or politics, for instance; dogmatism, attempted authoritarianism, inflexibility; extreme conservatism; intolerance; or an inordinate desire for perfection.

The keynote for understanding this behavior is the knowledge that fear is an element in it. When a person is baffled by a problem, he may respond by becoming terror-stricken, by having hysterics, by being unwilling to do or say anything decisive or even to think. His behavior may reflect his distrust of himself, coupled with his unwillingness to risk failure.

If an individual is certain of himself, he does not waste his energy in panic or ineffective action, in avoiding responsibility for his own action, in refusal to attempt anything new or even to complete a task that he has begun. To learn skill at a task, one must sometimes fail; for example, to learn what is the correct thing to say, one must sometimes say the wrong thing. However, some people dare not take these risks. They have known too much failure; they will not face a further reminder of their own limitations.

The indecisive individual cannot face the fact that we live in a world in which choice is inevitable. He will not choose because he is afraid that he will make the wrong choice. He is unable to take upon himself the responsibility of failure, therefore he substitutes the technique of attempting to persuade others to make his choices for him—then he can blame them if things go wrong. Blaming others for a difficult situation may sound reasonable because, necessarily, other people are usually involved in any situation. But this device can become a habit with the person who is afraid to undertake a new task on his own responsibility.

A person may delay a choice so long that, if the consequences are unpleasant, he can retreat into the safety of saying that this thing "just happened" to him, that life and the world are against him. Such a person should not have sympathy only; he needs a mirror. When "things always go wrong," one needs a good long look at oneself.

If a person makes no choice, merely allows the situation to drift, he is always in conflict with himself. He finds it difficult to concentrate on any other work. His emotions are dissipated in wondering what might have happened. He is denying himself the values that would have come from making one of the possible choices and taking the consequences, because he has refused to take the responsibility for any of the choices.

The individual who insists upon his own way under all circumstances is also confessing that he fears that he cannot handle a situation unless he can dictate the manner in which it is to be managed. He is also demonstrating incidentally that the amount of consideration that he has for other people is very meager.

The individuals who make decisions in immature ways—or fail to make them—need to learn that life is filled with circumstances in which we must take chances. Of course, a person should attempt to gather all the pertinent facts concerning a situation about which a choice is to be made. Advantages and disadvantages of any course of action should be considered thoughtfully. But evidence may be incomplete, for there can be no real certainty in a changing world. Some decision must be made—to do something, to believe something, to be something, or to buy something—in the light of the best knowledge concerning a particular question.

The person who exaggerates trivialities may be trying to keep the attention of others from the fact that he is not facing the real problem. Many individuals dissipate their energies by concentrating on a mass of details. When, for example, such a person must study for an examination or do some errands, it is not unusual for him or her to decide that first nails must be manicured, bureau drawers cleaned out, new clothes tried on, or a friend asked a question.

These infantile individuals have an amazingly long repertory of techniques of behavior with which to achieve their ends: they may cry, sulk, stamp their feet, whine, emphasize trivialities, blame others, or exercise various forms of self-pity if they feel that they are not being sufficiently appreciated. What is the real meaning of this behavior? When a feminine infantile reiterates, with violent sobs, how useless she is, this observation may be taken as a hint that she fears she cannot take care of herself and must be cared for. For anyone to pout, sulk, rage, or indulge in other displays of violent emotion is to confess frustration and inability to face the actual problem. Therefore, the person finds release for accumulated tension by emotional displays.

If someone fears that he has lost a friend or failed to win an argument in a club or fraternity meeting because he handled the situation poorly, he may be dissolved in self-pity. It builds up his ego and gives him satisfaction to picture to himself how sorry the friend would be if he moved out of town, how repentent his club or fraternity if he resigned. This seems so much easier than to confess that he handled the situation poorly and to learn from his mistake.

There are impulsive individuals who demand sudden change, yet resist any control. This kind of person can accept something only as long as it is new; he slavishly follows one new idea after another. He, too, is fearful. He cannot exercise his own initiative, cannot believe in or depend upon himself, therefore he relies on these types of external dependence. Or he may try to avoid depending on anything by the device of depending, in continuous and rapid succession, on a bewildering variety of things. He wishes to be and speaks passionately of being free, yet he does not dare to take risks. He does not trust himself sufficiently.

When he hazards an opinion or when he decides to act, instead of carefully working out the implications of his chosen course, he insists that his desires be met, his ideas accepted at once. He has not learned to wait. He may be afraid that people might not accept his ideas if they reflect upon them. Such infantilism is expected of children who cry if food is not forthcoming as soon as they express their hunger. But in an adult, an important indication of maturity is his ability to wait for what he wants. Life demands setting goals far ahead, then working gradually toward a final achievement, controlling day-by-day emotions and actions in the interests of future goals, not growing hysterical if the achievement of one's wishes is postponed.

The extremely conservative, dogmatic, and intolerant individuals are, in reality, those who fear change. Uncertainty makes them feel insecure. Moreover, all that is strange, whether people or ideas, is open to suspicion and is either to be fought or avoided. Psychologists say that such people may have lacked security in childhood. If a child is to be secure, the important details of life must be carefully planned and faithfully but casually executed to assure him care and protection. In addition, he must have the experience of a psychological routine. In other words, he must be certain of his own worth as it is proven to him in his parents' dependable but nonanxious care of him. If he has not had this experience, he must seek security in an outward routine. Everyone must have something on which he can count.

On the other hand, if a child is subjected to a routine so long a time that he does not have progressive opportunities to develop his own powers, to learn how to think or to act for himself, then he may remain dependent on routine in his environment far too long. He may fear a change in residence, a change in schools, a change in political, moral, or religious ideas. Insecure people always resist change. The violence of their resistance to some particular change will be determined by the degree of the threat to their personal prestige or economic security represented by the new idea, person, or action.

Let us examine those people who relentlessly demand perfection? Why must some persons idealize others? What is the significance of the uncritical "Oh, she's wonderful!" attitude? What is the appeal of descriptions of Utopia? The demand for perfection is correlated with a feeling of dependence and inadequacy. A small child is dependent because he is helpless; his parents seem perfect.

Gradually, however, a person should gain sufficient confidence in himself to find his security within himself. Then he will cease to seek perfection in the outside world or to torture himself by using perfection as a measure of the effectiveness of his own actions. For example, if a person can accept himself and his own limitations, then he knows that he sometimes makes mistakes. He grants the same fallibility to his friends. He does not demand a perfect friend or an infallible leader. Anyone who is seriously disillusioned either by the lack of perfection in himself or in someone else is still emotionally immature.

Hero worship, then, can be either good or bad, depending upon a person's attitude toward his hero. Hero worship may go no farther than imitation, or it may be the substitution of someone else's achievements for one's own. An individual may spend his days running errands for someone who is the kind of person that he wishes he were, who has the things that he wants. This relationship can be found even in marriage. If the hero should go out of the life of the immature person who feels like this about him, the person will feel thwarted, adrift, let down. His source of security has lain in that other person instead of having been developed in himself.

On the other hand, hero worship can be a significant phase in a young person's development. The heroes whom young people choose to follow are among the first voluntary choices that they make. These first heroes may be like the parents of the young person; but if the person is rebelling against his parents, the heroes will be very different from the parents. A person's heroes are very influential in determining the kind of adult he will become. Their ideals will contribute to the formation of his; their achievements will spur him to action.

Hero worship is advantageous if the individual has the capacity to achieve the goals thus set. It is pernicious if he is learning to be satisfied with the substitution of the achievements of another for the more difficult goal of achieving for himself, or if he is being constantly confronted with a sense of his own inadequacy because his goals are higher than he has the capacity to achieve. If a brother who is an intellectual giant is the hero of a younger boy who has only average academic ability, the younger boy may develop feelings of guilt and self-condemnation because of his failure to reach his brother's level.

Hero worship should never deteriorate into ecstatic abasement of one's self or into projection of one's ego to the stature of one's giants. It is unfortunate if, through a hero-worship experience, a person becomes accustomed, in all his relationships, to tend to bestow uncritical devotion on his friends. He misses the mutual respect, the real comradeship, which two individuals can have when each sees the other as he is, and enjoys him for what he is.

The Fighters

How can we analyze the behavior of overaggressive persons who meet their difficulties by bullying others, having temper tantrums, showing off, being dogmatic or sarcastic, being suspicious of everyone—the "chip on the shoulder" attitude—defying authority, stealing, or developing even more serious forms of antisocial behavior?

Such actions also include symptoms of fear. If an individual feels that he is not equal to a situation, he may threaten or otherwise attempt to terrify anyone opposing him so that the facing of the situation may be avoided. It has already been stated that temper tantrums disclose one's ineffectiveness in facing an actual situation. It is commonly recognized that bullying, too, is a cover for fear, that the bully is a coward at heart. Equally true is the fact that the individual who is the most dogmatic in his assertions is the person who is least sure of himself. He "doth protest too much." If he were certain of himself, he would not feel that it was necessary to impress everyone with the infallibility of his opinions.

Much ostentatious misconduct may be explained by the fact that some young people enjoy defying authority, breaking rules, or making problems of themselves, just as some children gain satisfaction out of chronic disobedience. These young people's real difficulty is that they doubt their ability to gain attention in a group except by spectacular behavior such as rebellion or extreme precociousness. They need to learn the skills, to develop the attitudes, that

will give them sufficient self-confidence to attempt to make
a place for themselves among their fellows in a socially
acceptable fashion. When they recognize their own worth,
they will scorn to do mean and petty things.

The above explanation is equally applicable to the
individuals who show off, who are bossy or sarcastic. They
too need to learn social skills and to gain self-confidence.
Showing off is usually done in a desperate attempt to gain
the notice of others. If a person knows he can carry
on a conversation, he does not attempt to talk all the time.
If he knows that he has good taste in clothes, he never
attempts to be the flashiest dresser in his group. The same
is true of the individual who resort to bossiness. He has
become so busy bossing a situation or talking about it that
he never has to do the actual work himself. Thus he hopes
that the feeling of inadequacy with which he faces the
situation will never be discovered. Again, a person can
become sarcastic and bitter about other people or a situation
in the hope that he may distract the attention of others from
his own real or imagined limitations.

Fearful also is the individual who has a perpetual chip on
his shoulder. He has been hurt so often that he now expects
people to insult, humiliate, or take advantage of him.
Unfortunately, as long as he retains that attitude, they may
do so. It is all too true that we live in a mirror world.
If we flash out hate and disillusionment to others, it is not
surprising if we are given that in return. And too much
unassimilated fear and rage can give us psychological
poisoning. Chronic fussiness and the piling up of small
peeves and frustrations are unhealthy symptoms. When
we allow our rages and fears to accumulate, the only result
is a splitting headache which may complicate our already
unsatisfactory relationships with others.

If we must have fears and rages, let us put them into
effective action. There are many conditions in society
over the consequences of which one could rightly become
fearful or enraged. Lincoln's interest in the freedom of

slaves had its origin in his presence at a slave auction and in his anger at the spectacle of human beings on an auction block. Our action toward social reform may be inspired by knowledge gained from personal experience on what being without money and a job does to one's self-respect. Instead of dissipating our energies in hatred and disillusionment, we can capitalize on our own experience by helping our society to achieve a really fundamental answer to our problems.

Stealing, truancy, and other antisocial behavior can sometimes be interpreted as protective phenomena, sometimes as efforts to fight a society that has given one a raw deal. Truancy, for example, may be an attempt to escape a situation in which failure seems ever-present, or it may be an action taken to punish adults who make demands. Stealing may result from a need to gain adult attention, from boredom, from the fact that debts have accumulated, from the desire for nice clothes, from mismanagement of one's allowance, or from a sense of adventure—to see whether one can get by with it.

More of us than one generally realizes have at some time resorted to some form of so-called antisocial behavior. The fact that children occasionally steal, cheat, lie, or play truant need not cause alarm unless the incident is handled in such a way that the behavior tends to become habitual. The individual must be helped to understand and face the significance of his behavior. He should not merely be punished or allowed to get by with flimsy excuses for himself.

When a young person resorts to belligerence or antisocial behavior, it is generally partly because he cannot face the difficulty directly. To understand how he can be helped, we must know the personality needs that prompted the behavior, then help him to face that which is his basic difficulty. If the young person needs money to spend, if he wants an opportunity to adventure, to excel, to have his ability recognized, he must be helped to satisfy those needs in a socially acceptable manner. He has a right to ask these things of society. Only as his needs are met can the actual causes of antisocial behavior be removed. When a young person's deepest needs have been satisfied, he will voluntarily relinquish the behavior that was the symptom of unfulfilled desires.

THE TIMID SOULS

Many of the timid souls are victims of circumstances which have repeatedly threatened their self-respect. Often their contacts with other people bring nothing but a feeling of inadequacy, of failure to hold up their end. Whatever the cause, this sort of person may tend to avoid situations in which he cannot be sure of success. He may be afraid of criticism; he may evade the assumption of responsibility because he dare not risk further failure. Various mechanisms of escape may be utilized. He may become shy, sulky, unapproachable; he may cheat, bluff, and blame other people or the situation for his mistakes. He may become dependent upon others or upon the opinions of others. He may escape into daydreams, into lassitude, or preoccupation with details, into drinking, into illness, into mental ill health, or even into suicide. He may exhibit jealousy; he may fail to finish what he has begun.

Such individuals must make for themselves sufficient opportunities to acquire the skills, knowledge, and information necessary for a feeling of adequacy. Learning comes to anyone only by ceaseless activity and effort, by trying many things for himself. As a person develops in ability to handle situations, he must know success and failure and must be willing to take the consequences of either. Anyone who wishes to become a more nearly adequate individual cannot retreat into the excuse of shyness; he cannot sulkily refuse to do anything or bitterly assert that it's no use trying. There are people, superficially called lazy, who are actually the victims of a paralyzing cynicism which keeps them aloof from others, makes them gruff and bitter.

Some people use daydreams as a retreat from difficulties. If they are afraid, disappointed in, or unsatisfied with their real selves, they can so easily become, in their imaginations, whatever they wish to be: the life of the party, a famous musician, a sparkling conversationalist. The danger is that a person may make little effort to achieve the ideal with which he is enamored. Daydreams are an advantage if they spur people on to attainable ideals. But if a person really wishes to attain the dream of himself, he must pay the price. For example, if he would learn how to reach the goal of becoming popular, he must meet people, talk, and attend parties; if he would become a musician he must spend many hours practicing. In other words, he must daily run the risks of an actual relationship, even though it may include the risk of making some social breaks or of executing his music badly.

Akin to escape into daydreams is absorption in unimportant details. It is not uncommon to find that a person has thought of numerous things to do before he answers an important letter, for example, or sees a person to whom he must apologize. Some persons may seem overworked or have nervous breakdowns not because their work has been difficult but because they have been haunted by feelings of inadequacy in facing their real problems. Therefore, they have spent their time in manufacturing endless details on which they could dissipate their energies. Yet they feel thwarted because they have been rewarded with no appreciation or sense of achievement.

Another method by which people seek to evade facing what is difficult is by cheating. The person who cheats in an examination may do so because of the pressure from his family to make good grades, because he was working his way through school and had insufficient time to study, because he was forced to take a course that he disliked, or because he has, from day to day, failed, out of inertia, to meet his responsibilities to the course and wants to avoid the natural consequences of this inertia. In any case, he is refusing to face an actual situation.   Moreover, cheating should not be interpreted as confined to a classroom or examination situation.   A person is cheating just as surely when he fools himself into thinking that he can gain courage by drinking, or when he breaks a date with one man or woman because he has discovered that he can go out with another whom he likes better, yet he tells the first that the date was broken because of his own illness.

The real question in every case is: Whom is he cheating? The more a person cheats, the more he undermines his own ability to face life as it comes.   Lincoln once said, "I am not bound to win, but I am bound to be true; I am not bound to succeed, but I am bound to live up to what light I know and have."

Not very different from cheating is bluffing.   It looks so successful until a person attempts it; then he discovers that it is difficult to live up to the pose that he has created.   He is insecure because he knows that he cannot do what he said that he could do, that he is not what he professed to be, that he does not possess what he said he had, nor believe what he said he did.   He has sacrificed integration of himself on the altar of a deceptive hope.   We lose ability to concentrate on real goals if we must constantly live up to fake ones.   How much wiser to accept our limitations, to develop whatever abilities we do possess, than to have our bluff called and to find that our unreal world has toppled!

Another timid soul is the person who compensates for what he cannot do or cannot have by trying to reform others in the very fields in which he has had his deepest conflicts.   For instance, the woman who has renounced, or been denied, marriage may become an ardent advocate of women's rights; the man who has sacrificed worldly goods for some kind of social institution, may become tremendously ambitious for that institution.   Reforming others may prove to be a very comforting task, since no one can feel the necessity of reforming others without assuming that he himself is better than the others.

We have all known at least one person who begins an enterprise, often with a great deal of fanfare, but has never been known to finish anything that he began. The secret of his dropping the project may be that he prefers to leave it unfinished rather than to submit himself to the evaluation that others may make of it. He is akin to the perfectionist who loudly demands that everything must be perfect. He can never admit that he has made a mistake; he cannot bear to have anyone criticize his work. Therefore he avoids entirely or postpones the evaluation as long as possible; he prefers to be blamed for not finishing a task. "At least," he consoles himself, "no one will ever know what I might, or might not, have been able to do."

Anyone who feels that he is not equal to a situation may develop a tendency to blame others for his own inadequacy. This reaction has already been discussed. This sort of person may blame not only others but also the situation. Perhaps he might profit by observing that the good fisherman will throw his fly where he is; the poor one wants to go to the next stream.

It is true that many radical changes may need to be made in any situation, yet a person needs to ask himself honestly why he is demanding such changes. It is sometimes very difficult to meet a situation as it really is. It might seem to be much easier, for example, when faced with an unfavorable personal situation in an existing organization, to withdraw and form a new organization rather than adjust to conditions in the existing one. It is well to remember that, even if the situation is changed, the person must take himself into the new situation; he will still have himself to deal with there.

There are also the people who rely entirely upon others or upon routine. They can make no decisions for themselves. They are the painfully submissive, "you know best" kind of people who are constantly going to others for advice. Unfortunately, there are many individuals who encourage the practice, who are most happy to dictate to others the day-by-day details of life—as well as political opinions or moral codes. Such individuals abet the cause of immaturity not only by allowing others to evade the responsibility for their own actions but even by praising their lack of initiative and their conformity.

This tendency to lean on another person is akin to hero worship. Any life can be enriched by sharing in another's life purposes, interests, and achievements, but the sharing jeopardizes the entire relationship when it is made a substitute for each person's achievements. A one-sided relationship leads to an uncritical admiration that is more resented than enjoyed by the admired person, since it seldom contains honest evaluation. Someone who admires another uncritically, who relies entirely upon that person, may be attempting to escape living his own life. Inevitably, however, living another's life leads to dissatisfaction, since a person cannot gain the deep satisfactions which can come only through his own achievement. For example, one can generally feel a subtle, continuous irritation in a household in which a son or daughter has renounced marriage to devote himself or herself entirely to a parent who wishes this undivided attention.

Moreover, one cannot live entirely in another person's life without becoming demanding and possessive, for he is unhappy apart from the admired person. As a result, the insecure individual, to whom only the admired person matters, begins making extreme emotional demands on that person. After all, he has closed other avenues of expression to himself. Simultaneously, he becomes jealous whenever the admired person spends time with anyone else. He may even begin to disparage all other persons to his hero.

Jealousy is always related to a feeling of inadequacy. The victim of a person's jealousy usually has something that he would like to possess, an attractive physical appearance, for example. Since he does not at present possess the appearance he wishes, the person may either shut himself up and give way to self-pity because he is homely, or he may study himself to catalogue his assets and determine how he can capitalize each one. To the extent that we will work toward something that we desire, the necessity lessens for being jealous of people who possess what we want.

The futility of such conduct as weeping, whining, and sulking has been discussed. Another way in which occasional individuals sometimes escape responsibility is by pretending illness. Illness in any form can be a powerful weapon; it looks real and its results are effective. No one expects a sick person to do anything difficult or to make any momentous decisions. Young persons have even, although rarely, been known to threaten suicide when life became too complicated.

In other words, when conditions of life seem insupportable, people may respond with despair rather than with determined courage. Statistics show that the incidence of both suicide and mental disease rises in periods of difficulty, notably of economic depression. Some people give up and adopt behavior patterns that attempt to force other people or society to take care of them, even to live their lives for them. The world owes no one a living unless he is willing to do his part in securing it for himself.

THE FROZEN PEOPLE

The younger a person is, the less he realizes the extent to which we are all bound by our fears and prejudices. He may recognize the origin of his own fears and prejudices; he may even discount them intellectually, yet emotionally he probably responds to them just as he did when he first acquired them. For instance, young people may be able to talk eloquently about the superiority of new ways of acting which they honestly believe they have adopted. Yet, when confronted with an actual situation, they are often shocked to find that the old automatic emotional response makes rational or thoughtful action difficult, if not impossible.

Consider, for example, a fear of night noises or of the dark. There are people who cannot go to sleep unless a night light is burning, people who leave the sidewalk and walk in the street after dark because they fear shadows lurking in doorways. They may even leave their beds to investigate the source of noises, although intellectually they are certain that a board was creaking or a curtain flapping.

Some people express, but cannot explain, their violent dislikes of whole groups of people. They designate an individual, with what is meant to be a term of opprobrium, as a radical, an economic royalist, a heretic, an atheist, a Fascist, a Socialist, a Democrat, a Republican, a Catholic, a Jew, a German, a Japanese, a Greek, an Italian—in fact, almost any group is the victim of someone's prejudice. People thus controlled by prejudice should have experiences in which they grow to know and respect individuals of nationalities, races, religions, and political creeds different from their own. Becoming acquainted with and appreciating the people on whom formerly they had merely pinned labels, seeing them as individuals, each with needs and desires and ideals akin to their own, usually results for intelligent people in their reexamining their unreasonable, purely emotional feeling, in questioning it, and in finally displacing it by the tolerant attitude toward people different from ourselves that is characteristic of our democracy.

Some people have scruples or inhibitions which in their effect are as paralyzing as fears. Especially is this true in the field of sex and of religion. Several studies have shown that fear operates, especially in women, to cause frigidity. Almost everyone knows individuals, reared to believe that dancing or card playing are somehow "wrong," who find it difficult to enjoy themselves without feeling vaguely but uncomfortably guilty. Other individuals find it impossible to enjoy the beauty of the architecture, the ritual, or the music of a church of a denomination other than their own because their "conscience" tells them that it is "wrong" for them to be there. Such warnings of "conscience" and such unexplainable prejudices as those cited above are often, in reality, the voice of environment. Feelings such as these, when expressed by children and young people, usually reflect the attitudes of adults and of a community.

A child absorbs the attitudes of adults surrounding him; his prejudices are seldom the result of actual experiences of his own. A prejudiced child does not understand why he feels as he does about certain groups of people; he merely realizes that the adults around him and in the community express horror, displeasure, or fear if he is "too friendly" with some group of which they do not approve. They make him uncomfortable by their violent disapproval, and gradually the child learns to guide his behavior in such a way as to escape these unpleasant reactions. However, as the child himself becomes an adult, he can, if he will, question instead of accept these attitudes and help to break down the prejudices that bind him and his community. Thus, he, as a citizen, can contribute to the ideal to which this country has pledged itself: equal opportunity for all to enjoy life, liberty, and the pursuit of happiness, regardless of color, creed, or religious affiliation.

There may, of course, be some real basis for an individual's fear of unfamiliar people, experiences, and ideas. Generally, however, the situation upon which the fear is based is not so serious as the depth of the fear would indicate. For example, one young man could not conquer a fear of the water, yet could not account for what seemed to him an unreasonable reaction. He finally connected his fear with an experience that he had had as a five- or six-year-old. He was visiting in the country. One day he and four of his companions stole away and went swimming. He dived and struck his head, but not seriously. The other boys ridiculed him so that, in his humiliation mingled with fear, he got out of the water and never reentered it.

Another example is that of a girl who refused to accompany a group of her friends on a visit to a night court. She confessed to an overpowering fear of policemen. She said she was in constant terror, when on the streets, that one would approach her. When she was a small child she had run out into the street after a ball. A policeman had seen her and, in order to warn her, had gruffly threatened that the next time he came around he would put her in jail and feed her crumbs through the bars. When she told her mother of the incident, her mother reinforced what the policeman had said, telling her that the policeman was right.

To a great many of us, making a speech is not an easy task. Yet, given adequate preparation, we can usually manage to acquit ourselves rather creditably. However, most of us are acquainted with people for whom making a speech is a grueling ordeal. As they try to explain why it is more difficult for them than for the ordinary individual, they usually relate a childhood experience in which they remember having been humiliated because they arose to recite some speech before a large group of people and then either forgot some important lines or broke down entirely and retreated in failure.

It is important to recognize that the response that a person makes to an experience is in proportion to the amount of fear that was engendered by a previous, similar experience, not in proportion to the danger involved in the experience that he is facing at the moment. Of course, a person should learn caution from all experiences involving actual danger, but if he allows himself to be controlled by numerous unreasonable fears or prejudices, it becomes almost impossible for him to profit by new experiences.

All of us are inhibited to some degree and bound in some ways by fears and prejudices. How are we, then, to learn to release ourselves and to help to release others from these fears and prejudices? We must all be helped to understand the origin of unreasonable behavior and to see the significance of early crucial experiences. Then we must be provided with happy experiences out of which we can gradually gain new attitudes and new insights which will finally displace the unhappy fear-producing attitudes.

If, as a child, a person had immediately had a successful happy experience to counterbalance a fear-producing, unhappy one, fear and prejudice would never have developed. For instance, the young man who could not conquer his fear of the water might have gained from rather than have been harmed by the early experience if he had been coaxed back into the water, had been shown where to dive, and had done it successfully. In the case of the girl who was afraid of policemen, how much better it would have been if her mother had explained that the policeman meant only to warn her, not to frighten her.

This same principle applies to anyone in the grip of prejudices and fears. People must first be helped to recognize their unfortunate experiences and their prejudices, helped to ask, "How did I get to be this way?" They must recognize the origin of their prejudices and be allowed to relive the unhappy experiences by relating to a sympathetic person all the details connected with them so that the original emotion is released. Parenthetically, it should be said that the person who helps to effect this release should be skilled in handling personality problems if the experiences involved deep emotional upsets. Finally, new experiences that will wipe out unhappy memories must be provided and the individuals helped to take advantage of and to see the significance of these new experiences.

CHAPTER III

ADJUSTMENTS IN FAMILY RELATIONSHIPS

Maturity presupposes changes in an individual's habits and ways of living, changes involving serious personal and social consequences. The process of achieving maturity involves changing from a life externally supervised to one that must be self-supervised, of changing from a relatively stable to a relatively unstable environment, from an environment fairly well understood to one full of the unfamiliar. To become psychologically independent, a person must develop certain essential habits. Principal among them are: intelligent analysis and experimentation, learning from experience, objectivity in the consideration of a problem, ease in personal relationships.

An individual's home is his earliest and best instrument for acquiring habits and attitudes. It is the focal point from which he interprets the world around him. Here his basic habit patterns, those powerful instruments of adjustment, are learned. The broader his contacts are, the better he is prepared to meet the varied situations in life. In his home, he is given practice in the use of skills. Here his potentialities are first developed. Those qualities that an individual ultimately possesses are the result both of innate ability and of opportunity. The family group can help to create opportunities for abilities to develop and to direct them into appropriate channels.

In the family circle, an individual should from his infancy have found opportunities for freedom of choice and for carrying responsibility without too much pressure, dominance, oversolicitude, or overprotection. The freedom should have included responsibility for making his own choices and also responsibility for what happens to others— as well as to himself—because of those choices. If freedom does not include responsibility, it is ineffective as a basis for conduct, since it gives a person no measuring stick by which to judge the results of his conduct. Ideally, responsibility includes opportunities for an individual to make his own decisions, to handle his own money and time, to make his own friends and social adjustments.

With such a background, an individual gradually learns to meet emergencies and new situations with security, poise, and stability. As an aid to developing these qualities, he needs the knowledge that he is loved and cherished by his family group. A person is most fortunate if he has been brought up in a family that has known how to free him to develop, yet has stood by, a family that has looked ahead with genuine pride in his growth and has not held him back by its own too great satisfaction in holding onto him. It is this type of home influence that is most helpful to young people.

PERSONAL EXPERIENCES: HAPPY FAMILY LIFE

The importance of a happy home background is abundantly demonstrated by the following testimony given by young people. The statements that their homes had been among the most important influences in their lives become even more significant when we realize that many of these young people had been living away from home for two or three years at the time when they expressed this opinion. They had had an opportunity to look back with some objectivity on their lives with their families.

My father is a controlled sort of person. We're awfully close friends. In the matter of making decisions, he is very helpful. There's nothing I wouldn't tell father. Mother is very important in my life, too, but in quite a different way. She is impulsive and artistic and very lovable. She tries hard to fan my dying musical ambitions. I'm more like dad than she wishes I were, I think. I have three younger brothers of whom I'm terribly fond.

I don't get home very much but I do see quite a little of dad at his office. We're sort of in business together, you might say. I'll really be in with him next year. Father tries to act merely in an

advisory capacity, trying to get me to use my own judgment and
make my own decisions. He's not very well right now and we
children try to be as considerate of him as possible. I reserve
some time every week to play golf and swim with him. The
doctor says he needs it and if I make the definite appointment to
exercise, dad goes with me. Father is the head of the house, and
no mistake. I have a great respect and love for mother, but she
has never had a great deal to say because father is such a strong
character. This is the sort of father he is: When I was fourteen,
he created a trust fund of $25,000 for me. I've had my own
income from that time on. All checks have to be countersigned
by father, but he only asks me what the money is for and never
really questions my spending whatever I want. He has supervised my investments of the money, and under his clever guidance
I've increased the fund to about $40,000. Every day I see him
we go over financial reports together and he tells me what he
thinks is going to happen to various stocks in which we're interested. Recently, just before a big break in the market, he called
me up and told me to sell out everything. He's about the only
person I've heard of who guessed it so close. He really is quite a
remarkable man. He finished college at nineteen, having earned
every penny of his expenses and found time to be wrestling
champion. Dad is having me sit in on many of his business
conferences. I think he's about the smartest man in the world.
He's made college seem a bit insipid. I've majored in economics,
but I can't be expected to listen very seriously to what my
instructors have to say when I have the constant tutelage of a man
who really understands the economic system well enough to make
it sit up and take notice.

My family straightens me out when I get all mixed up. I had
a very radical instructor in my freshman year. I'd have been
bowled over if it hadn't been for dad and mother. I get a lot of
good from them by a process of osmosis all the time. A brother
who went through college just ahead of me has had a lot to do with
sobering me up when I needed it.

Father and mother maintain a definite tradition as to what a
member of our family should be expected to be and do. Our
whole family is pretty nonconformist, though. Father and
mother state their opinion, but we children have always done
pretty much as we pleased. I have two older brothers who are

not much concerned about public opinion. Their precedent has had considerable influence on me, I think. I've profited somewhat by some of their sad experiences.

My father seems to know just about everything. He leaves me pretty much alone, though, and just advises. Mother is quite an influence in social and practical ways. I've needed a lot of help along those lines because I used to have a severe case of inferiority feeling with regard to almost everything. This was probably due to a bad case of acne which I had for several years which made me self-conscious. My younger sister is here at school now. We have pretty much the same ideals and discuss everything with each other.

I suppose my love for my parents controls my conduct more than anything else. I have a younger brother whom I write once a week regularly. I hope I can be of some help to him. But I feel pretty sure that just at present I am getting more out of it than he is. I have a little sister twelve years old, too. I want her to be ideal. I write her frequently too—particularly about boy friends in whom she's beginning to be interested.

The influence of my home on me has always been very great. My mother is more interested in me than my father. I have three brothers and two sisters who are older and one younger sister. My brothers and sisters have had more influence on my development than either my father or mother. In fact, they are the most important influence I have had thus far. The influence of the older ones has certainly had an effect; and my attempt to influence my younger sister has been quite important.

My father and mother never dictate to me, even as regards the kind of friends I pick out, but they certainly do exercise an important influence. They control my environment to a large degree and thus, I suppose, they determine my standards. I have an older brother and a younger brother and a very irresponsible sister. I think that feeling a sense of responsibility for my younger brother and my irresponsible sister has had quite a steadying effect on me.

One boy who had returned only a few days before from his mother's funeral was, naturally, deeply affected by this experience, but well-poised and controlled withal. He said:

My home has probably been the strongest influence I've had. I have four brothers and all of us have always felt strong family ties. We've always had a habit when we were home of spending Sundays together off up in the mountains with a basket of lunch. It's done us all as much good as church could have. Dad has always given each of us a kind of companionship. We all feel closely in touch with him. From mother we've always had close companionship and friendship and help. We all know how she worked and sacrificed for us, but you could never get her to admit it. My two older brothers have certainly influenced me through companionship and admiration of them. I feel a real sense of responsibility to act as an example for my younger brothers. Then, too, my brothers have always felt perfectly free to criticize me for things of which they did not approve. I'm sure this has had some effect.

My family is by far the most powerful influence I've had during these years and before that. My parents tell me how they look at things and how they hope I'll look at them, but they let me decide for myself always. They never did punish me by other than a half hour to think things over. They haven't said "No" for many years. I try to make it unnecessary for them to. I haven't any brothers but I do have a sister. Because she could be popular and still stick to her ideals I didn't see why I couldn't too. She's spoiled a lot of dates for me because I compared her with other girls.

I feel almost as though mother and dad and I were contemporaries. There are no other children in my family. They've always made it a practice to talk everything over with me. We write each other frequently. They are my balance wheels.

My parents are real companions for us children. They are not authoritative but we can always go and talk things over with them.

My parents are French and Italian. I've had to teach them English. They don't understand my life but they are very sympathetic always. We have a most affectionate relationship. They have kept me in the practical, working world. It's good to keep one's feet on the ground.

When I came here to college, mother and daddy had a long talk and told me that they had been trying to do all they could for me and that my conduct here would reflect their training. Well, naturally, I try to do as well as I can by them. Daddy writes me quite frequently. One letter I had from him I shall always keep. It was especially helpful.

I talk things over with dad more than most boys do. Talking with me will be almost like quizzing my dad because I take most of my ideas from him. He's a policeman and a very observant man. He's invented some things. At least *I* think he's brainy; of course, he's my dad. He's very liberal-minded. He doesn't care what I do, but he wants me to think of what I'm doing and profit by the mistakes I'm bound to make. Mother always wants me to do right, but she doesn't try to tell me. I wouldn't hurt her for the world. I have two younger brothers and two younger sisters. I try to set them a good example. I suppose that's good for me.

My father and mother have quite an ideal relationship. I've become rather conscious of this during my last few years and I'm terribly thankful for it. Not every girl can feel so happy about her father and mother.

One boy who emphasized the importance his home had played in his development was the son of a widow, with one older sister. They had been desperately poor during the time he was in college. The boy had felt the keen sacrifice that his going to college had meant for his mother and sister and had worked desperately to increase the family finances all during college, wearing cheap, almost ragged clothes in order to be as economical as possible. He says he will never forget the evenings his sister and he met in the kitchen late at night, sitting on the edge of the kitchen table, drinking hot chocolate and eating crackers and talking.

PERSONAL EXPERIENCES: FAMILY LIFE WITH COMPLICATIONS

Some young people report less happy experiences with their families than those given above. Specific problems such as illness, a second marriage, or meager finances may complicate family relationships.

It is not surprising that the difference in age between young people and their parents is accompanied by differences in viewpoint. These differences are implied when a young person speaks of his parents as "strict" or "old-fashioned," or when he mentions "gaps between their ideas and mine." As a result, some young people have expressed themselves as being "disillusioned" about their parents. Others have felt that they had to choose between rebelling against them or "knuckling under" to them. It is often reassuring to the young person who is having difficulties at home to know that others among his contemporaries have found it necessary to take issue with their families. Opposing parental beliefs may seem very important to the young person who feels strongly about certain issues yet cannot stand by his own decision without opposing his family.

The following statements of young people describe or suggest certain difficulties that may arise within a family:

There are many ways in which I don't agree with mother and dad. They have set me a wonderful example, though, and I'd like to be as successful at living as they have been. They're pretty good at talking things over with me and reasoning things out with me. I had only one sister. She died two years ago. It affected me terribly. A friend talked to me and made me realize that I must be courageous and go on—that I must mean all the more to dad and mother on account of it.

I'm rather disillusioned about my parents. I've tried to get them to treat me like a responsible adult but just recently they failed to trust me with regard to a rather small thing. I hardly know whether to waste any more time on them or not.

We've had a rather mixed-up family. My father was seventy-eight when he died last month. He had been married before and had daughters old enough to be my aunts. Mother was about their age. My stepsisters were terribly opposed to mother when dad married her. She's had a lot to work out. Both father and mother have had a deep influence on my development; and I'd say that my stepsisters have, too.

My father and I have never been very close. My mother and I, on the contrary, have always been extremely close to each other. I guess I had a mother complex. During my sophomore year, my mother began to go through the change of life. She had an awful time with herself, poor dear. She went all to pieces and even turned against me sometimes. I used to go to the college physician for advice as to what under the sun to do. She persuaded me to live here at school in my junior year and to have my mother sent to a sanitarium. Mother was happier there because she had never liked father very well anyway. I went all to pieces myself after I moved into the dormitory. I got straightened out, however, largely through the help of the college physician. Mother got better and they let her come home. She committed suicide. I know I have to stand on my own now. I'm terribly dependent. I even have to have the approval of the girls on my corridor of the new shoes I get before I feel comfortable wearing them. They're kidding me out of it and I hope they succeed. I'm trying to get closer to father now. I think he and I could mean something to each other if he would only thaw out a bit.

My parents are the biggest influence I've had during these four years. They're Victorian type of folks. I'm a modern student trying to be modernistic. I go home every once in a while just to get checked up. My father is awfully strict with my two younger sisters. I doubt whether he can get away with it. I try to talk to him some about it and try to help my sisters to understand it and take it the right way. I thoroughly enjoy going home—more than anything else I do.

My family has awfully strict ideas about dancing and cards and sex. When I came up here, other ideas than theirs were suggested to me. I still maintain my strict standards with regard to relationships with men—tempered somewhat by advice I've had from the nice family with whom I live here—but I have gained my parents' consent to my participating in dancing and card playing, and think they add quite a bit to my fun. I don't know whether you'd say one of my older sisters has influenced me or not. She goes with an entirely different crowd and it has always been very helpful to me to watch them and get their different points of view.

Daddy isn't a college man, but he's had good experience with the world. I've thought a lot more of him and respected him a lot more in about the last two years than I ever did before. I ask him about quite a lot of things and respect his advice. Mother doesn't get out into the world the way daddy does. She didn't have a college education, either. I really can't look to her for much help. She has influenced me mostly through my feeling rather sorry for her that she can't play the role I'd like to with my daughter if I ever have one. I have a younger sister in high school. I think a lot about her future and wonder if she will have to go through all I have. I want very much to help her if I can only get myself straightened out.

Father's a hypochondriac. He's unconsciously influenced me to dislike that kind of thing very much. I am trying to make myself a better balanced individual. Mother has always preached doing what other people think is right. I've begun to question that absolute reliance on what other people think. In the past two weeks I've had some experiences that I think will eventually serve to make me more independent. My older brother has influenced me more than any other member of my family and more, I guess, than anything else I've known. He has very high ideals. Somehow he is able to criticize from an objective stand-point. I can take his criticism and I really want to please him.

My father is old-fashioned. One can't disagree with him without his getting excited. He's quite a trial to me at times. Mother has really helped me more than father. I have two older sisters and an older and a younger brother. I try to tell my little brother—especially—what he should do and be. Occasionally, I've had to do some tall thinking to try to see what I should advocate for him. I expect this has influenced me quite a lot.

My father was a conservative Frenchman. He was the protective sort. He had very definite ideas of right and wrong. My mother is French, too. She's extremely brilliant. She tried to bring me up according to Rousseau's *Emile*. She tried, in spite of my father, to give me freedom to experiment and make my own decisions about everything. Everything, that is, except sex, about which very definite taboos were rigorously maintained and with which absolutely no experimenting was to be done. I was even to work out the concept of honesty for myself. Last fall while driving father to business on my way to school our car was wrecked, he was killed, and I was badly hurt. I've been through a lot since then. I would say that certain of my teachers had helped me more in my recent struggles than my home, but both mother and father figure rather largely in the growth I have made.

I don't see much of father. Up until last year I was practically controlled by my mother and my sister, who is eight years older than I am. I've always idealized my sister. During this past year, I've deliberately tried to break away from my complete dependence on home. My study of psychology and being in love determined me to do this. I realized that I must learn to rely more on myself and not be so completely at the mercy of my mother and sister. Psychology really deserves the credit for the development I have achieved during the past year, but my home has played an important part, too.

My father died when I was quite young. Mother is a physician but she gave up her practice to devote her life to me. She thinks she handles me pretty subtly, but I understand her pretty well now. I don't tell her too much because it would worry her. She'd devote herself to me even harder. She really means well but I'd be glad if she married again. She's given me plenty to think about and really put me more on my own than if she hadn't taken such an overwhelming interest in me.

My family are orthodox Jewish. I conform but I do not consider myself an adherent. I conform simply out of consideration for my home. I hesitate to take any drastic step until I am older because to me it is a deep philosophical problem. My brother, who is a year older, takes the same attitude. He tries not to influence me with regard to it. He's quite a wonderful boy.

My whole family have always been farmers, but I wanted to study medicine. I had to almost break with them to come here. I've been entirely self-supporting for six years. My family is partially reconciled now. It has made me very careful and conservative, knowing that I was acting against their wishes and judgment and that I couldn't have them to fall back on

My father married my mother against his family's wishes. My mother came from a sort of *nouveau riche* family. Her folks were all for the match. Mother died when I was seven years old.

I'm living with dad's family now. They think they are very aristocratic and they do have a long family tradition. They've had financial reverses, though. My grandparents are strong-minded people, to say the least. The women in the family are more strong-minded than the men, if possible. But I'm one of the women and I'm strong-minded, too. I really get along with both sides pretty successfully simply by being independent. My younger brother doesn't get along so well and I have to fight a lot of his battles for him. I'm sure the influence of my family life is the most powerful one I have had."

Father is very conformist, nonaggressive, and retiring. He's not a money-maker. He has checked my tendency to rashness considerably. I used to be conservative like father, but I've changed considerably. It worries father because he thinks I get off the track a little—for instance, in my socialistic tendencies. Mother has a mind and ideas like father's, but she is more aggressive. Both father and mother let me do about as I wish. I'd displease father with fewer compunctions than I would mother. My brother, four years older, is a big influence on me. He worked for several years and then worked his way entirely through college. He's an architect now. He's terribly anxious for me to make good.

There have been some pretty serious gaps between my home and myself. I have no brothers and sisters. I think I've become more tolerant of my home, due to college influence. I don't particularly admire either my father or my mother. Father has never had a salary of more than $3,000, and we've gone through some pretty difficult times together. Conflicts with regard to my feeling about home and father and mother have kept me in constant turmoil. In the studying I have done here at college I've found quite a bit of help for my trouble. My home certainly has been a big influence in my development through these past years.

My father and mother exercise a sort of restraining influence. They try to modify my career always to conform to their desires. They succeed to some extent, but I always have a sense of sitting back and watching what they try to do to me. It's kind of funny. I have an older brother who is a peach. He takes a friendly interest in me.

My father is the sort of man who is really in control of his home. I admire him very much. He is a patriarch. He and mother and I had some difficulty about a girl I was in love with last year. It upset dad some not to have me knuckle under but it did me a lot of good not to.

I've one older and one younger brother. The older one began drinking when he was about fourteen. He flunked out of one college, but finished at another. He and I have traveled a good deal together. He's really very brilliant. Dad thinks he'll come out all right. He isn't very much interested in business, though. My younger brother and I are better friends. He's crazy about horses and not much else. He's very lovable. We boys have had mighty good times together.

Well, we've been through quite a lot together but we all try to stand on our own feet. Mother has worked for 15 years. My sister worked her way through high school and then took a nursing course. She's made good, too. Father was hit pretty badly by the financial depression. In addition he has had to have two operations. My mother and sister have influenced me especially, I think. They have been the ones who have held me to college when it seemed pretty hard. I'm getting through in three and a half years. In addition, I've been entirely self-supporting. I started in with a debt of $140, but I've cut that down to $50 and have bought a small piece of property in addition. I want to do as well, if I can, as my sister has. She gives me advice every once in a while but only if I ask for it. Then she gives it to me straight and makes me like it, too.

One boy who said that his home had been of great importance during college years lived in a dormitory, although his home was in the same town. This boy, Charles, evinced a very strong sense of rebellion against his parents. He said that he had put up just as many barriers as he could between himself and his family; had tried to be just as independent as possible. He usually went home Sunday noon to dinner, got some money, left as soon as he could to see his girl, and after that returned to the dormitory. Just recently he had had a phone call telling him of the dangerous illness of his mother. He had had to go home, take charge;

see to getting her to the hospital, and notify his father, who was out of town on a trip.

Now his mother was recovering, and already the boy and his father and mother were having some really good talks. He was finding that they were not so opposed as he had thought to the girl of his choice but that they very much wished he would take one year's study at business school before going into business, marrying, and settling down. Charles felt that his father and mother were a little too shut off from each other. He was beginning to acknowledge a strong attachment for his little sister, who was a diabetic. He seemed to be more willing to take some sense of responsibility for his family, and he was coming to acknowledge that they did deserve some consideration, that his former struggle was puerile and cowardly, and that he need not fear them as he had thought he must.

PERSONAL EXPERIENCES: MORE DIFFICULT FAMILY SITUATIONS

In some homes, young people face even more difficult problems than those mentioned in the preceding section. Parents may be unhappy together—they may even refuse to speak to each other. A young person may find that if he is to create an opportunity to fulfill his ambitions, he must make a complete break with his family. Some young persons feel that they are hindered by domination; others resent overprotection on the part of their parents.

Such experiences can, however, prove valuable in the end. One young person said, "I suppose my struggles have made me stronger—they certainly have made me wiser."

In spite of the tragedy suggested by some of the following statements, it is reassuring to see that even in situations as difficult as some of these, the young person has, in most cases, been able to keep an objective viewpoint.

The relationship between my parents is tense. They don't talk to each other for months. The effect of this on us children, of course, is great. My father disapproves of any college education for me. I have felt rather frightened all along of what he might do and I've a sense all the time that I must show him it is the right thing for me to be here. I have six younger brothers and sisters. I have been worried about myself; and I haven't been able to do much for them.

My father always attempted to dominate me by companionship. I gradually grew up and resented his clever domination. He is no longer my hero as he once was. He resents this and says it is all my fault. Mother is pretty much occupied with trying to "express herself," as she says, but she has helped out in the trouble with my father. We may get things straightened out eventually, but I want things on a different basis than they have been.

I've just been through a rather serious illness. Father and mother have been very complicating factors. They nagged me and nagged me about my health until I tried to totally disregard how I did feel. I never want to live at home again. They feel they were at fault in not getting me to a physician sooner. I have to defend myself vigorously from their too-kind ministrations. I have hated my father since my twelfth year. During my illness he used to figure in my nightmares and still does. I want to be like anything but what he is. I get along with mother very well except that I have to lock myself in my room to get her to promise not to harp on how I feel and how my heart is acting. I have a lot of relatives who seem to revolve around the state of my health.

None of us is very happy at home. I used to weep over the home situation. Perhaps the thing that is wrong is that there is no religion in my home and Jewish families are usually held together by religion. My brother and I are always glad when we don't have to go home. We have never had any discipline in our home. We could always have everything we wanted. But things weren't right. I have a strong emotional attachment to my mother but it only serves to make me unhappy. I'm very fond of my brother. He and I sometimes talk very frankly about the ways things are. I never have talked with anyone else about it. Mother wanted me to study medicine but I didn't want to and I made terrible grades. My brother went to law school and he persuaded me to switch to that. I've done very well since I changed to prelaw. College has been the happiest four years of my life. It has been a place of refuge for me.

All during high school I was far too much in the control of my family. Why, up to the time I was almost twelve mother had me wearing white sox and little Lord Fauntleroy clothes! When I came up here I made a big fight to get away from home. I feel that I have. I've tried to get across to my parents that their policy must be one of hands off. My mother has always tried to shelter me and safeguard me to an extreme. Part of it may be due to the fact that I used to stammer badly and she felt I needed her protection. I've spent four years freeing myself from their control. Incidentally, with the help of a teacher here, I've cured myself of stammering. I have a younger sister who is very pretty, and who gets into jams quite frequently. I have tried consciously to act as peacemaker between the younger and older generations. I think that a lot of my sister's conduct is an unconscious protest against the hovering my mother wants to do all the time.

Yes, I guess my home has had some influence. I haven't had a great deal of contact with it for seven or eight years and never want to much again. I come from the hard-coal region of Pennsylvania. My father is a coal miner. The whole community and my home are not the sort of things I enjoy. I love mother; she can't help the ways things are. I have five brothers and sisters. I've kind of lost touch with them. If things hadn't been so bad at home, I would never have had the incentive to get out and come here and work the way I've had to in order to get through college on my own hook. My home gave me a taste of a kind of living that isn't worth the name. I wouldn't say that home had been one of the paramount influences during these four years, but it certainly can't be overlooked.

A girl who had tried to commit suicide told about the experience dispassionately. She had been a member of a family of eight children. The parents were very much interested in all their children, loved them, tried hard to make them happy, strong members of society. Each child had always had an allowance—a very small one, to be sure, but the parents had wanted each to learn the value of money. From an early age, each child had been allowed to decide for himself, for instance, whether to spend part of his allowance for a movie or to forego the movie in the interest of getting some new shoes that would be needed later.

This girl had thought that she would be able to work her way through college, because she did know how to economize, and she was considered competent and self-reliant. At the end of her sophomore year, however, she was simply so weary and discouraged that she didn't see how she could carry on any longer. She had managed to support herself and had, by a great expenditure of energy, made good grades, but she never had any money, could never dress well, and was so tired that she could not see what difference it all made anyway.

At the beginning of her summer vacation she decided quite coldly—not as the result of an emotional crisis—to commit suicide, whereupon she stopped eating and began to take small doses of poison. At the end of three days she was very ill, and her family called a physician, who discovered what she had been doing. Her family begged her to get well and told her that she would not need to go on trying so hard, that she could do anything she wanted to. She finally did get well, and her family managed to send her to Paris for a trip. She doesn't study so hard any more— although she does write extra papers for one course she is interested in. She isn't earning any money, and she has a sense that her family is happier for being allowed to provide her with money.

Significance of These Experiences

There can be no doubt of the sincerity of the statements quoted. On the basis of this evidence it is apparent that the home has by no means ceased to have a determining influence on the development of personality during the years of late adolescence. It is interesting to note the variety of ways in which these young people say that their homes have furthered their development. The most effective influence that a home can wield seems to be that which emanates from parents who give independence, freedom, and responsibility, yet stand by as advisers. Equally

important for an individual's development seems to be
the fact that he is attempting to influence or to be an
example to younger brothers and sisters.

Another type of influence that binds young people to
their homes is admiration, respect, and love for their
parents and a desire not to hurt or to fail them. This kind
of control might be termed undesirable by psychologists
who feel that, although it is well to have individuals
influenced by consideration for others, such influence should
not constitute control. When, for example, an individual
unquestioningly accepts orders from his parents who dictate
exactly what he is to do or think, his development is
probably hampered rather than furthered. Fortunately,
this type of relationship is probably unusual; it was mentioned only a few times in the statements quoted.

Older brothers and sisters who are admired and from
whom help and criticism is sought or accepted also contribute to adjustment. However, many individuals state
that they have matured more by attempting to influence
younger brothers and sisters than by following the advice
and example of older brothers and sisters.

The fact that they either do or do not have a happy home,
a happy relationship within the home, and the companionship of their parents is very significant to these young
people. An important relationship apparently can as surely
be built by means of conversations over crackers and cocoa
in the kitchen as it can through lessons in economics and the
management of a trust fund, judging by what these young
people say. It is the quality of a relationship that is
significant for a person's growth.

According to these descriptions, many young people are
having an experience of rebellion and struggle against their
homes, and for many their homes are a source of deep
concern. In a few cases, there is absolute, direct control of
the individual and of the environment by the parents.
In such cases, rebellion is not surprising. Studies of late
adolescence have shown that such relationships are to be
expected and even desired when parental control is over-

strong at this time.[1] Struggles against their homes are often interpreted by these young people as contributing to their growth, since struggles force them to evolve ideals and life plans of their own.

A declaration of independence by young adults is a rather frequent occurrence. It is extremely difficult for parents to know how to give a young person enough freedom to make rebellion unnecessary, yet not to give too much freedom or to give it so fast that the individual's security is undermined. Parents who grant a sufficient amount of freedom and independence and are successful in getting young people to assume responsibility for themselves by that very process seem to avert open rebellion.

Although a person may question occasionally whether the home has been as good an influence on his development as he might have wished, there can be no question of its importance in bringing about whatever state of development he has attained. There are necessary hazards in growing from childhood to maturity; often grave importance can be attached to seemingly insignificant outcomes of a person's attempts at adjustment. For example, the ultimate effects of someone's experience of defeat and the sense of inferiority engendered by it may often be so serious and permanent as to affect an individual's estimate of himself from that time on.

SPECIAL PROBLEMS OF ADJUSTMENT

Since it is often from the viewpoint of his family's customs, habits, attitudes, and standards that an individual interprets the world around him, it is important to examine in detail the types of relationships that young people have with their parents, the attitudes that their

[1] HOLLINGWORTH, LETA S., *Psychology of the Adolescent*, D. Appleton-Century Company, Inc., New York, 1928.

TAYLOR, KATHARINE WHITESIDE, *Do Adolescents Need Parents?* D. Appleton-Century Company, Inc., New York, 1938.

WILLIAMS, FRANKWOOD E., *Adolescence: Studies in Mental Hygiene*, Farrar & Rinehart, Inc., New York, 1930.

parents display toward each other, the effect on the young person of the size of the family, of its social, economic, cultural, and racial background.

At birth the family provides the entire environment of an individual. Certainly life does begin at home, and most of us are in the main what our homes make us, even though home may provide an example of what we do not want to become rather than an example that we wish to imitate. Nevertheless, in the home the unformed complex of possibilities first makes its appearance. Here the processes of development and direction begin to work. The outlines and limits may become so fixed during the time when the home is the dominating influence that only minor changes within these limits and outlines are possible as one grows up.

Although the home may not change, mature adjustment demands that the individual be prepared to live in a world of change. This can be accomplished by living fully and satisfactorily at each stage of development, by living in the midst of change in such a way that habits and attitudes for meeting it are developed. At times, however, parents and home conditions make this development difficult.

At some time during the years between sixteen and twenty-four most individuals leave home to go to school, to start a vocational career, or to establish homes of their own. This change often means that a person is taken from an environment to which he has become more or less adjusted into an environment in which he may find that he lacks habits and attitudes necessary for adaptation to customs that are acceptable there. If an individual finds that he does not possess the habits and attitudes that will help him to find satisfaction for his basic desires in ways approved in the new environment, then either he must learn quickly how to satisfy those needs and desires—how to realize his ambitions in ways acceptable to the new group —or he can expect to find himself rejected by the group.

Everyone encounters problems in the process of adjustment simply because each of us is the product of a particular environment, an environment that is not alike for any two individuals, even in the same family. Our total range of experiences has made us what we are to date, has conditioned us to what we may be able to accomplish. For each of us, a life pattern has developed out of interests and purposes, habits and attitudes, interrelated with the satisfactions, frustrations, and tensions of a social setting. This life pattern determines the direction of the future.

Unfortunately, some people who have adjusted most perfectly to their early environments find it very difficult to vary their behavior patterns or to adapt them to new situations. Their most severe difficulties usually arise at the points where the new environment differs most from the old, at the places where they are unable to accept the new ideas, circumstances, and habits of living, or where they are unable to develop a satisfactory outlet for their basic needs. For example, a person may be so conservative that he cannot make friends with a new group because he feels too keenly that he is different from its members.

When a young person is attempting to make adjustments that will help to make him more independent of his family, conflicts of one kind or another are almost inevitable. For example, when there is illness or economic strain in the family, a conflict may arise between the good of the family group and that of the young person as an individual. A family's social or cultural limitations may bring about in the children a sense of inferiority that makes them fear to leave the protection of their homes. Some young people feel that overprotective or oversolicitous parents have made them overdependent on home contacts and therefore bewildered and uncertain before new problems. Others feel that resistance by parents to new ideals and religious beliefs— parental insistence on the old—has driven them to open rebellion.

Whatever difficulties are involved in accomplishing it, a mature adjustment to one's family is important for personality development. There should be the kind of mutual respect and consideration in which parents and young people see one another as persons with interests and ambitions and adjustments to make, some of them apart from family responsibilities. Under such conditions, each person involved is able to permit the others to grow.

Since our problems are always related to our earlier experiences, what constitutes a problem for one person may be a familiar situation to someone else. The degree of difficulty that one has in adjusting in a new situation is in proportion to the amount and quality of his previous experience in meeting similar situations.

We recognize as a problem anything that thwarts or blocks us in our attempts to secure what we want or need. The seriousness of the problem is determined by the type and power of the drive involved and by the difficulty of its solution. It was stated earlier that problems, as such, are not disadvantageous, since they may necessitate a type of effort and achievement conducive to growth. But if there are too many problems or if they are too difficult, then we may be overwhelmed by them; we may yield to discouragement, even to defeat. We may be driven to desperation and find ourselves doing ridiculous things at which even we are surprised. Or we may live on at a low level of efficiency, constantly unhappy because we feel that we have failed to develop our potentialities, confused and misled by the overwhelming multiplicity of problems.

No one can meet, without bewilderment, too much newness at once. In order to adjust successfully in any new situation, an individual must have learned, consciously or unconsciously, the technique of adjustment. He must know how to analyze a problem; he must have had opportunities to explore facts relative to it, to consider various ways in which it can be met, then to come to his own decision and abide by its consequences.

To turn first to the behavior that previously brought the desired result is characteristic of most people. The momentum of habits and attitudes that a person has developed early in life carries on. The life pattern that he has evolved determines not only the quality of his adult adjustment but also the degree to which he is fitted for adulthood. In order to get along successfully and "be his age" in an effective way, a person must seize every opportunity to develop positive, constructive ways of attacking problems to replace infantile techniques such as evasion, withdrawal, aggression, or various other forms of compensation. Every new situation can serve as an opportunity to improve techniques of adjustment.

MOTIVES FOR PARENTAL CONTROL

Some parents are able to stand back and watch their children grow up. However, many parents express their deep concern for the welfare of their children by attempting to retain control of some kind over them. These parents may, for example, believe that they are protecting the young people from harm if they can force them to behave in certain ways that the parents believe are right and best for them.

This attempted control may be prompted by a variety of motives, perhaps a desire to make life as happy as possible for the children or a reluctance to let young people face a world that parents have found cruel and harsh. Whatever the reason is, it usually arises from a deep love. Consciousness of this fact will help young people to understand and respond sympathetically to what those less wise might call unfair discipline. Moreover, the fact that they are the objects of this affection should give them a deep security. We all need the assurance that somewhere we belong, are wanted and valued for ourselves, no matter what we may do or be. We need the stability that probably can best be provided within the family. Emotional development usually suffers when a person has been uprooted from his family group.

Young people are, therefore, acting maturely when, in response to questionable disciplinary measures used on them by parents, they do not rebel or make their home life unpleasant but instead learn from whatever they experience in their homes. In this way, they establish and maintain as cordial relations as possible between themselves and their parents.

Parents who desire most earnestly the happiness of their children are often the ones who demand unthinking obedience. Many of them are fearful of the world that young people are entering because they themselves have found it not altogether pleasant. They believe that they know what young people should do to avoid difficulties; they think that they can show them the road to happiness. They do not want young people to be as unhappy as they have sometimes been. Therefore parents attempt to choose for young people their friends, their schools, their churches, and sometimes even their vocations and their life partners. They ask of young people a blind adherence to ideals and standards that they dictate. They feel that young people have not the wisdom that their parents, the church, or these ideals represent. Because the parents are sincere in this belief, they may even hurt or shame a young person into obedience. The whole structure of their lives is built around the wisdom that they have accumulated and have expressed by means of these ideals or beliefs. They make no preparation for young people ever to become independent of outside authority.

Other parents who themselves are unhappy may need desperately to feel necessary to someone if they are to believe that their lives are worth living. This feeling may arise because two parents are incompatible, because parents have so completely built their lives around their children that they have few interests outside their homes, because they feel that their failure to meet certain goals may be atoned for in their children's success. Such parents desire to keep a young person dependent on them as long as possible; they find real joy in making the young person's decisions, in helping him to solve his problems.

It is natural for such parents to give children too much care. From the time they go out to play, the parents may literally fight their battles for them—allow the children to come in crying if their feelings have been hurt or if they have not been given their own way. Even after young people are in college or in vocations of their own, the parents may still choose clothes for them, may worry about the amount of money they must live on, or may be overly concerned about the state of their health. Overprotection makes for unhealthy dependence of the young people on their parents. It is so easy for young people to live in this way and to accept the parents' continued control. It temporarily simplifies life when one is not forced to make decisions; then often, when difficulties arise, one can fall back on the alibi, "It wasn't my fault; mother or father told me to do it."

Some parents exercise control over young people by appealing to their sympathy and love. There are a few cases where a parent requests a young person to do or not to do or to be something that the parent wishes, merely because refusal to conform to the parent's demands will hurt the parent's feelings, cause a sick headache or a heart attack. This kind of appeal makes it very difficult for a young person to weigh an action or to make a decision on an objective basis. It tends to blind him to more important implications of his decision when he considers not, "Shall I marry this man?" or, "Shall I leave home to take this job?" but, "Would it hurt mother or father too much if I married or if I left home?"

Occasionally we hear of parents who constantly remind young people of the debt that they owe because of the parents' early care of them, because of the sacrifices that parents made for them. One young person stated that she had even begun to feel that her parents considered her merely as an investment for their old age; the idea was kept constantly before her that she must discharge her debt to her parents by taking care of them. Parents do give a great deal to their children, but many parents feel that the joy and satisfaction that they gain from the child in the process of his growing up has discharged that debt.

Too much parental pressure may imperil a young person's power of decision and his belief in the soundness of his judgments unless he is constantly on guard. Each decision that a young person makes should be made primarily on its own merits, on the basis of what is best or right for all concerned, not on the basis of an emotional appeal from a parent. The latter method of making decisions may be responsible for developing unwarranted feelings of guilt in later life.

Unsatisfactory Ways of Responding to Discipline

To any form of discipline that involves domination, young people may respond in several ways. They may rebel constantly. When this becomes the pattern of behavior at home, it soon becomes a habit, and overaggressiveness characterizes all of the individual's relationships. This sort of person is always fighting because he never seems to be able to finish the quarrel begun at home. Such individuals are not happy. They feel guilty about their behavior and insecure about their lack of adjustment in their family groups.

Other young people may seem to conform to imposed discipline. Yet their submissiveness hides cynicism. Their ideas and decisions—even they themselves—"did not count at home," they will say. They have been humiliated or scoffed at. They have lost their initiative, their fighting qualities. They cannot be certain that they will ever amount to anything because they have had no opportunity to develop confidence in themselves.

Still other young persons may set out to fail because they think that in this way they can punish those who forced them to do something that they did not wish to do. There are instances of individuals failing in occupations chosen for them by their parents. Many of these failures are caused by reasons other than lack of ability. Even a marriage sometimes fails because a young person has been induced to marry someone who is the parent's choice.

Consciously setting out to fail is, of course, a means of evading the issue at hand. Other evasive reactions are blaming someone else, lying, and developing the capacity to be ill when something difficult should be done. None of these evasive responses is adequate in meeting situations. Nor does such behavior tend to build up an individual's respect and confidence in himself. On the contrary, its repetition brings on the habit of evading rather than facing difficulties. Thus the person is gradually robbed of the best method for learning his own ability—through the process of actually meeting and solving problems as they come up.

These types of responses are displays of emotions that belong to the infantile stage. They are poor ways of meeting the problem of discipline. Behavior such as this may eventually lead to a break between the young person and his family. It should be kept in mind that to break immaturely with his family is usually dangerous to a young person's stability. Because of the break, he may develop a sense of guilt that will bind him to his family more firmly than even their domination of him could.

ESTABLISHING ONE'S INDEPENDENCE ON A SOUND BASIS

By the time a young person has reached his twenties, it is important that his relationship with his father and mother be fairly well established on a basis quite different from the one that was effective when he was in his teens. This new relationship should be one of genuine companionship, one in which adult meets adult on a basis of comparative equality, in which there is no longer any need on anyone's part to attempt or accept domination. The infantile ways of reacting must be replaced by ways that will bring permanent satisfaction.

Young people often need to take the initiative in establishing this new relationship. They may attempt to understand why parents resort to a particular kind of discipline. They may try to work out with their parents better ways of dealing with difficulties; for example, they may use their

influence to develop in the home a habit of periodic family
discussions. During these meetings, things that may be
causing tension within the group are considered—the use
of the living room, the car, or the radio, the doing of household chores, the fair disposition of the fam ly budget,
friends or ideas considered by the parents to be unacceptable
or dangerous. Any member of the family is allowed to
present his grievances, desires, or problems; and the entire
family group attempts honestly and intelligently to bring
about an adjustment. Every member of the family is free to
take part in the discussion; no one person dominates it. As a
result of this process, not only does every individual in the
family feel that, at least, his wants and needs have been
made known and given fair consideration but, also, parents
and young people find that there is less need to attempt to
solve problems in some arbitrary manner.

If parents and young people habitually discuss their
problems, trying earnestly to understand all points of view,
then discipline no longer need be imposed by some outside
compulsion, such as a parent's demand for obedience.
Discipline becomes inherent in an experience itself; it comes
as the inevitable consequence of each person's action. To
the first kind of discipline young people may respond with
a desire to get even with the parents who punish them
when they do not obey. This kind of discipline may become
to young people merely a symbol of the parents' irritation,
disappointment, or frustration at the conduct of the young
person. The second kind of discipline—being forced to
accept the inevitable consequences of his action—the young
person recognizes as fair. He soon learns to profit by his
mistakes; he uses that knowledge to prevent his making the
same mistake again.

Too much parental discipline is perhaps a great deal more
common than too little control. However, the latter situation can cause equally trying complications. Some parents
say that they do not care, for example, when and how young
people use the car, whether or not they drink, what they

believe about relationships with the other sex, what life values they wish to make their own. This viewpoint may be a result not of failure to take responsibility but of a conviction that young people should find their own way unguided. It may result from an eagerness to keep the children from being inhibited. In some cases, perhaps, it indicates merely a lack of action or philosophy on the part of the parents.

As a result, young people are often forced to make decisions about which they have too little knowledge, to take responsibilities that they have not been trained to assume. Young people need for security whatever amount of care from parents is necessary to give them a stable, consistent environment. External control psychologically precedes and is necessary for internal control. The baby, for example, must be put to bed. Gradually, the areas for internal control are widened: a child learns to take care of himself, to choose the clothes he will wear, even to stay in bed when he feels ill.

Young people know that they need some guidance as they are learning. They seek and respect the help of adults when it is offered in a cooperative spirit. Young people seek out the adult who will, as one boy put it, "give me six or seven sides of a question and then let me make up my own mind."

Making Choices

That young people in their twenties should make many of their own decisions is generally agreed. The question arises, however, as to how the transition should be made from the stage of development during which parents and teachers say "you must" or "you must not." Everyone should begin early to learn how to choose in small matters; making important decisions later will then come more naturally.

One must be able to take the responsibility for the consequences of his decisions. Moreover, before one can be effectively free, one must pay the price of freedom in training and discipline of himself. For example, if he stays out late the night before an important tennis match, he has no right to bemoan his loss of the match. If he fails an examination because he preferred attending a dance to studying, he must accept the verdict. If he was speeding, was caught, and was fined particularly heavily because there was liquor on his breath, he must face the connection between liquor and driving a car. Punishment that is just and consistent with the act must be recognized as the inevitable consequence of an ill-advised action.

Before making a choice, it is important to know the restrictions involved in the situation. For instance, young people attending a church school whose endowment will exist only as long as dancing is forbidden cannot choose to have a dance unless they will also choose to raise an endowment. A family cannot make the decision as to whether they will smoke at a summer camp where they are staying if the local fire laws forbid smoking. When a situation is entered into, the rules that govern it must also be accepted.

Before young people make a choice, they need to ask themselves, "What is it that I really want?" Suppose that a young person's parents are choosing his friends because, they complain, his choices are poor. By the time that he leaves home every person must be ready to select his own friends. Therefore, he needs experience in knowing all kinds of people. In the process, it is not at all unusual for him to choose for a friend someone whom his parents consider the wrong person.

What is the real issue involved in this choice? In the process of growing toward maturity, one person may see in another qualities or abilities that he would like to possess. Until he possesses them or until he gains the confidence that he can possess them, he may choose as friends people who represent what he would like to become. Therefore, we need to ask ourselves in regard to a friend, "What is it in me that he appeals to?" If we are interested in gaining a name in football, campus activities, or music, we may be very proud of our friendship with the football captain in spite of the fact that he has bad manners, with a person well-known for his campus activities in spite of the fact that he is conceited and overaggressive, or with a girl who is an excellent violinist, although she lives on the "wrong side of the tracks." When we are looking for something specific in an individual, it is inevitable that we shall overlook certain other things that may be important to other people.

Parents would probably be greatly relieved if they remembered that, when we once achieve our goals or gain the confidence that we can achieve them, then, if our friends really are the wrong kind, we shall naturally drift apart, since we no longer need that kind of friends to bolster us. It would be well for all of us to ask ourselves occasionally whether our friends are stimulating us to struggle toward our own achievements. Unless this is happening, we are probably not making the best of our new-found freedom.

Does freedom mean having everything that we want? Mature people realize that they cannot have everything they want, and that, inevitably, more privileges are accompanied by more responsibilities. They know, too, that their privileges end where rights of others begin; that, for example, if they live in an apartment, they must consider the bedtime of the families above and below them when they plan their parties.

INDEPENDENCE MUST BE LEARNED

The goals in the psychological weaning of the young person from his parents have been described in the two preceding sections. It would be a mistake, however, to assume that developing independence is a simple process. An individual has to learn gradually to do the things required of an adult, such as acquiring the ability to weigh relative values, making his own decisions, expressing his own opinions, and finding answers for himself to questions in the field of vocations, relationships with the opposite sex, and life values.

The process is complicated by the fact that both the young person and his parents are combinations of opposing tendencies. Each wants to do two things at once, to "eat his cake and have it, too." Parents want the young person to become an adult, yet they regret losing their baby. They want him to take responsibility for himself, yet they fear what may happen to him if he does. They wish to have him make his own decisions, yet they are apprehensive because he may make a wrong decision; and they know how serious can be the results of some wrong decisions.

Young people often shift uncertainly between their desire to grow up independently and their desire to have someone protect them from themselves, between their enthusiasm for and their utter indifference to work that has to be done, between their self-confidence and their self-deprecia- tion, between their desire to work and their desire to be lazy, between their happiness and their depressions, between their vows to altruism and their total selfishness, between their sensitivity and their hardheartedness. Decisions that a person is forced to make begin to give him a working stability. They become an intellectual framework in which thinking can be done, an emotional framework against which to evolve ideals.

The problem of psychological weaning involves, then, both young people and their parents. It cannot be avoided unless a person is to remain emotionally immature and dependent like the young married woman for example, who trusts her own decisions so little that her mother must manage her home or like the young married man who finds satisfaction in criticizing his wife to his mother. Becoming independent of one's family does not, however, presuppose open warfare with them or even leaving home. It involves a relationship in which parents and young people treat one another as responsible adults, each with interests, desires, and abilities of his own, and the capacity to handle the fulfillment of them intelligently.

If parents and young people have gradually adjusted their relationships on the basis of the young person's growing into adulthood, then there is no sudden or final transition. All can live together happily, consulting one another, to be sure, confiding in one another, but each trusting the other to take charge of his own life. Respectful comradeship has been substituted for dependence.

Such a relationship is facilitated if young people can demonstrate to their parents that they have attained a sufficient sense of responsibility that their parents need not feel too concerned for them. Young people have not yet assumed responsibility for themselves when they have merely replaced the authority of their parents with dependence on the dictates of their social group—when, for example, they adopt excessive swearing, smoking, drinking, late hours, and excuse themselves for following certain behavior patterns because "all the gang does." They cannot rely on themselves. They have merely substituted the group's commands for their parents'; and they are probably obeying the dictates of the former even more slavishly than they ever obeyed those of their parents. These young people have no steadiness or security; they have not learned to make decisions for themselves. It is not to be wondered at that parents fear for them and attempt to continue to control them. Parents know that they have not yet learned self-control.

Young people who in late adolescence become skeptics in religious matters or radical in political beliefs may also be immature. They are usually merely protesting against whatever has been accepted in their home. They may be taking this way of declaring their independence of their home, their desire to think for themselves. It is well for them to do so, provided they take the next difficult step and attempt gradually to work out a life philosophy that they can accept. However, if they merely embrace hur-

riedly another creed, code, or political belief, they are again
demonstrating that they have not grown up. They are
testifying to the fact that they must remain dependent on
something. Or if they work out nothing for themselves, if
they merely continue all their lives rebelling without
attempting to make any contribution on the constructive
side, they thereby betray immaturity.

Equally immature is the young person who asks no
questions, who continues, as one girl stated, to accept her
parents' decisions as her own—to believe that the world
actually is as her parents see it. Such an individual may
sometime wish fervently to find out for herself what the
world is all about. No automaton mechanically obeying
directions can have as good a time in life as a human being
who will take the responsibility for his own life, even though
this involves taking risks.

Very often a young person quite sincerely disagrees with
his parents in his appraisal of a decision or a belief. Then
he needs sympathetic understanding and help in getting at
all the facts available on which to base an eventual decision.
He needs to be sure that he has explored all possible positions. If he is allowed to come to a decision gradually in a
sympathetic atmosphere in which he feels no compulsion to
make certain kinds of decisions or to adopt a certain belief,
he is more likely to decide wisely and rationally. And,
painful though it is when a young person finds that he must
disagree with his parents, it may comfort him to know that
he who has the courage of his convictions may in the last
analysis be a stronger person and more respected than he
who unquestioningly accepts the opinions of others.

Let no individual suppose, however, that the decisions
that he makes or the beliefs that he professes at any given
time must necessarily be permanent. If an individual
would be mature, he will think of these conclusions as the
best at which he can arrive at the time, but as subject to
revision in the light of new experiences. His explanation
of this point of view to his parents may comfort them and

reassure them concerning his maturity. What is important is that he himself has made his decisions and is willing to abide by the consequences.

ATTITUDES TOWARD ONE'S FAMILY BACKGROUND

That young people sometimes allow themselves to feel inferior or frustrated because of their family background was evident from some of the statements given earlier in the chapter. However, few of us escape family difficulties of some kind or degree. Let us look at statistical evidence suggesting a few characteristics of our society.

The United States census for 1930 indicated that of the youth between the ages of sixteen and twenty-four almost 81 per cent were not in school. Studies have shown that many of these young people are no longer in school because it was economically impossible for them to continue. For example, in Maryland, economic reasons accounted for 54 per cent of the withdrawals from school.[1] In the year preceding June, 1936, one person in eight of the young people studied had received some form of public or private relief.[2] During this same period between 40 and 45 per cent of the sixteen- to twenty-four-year-old population were unemployed.[3] The 1930 census shows that almost 30 per cent of the youth of sixteen years to twenty-four years are of foreign parentage and that almost 13 per cent are Negroes. The large families, in general, are those with the least economic security. It is reported that in one year during the depression 233,822 children were born to families on relief.[3] The percentage of homes broken by the death of one parent is between 25 and 28 per cent. In 1935, there were 218,000 divorces, or almost one for every five

[1] BELL, HOWARD M., *Youth Tell Their Story*, p. 64, American Council on Education, Washington, D. C., 1938.

[2] RAINEY, HOMER P., and others, *How Fare American Youth?* p. 137, D. Appleton-Century Company, Inc., New York, 1937.

[3] BELL, *op. cit.*, p. 13.

marriages.[1] President Roosevelt says that one-third of the
nation is ill housed. Many individuals have never enjoyed
proper public health or recreation facilities.

These statistics suggest conditions that make for difficult
adjustments on the part of many young people. For example, when the family has no assurance that the standard of
living that it regards as necessary will be maintained,
tension results. Lack of privacy, noise, and difficulty in
keeping out of one another's way are some of the inevitable
results of living in crowded quarters. These conditions
may produce quarreling. The question arises as to how to
meet the situation. Contributing to the tension and joining
in the quarreling are one way, but the situation is not so
hopeless. The members of the family might sit down
together and talk over grievances. For example, a schedule
might be worked out by means of which the radio would be
turned on only at stated times, and everyone might be
given his opportunity at exclusive and undisturbed use of
the living room to entertain his own particular guests.

In describing a situation in which the family was in
desperate straits financially, one youth said that he felt
"caught in it all." It may be true of some of us that our
families have not provided us with the advantages that make
social adjustment easy. Possibly there has been no opportunity to acquire a knowledge of social customs and practices; the family may not have owned books, played music,
or had an interest in art. Or we may feel because our
parents are of a race or nationality different from that of
most of our friends, that we should be ashamed of them.
Some young people respond to this situation by self-pity,
by bitterly resenting their families and the circumstances
which, they assume, have prevented them from acquiring
prestige in their own groups.

On the other hand, many young people have triumphed
over circumstances. "Getting out from under" and going
to college, as did the boy from the Pennsylvania coal mines,

---

[1] RAINEY, *op. cit.*, p. 138.

may be a mirage for some of us—besides, we may not wish to go to college—but fatalism and doing nothing about a situation is equally as destructive of personality as chasing a rainbow.

The mature individual knows that difference does not mean inferiority, that, for example, his cultural heritage from his national or racial group is a precious one, whatever his ancestry is. He knows and is proud of the role that his race or nationality has played in history, of the contributions that it has made to industry, government, music, art, and literature.

Nor does the mature individual waste his energy in unhappiness and embarrassment because of his unfamiliarity with the social graces. He knows that the situation is not irremediable, that the lack of early opportunities need not handicap him permanently. He sets himself the task of learning the accepted ways of doing things; he practices until he acquires a feeling of ease in all social situations. He knows that at first he will make mistakes but that, if he is observing and willing to learn, any intelligent, adaptable person who is basically considerate of other people can acquire social poise. One can similarly set himself the task of gaining knowledge and appreciation in the field of books, music, or art.

It is well known that there are thousands of young people living in homes where parents are not happy together, where parents may not even speak to each other, or where they use the young person either as a go-between or as a buffer, where each parent vies for the young person's affection or assent to his particular viewpoint. Overt conflict, however, is not so disturbing to young people as is the more subtle but constant tension experienced in some homes in which the parents are not happy together.

The insight and intelligence with which young people can face such a situation is amazing. An example is reported here. Two eighteen-year-old girls and one sixteen-year-old girl came to an older friend to discuss this question. They

were friends.   Two of them, whom we shall call Mary and
Sue, were sisters who lived in a very unhappy home; the
parents of Ruth, the third girl, had been separated for four
years, the girl dividing her time between her parents.
Her father had remarried.   Mary, the older sister, said:

Our parents never quarrel, but we know they aren't happy.
They don't belong together.   They're just different.   And what
makes it worse is that we know that they're staying together
because of us.

Sue burst out:

We don't want them to.   Knowing them both, we know that
they shouldn't live together.   Parents ought to be happy, and
they're not.

Ruth interrupted.

I know.   It's like living with something that's dead, when it
ought to be alive making the world wonderful and beautiful.   I
used to think I never wanted to fall in love and get married.   Now
I don't see why people can't admit that you may love the wrong
person.   We all make mistakes.   I love my father.   I know
mother didn't, but I love her, too, though I feel sorry for her
because really father outgrew her.   I'm glad my father kept on
trying.   Now he's found someone who can take his love and keep
up with him.   It's wonderful to see them together—it kind of
makes you glow.   It's one of those rare marriages where just being
in the room with the two of them makes you feel good.   It's just
as if two people were each bigger because they had each other.
Daddy's a different person when he's with her.

When she was asked whether she, the only child, felt that
she had been hurt by the separation, she said:

Oh, no, I'm glad they had the courage to face it.   Of course, I
couldn't help but know how they felt about each other.   But we
talked about it together when the time came—when daddy
decided he must go.   I knew it was the best way out and that
both mother and he were thinking of my good, too.   They'd both
do anything in the world for me.   And I always feel that I can

go to either of them whenever I need to, though when I want real advice I go to my father.

This undoubtedly is an exceptional case, and everyone concerned acted in an unusually intelligent manner. However, it illustrates how constructive can be the attitude of young people toward relationships between their parents. It seems to imply, also, that even if the parents of young people have separated, young people need not allow that fact to become a threat to their security. The important thing seems to be the extent to which young people can really understand their parents and the soundness of the relationship that they are able to maintain with them in spite of the parents' various difficulties. If the young person feels that he is really loved by them, that they are both cooperating to help him to establish himself as a self-confident, well-adjusted individual, then it is possible for him to feel more secure than he might if he knew that they were living together unhappily because of him.

Any particular feature, whether it be good or poor, of the home environment is less important for the development of an individual than is the character of the entire environment and the way in which he is able to convert it to his own constructive use. The home may be poor, the parents without racial or cultural recognition, the parents even separated, yet the family group may provide a genuine security to the individual.

FUTURE OF THE FAMILY

Just as changes within a family can change an individual, so changes in society are gradually changing the family. We cannot close a discussion of the family without recognizing this fact. A recent study makes the following prediction as to the future of the family:

Although other institutions have taken over some of the functions of the home, those which remain are becoming more crucial—the physical reproduction of the race, the care and basic habit-training of the young child, and the providing of personal security, enduring affection, and healthful emotional life, which for a majority of people is the source of mental health and happiness.

For the large masses of people, family life may have to be relied upon for a greater proportion of life's situations and satisfactions than formerly. . . . Most youth can no longer hope through mere effort and industry to become a ranch owner or railroad president; they can reasonably expect a modest living with increased leisure, affection, and happiness within a family as their chief source of enduring satisfaction. While this new situation does not mean that we should abandon effort to make jobs more secure and more challenging, it does mean that life in the future may be less job-centered and more home-centered.[1]

[1] RAINEY, *op. cit.*, p. 135.

CHAPTER IV

MEN, WOMEN, AND LOVE

In one sense every man begins to make his adjustments to the opposite sex before he is a year old. In the feeling he comes to have even at that age for the woman-person who means so much to him, in the stimulating regard that he as a baby is able to attract from his mother, in his recognition of his ability to influence and control her, there exists the first faint foreshadowing of a relationship search which, twenty years later, will have altered and focused to seek out a contemporary as its object. Girl babies, similarly, begin to learn to attract love and to give love long before they cut off their pigtails and face up squarely to the fact that to find, to love, and to be loved by "the one man" is one of the most important objectives of their young adulthood.

It is of critical importance to the happiness and life fulfillment of most individuals that they should so develop that they will be able to attract the favorable attention and affection of members of the opposite sex. It is also important that they so develop that they are able to give their own wholehearted interest, affection, and loyalty to a selected member of the opposite sex. But not only is it critically important to each individual to accomplish a happy, lasting relationship with some member of the opposite sex; it is also of serious and persistent concern to society that each individual shall find some other individual of the opposite sex with whom a lasting, happy relationship can be established.

Society expresses its concern by attempting to exert in this area especially heavy pressures on individual conduct.

It attempts to regulate development because it has long
recognized that there are large social as well as individual
values at stake.   Because the whole matter of men, women,
and love is of so much importance both to individuals and
to society as a whole, people are inclined to have strong
feelings about different aspects of the relationships of the
two sexes.   There is, perhaps, no other area of human life—
unless it be religion—around which more emotionalized
points of view have developed.   Any young person—or
anyone who knows young people at all well—knows that
most of the really compelling problems and questions of the
late teens and twenties are to be found in this area.   The
emotions of hope, desire, fulfillment, frustration, disappointment, and bitterness accompany, in varying proportions
but consistently, all but the most superficial social contacts
between young men and young women.   Whenever young
people are completely frank they express questions, baffle-
ment, ignorance, and even a sense of mystery in relation to
experiences they have or have not had in this area.

Since the authors are fully aware that practically everyone has some strongly emotionalized attitudes in this area
and that society also is far from dispassionate in passing
judgments on everything that touches the relationships
between men and women, there is little question that whatever might be said in this chapter would constitute the
basis for all kinds and varieties of strong emotional reactions
on the part of those who read it.   Out of their counseling
experiences, the authors believe that they have come to have
a comparatively broad, realistic appreciation of the many
problems that young people face in this area.   In addition
to learning about the problems of young people firsthand
through interviews, the authors have studied and weighed
as carefully as they could the many stereotyped points of
view, the social taboos of our culture, the individual and
social values to be conserved, and all the systematized
arguments concerning the many questions that arise out of
men-women relationships.

The question arises as to which of several approaches it is best to adopt in writing about men, women, and love. Should one attempt to "pussyfoot" in order not to create new storm centers? Should the presentation be keyed primarily to an attempt to keep it completely neutral? Should an attempt be made to present all the angles of every question, carefully avoiding, however, any indication of the authors' preferred positions? Or might it be better, in spite of the emotionalized reactions that will inevitably result, to give as thorough a presentation as possible of the outstanding problems in this area, indicating, without equivocation, the points of view that the authors themselves hold?

After careful consideration of the advantages and disadvantages of each approach, it has been decided to adopt the last.

In the area of men-women relationships, there are important data from the biological sciences. There are also important findings from psychology and sociology. These facts, more or less scientific and constant, can be used as guides to conduct in relationships between men and women. But there is, in every successful human relationship, an additional area to which scientific data thus far have made little contribution. The beauty that two people are able to build into a relationship may depend more upon artistic appreciation and artistic skills than upon scientific knowledge.

There is, furthermore, in every human relationship, another qualitative aspect that has to do with ethics. In every relationship the question of what is good and just and fair arises in addition to questions of what is scientifically true and what is aesthetically satisfying. Since scientists never expect to agree permanently on any fact, even though it is at present assumed to be true, since aesthetics has never been assumed to be exact and absolute, and since ethics vary with both time and space, no final answers to problems about men-women relationships can ever be attempted.

Under these circumstances the most honest course seems to be to describe the persistent problems that young people say that they face in this area; to illustrate some of these by verbatim quotations from young people with whom the authors have worked; to summarize the findings of various youth surveys concerning youth's problems; to cite scientific fact where it is available and pertinent; to suggest considerations which, to the authors, seem to relate to beauty; and to present a point of view that calls attention to certain ethical aspects of relationships.

Of course, not all readers will agree with the authors' presentation. Nor is this important. But perhaps the discussions here will help each individual to think through more clearly for himself the facts by which he will be guided, will suggest to him how he may cultivate beauty in his relationships, and will present questions concerning values that cannot wisely be ignored.

How Problems Arise in This Area

Conflicting ideas regarding relationships between men and women, marriage, and the home are being freely discussed. As it has become more customary for young people to leave the protection of the home, to spend time with groups outside it, or to live away from home—perhaps at college— they often find that the ideals and standards in the outside group differ vastly from those of their homes. Conflicts are precipitated, especially when new ideas run counter to old beliefs; when, for example, a young person is urged by the new group to be "a good sport" in smoking, drinking, or petting. Consequently, an individual may feel forced by social pressure to experiment in an unfamiliar field.

When experiences of friendships with members of the opposite sex are relatively new to young people, they may feel obliged to follow slavishly the dictates of their contemporaries about "what is done." Because of lack of confidence in this new realm, because of a desire to be secure, or because of the sarcasm or jests of thoughtless friends or members of their family, they may pretend a sophistication that they do not feel, or ape the behavior of others who seem to be succeeding in relationships with the opposite sex. They may be confused by feeling that somehow a friendship with a member of the opposite sex must have different components from other friendships. Or they may venture only a short distance into this strange new world of the other sex and then cling desperately to the first individual who accepts them and who furnishes a feeling of security.

In any one of these instances, young people lack the ability to describe the quality of their feeling for the other individual in the relationship. They may suspect that, though they call the relationship love, actually it is only gratification in having someone to count on, someone who gives some of the security and prestige that they crave. Should the relationship be based on doing what is "being done," especially in the realm of sex practices, then they may well ask, "Is sex love?" If they know well only one member of the opposite sex, they ask with justification, "Do I love him—or her—or am I only accustomed to him?"

Young people seek eagerly to gain insight to guide them in making their experiences in this realm as valuable as possible. They want desperately to have something to cling to, some focus for life in terms of which they may appraise, motivate, and direct day-by-day actions and broaden their perspective. They want to know where they are going, so that long-range planning can lend significance to daily actions as they see the daily decisions in relation to what they consider most valuable in life.

They want to know how to think clearly in this sphere of action, how to make choices when there are several alternatives to be considered, how to see the cause and effect relationships between choices and consequences. They are eager to be honest with themselves about the results of possible courses of action. They want to face situations rather than to evade them. But in order to guard against a tendency to act first and find a reason afterward, they want to secure pertinent facts. In this way they hope that they may not make too many mistakes or yield too often either to blind prejudice or to impulse.

WHAT THESE PROBLEMS ARE

Some information concerning problems of men-women relationships has been gained from youth surveys that have taken into account young people all over the country. A well-known national study quotes the fact that in 1935, in Orange, N. J., there was held a "Trial by Jury in the case of Youth versus Society," at which time society was indicted by young people primarily because it gave youth "inadequate sex instruction and inexcusably little help in the subject of choosing a mate, and it allowed conditions to exist whereby the marriage of young people of marriageable age was delayed because they lacked employment."[1] This last fact was substantiated by other studies. In spite of the fact that numerous surveys have shown that the great majority of young people in this country wish to be married and wish also to have children, "the unemployment and poverty accompanying the depression period brought down the marriage rate from 10 or 11 marriages per 1,000 population during the 1930's to 7.9 in 1932."[2]

In the Maryland study,[3] one out of five of the twenty-year-olds reported that their marriages had, for economic reasons, been delayed.

One of the problems of young people has been the slowness with which society has provided them with information and counsel in an area so important to their lives. Five older men students were speaking to the head of a large

[1] RAINEY, HOMER P., and others, *How Fare American Youth?* p. 143, D. Appleton-Century Company, Inc., New York, 1937.

[2] *Ibid.*, p. 139.

[3] BELL, HOWARD M., *Youth Tell Their Story*, p. 43, American Council on Education, Washington, D. C., 1938.

Middle Western university. "Mr. President," they said, "we have been getting a fine technical education, but no preparation at all for what we consider one of the most important relations in life; we mean marriage. We know how to build bridges, but not a happy home life." They had a plan, and it was approved by the president. That was five years ago. Since then a course of lectures on marriage has been given each year with gratifying success.[1] The demand for this type of education is increasing. Numerous colleges, community centers, unions, and social agencies have instituted courses which offer some help; many high schools offer the information on a more elementary level.

Young people, almost without exception, seek friends of the opposite sex. There is a driving power within them that propels them toward the building of genuine relationships, one sex with the other. The importance of these friendships as influences in their development is apparent in all the testimony that young people have given the authors about their lives. Such friendships are rated by them during their late adolescence as second in importance only to the influences that their parents have had upon them. The following random samplings of the word-for-word comments of young people give some further indication of the types of problems that young people face during their late adolescence and early adulthood.

I had a love affair for four years with a man three years younger than I am. Our families are very good friends and they were all for our being engaged until last year they suddenly decided that we should break it off. At the same time last year father had a nervous breakdown and the position of the family became very precarious. Then I started going with the boy again but fell in love with another man to whom I became engaged last Easter. The two families still want me to marry the first man. I can't seem to make them understand that I don't love him. The whole situation isn't very conducive to happiness right now.

[1] RAINEY, *op. cit.*, p. 134.

I fell in love with a man two years older than I am and went with him for over a year. I came to love him very much. He didn't seem to be interested in marriage, though. I decided that I would have to break it off because it was so hectic to care about anyone so much and always to meet with a kind of stone wall. After breaking it off, though, I had a nervous breakdown. I didn't know what to do. I finally talked it over with one of my professors who had his students write autobiographies for him. He advised me to see the man again if I wanted to so much. I knew that my family would think I was utterly without pride to tell a man I wouldn't see him any more and then beg him to have another date with me because I couldn't endure not seeing him. So I didn't tell them. It grated, having to keep it from them. I had one more date with him but decided again it just wasn't any use and I'm not going to see him ever again. I plan definitely on being married; I want a happy marriage more than I want any other thing. But I just haven't found the man yet and I'll have to wait until I do.

I was married two years ago. I don't know whether or not it is so much my husband who has influenced me as it is the whole situation of marriage—if you have any idea what it is I mean. Marriage has made everything else seem less important. Before my marriage I was very mercurial—everything upset me—I was given to being affected emotionally. Now I have a feeling that nothing can really bother me as long as my marriage is so secure and comfortable. I never get upset any more. Of course, my husband figures in this whole effect.

I am really engaged but we aren't going to announce our engagement until next year. Then we'll be married and I expect to keep on working for two or three years after we're married. The course of our love hasn't run entirely smoothly, though. My family has met my fiancé only twice and doesn't approve of him. They are trying to influence me to break my engagement, but the thing that is happening is that their attitude is influencing me to break away more and more from them.

I've been in love with a girl for some time. Now another fellow has fallen in love with her too. I don't know what in heck to do about it. I'm pretty much in debt—the other guy has no debts and a good job. The girl herself is earning $45 a week. If she marries me she'll have to go with me to Maine to live and give up her good job here. She might or might not be able to get a job up there. I hate to ask her to try to live on what my job will pay next year, especially since I have these debts to wipe out. I really think she loves me; but, the question is, will she reproach me for letting her in for something if I let her go ahead and marry me? On the other hand, I don't see how I can stand by and see her marry the other fellow. I think this situation is by far the toughest I've faced and I spend most of my spare time thinking about it.

I've been in love with several men in the last few years. I've learned that I'm not interested in men only—love is not all. A man from now on has to have more than good looks to get my time.

Falling in love—or at least thinking I was in love—has been very important to me. The girl was a leader, and very brilliant, but as I see it now she lacked poise and steadiness. It took me only about two weeks to get over the affair when it broke up, so I guess it wasn't as serious as I thought at the time. That experience changed my idea of the "desirable woman" considerably.

I was awfully in love with a man. He didn't love me as much as I loved him and was trying, I realize now, to let me down gently. I sent an awfully dumb letter to him. I've reproached myself for it for the past two years. I've gotten over it now but it certainly shook my own self-respect for a while to have done a trick like that.

I fell deeply in love my sophomore year with a man who was a big disappointment. He has been a shocking and regrettable revelation to me of how nice something may look on the surface and how rotten it can be underneath.

There is a girl who really has had a bad effect on me. I gave up everything for her for two years—all my other friends, athletics; I even sacrificed the best grades I could have made in order to give her more attention. I'm beginning to come to my senses now—largely through the efforts of my brother. I suppose I've learned something from her, though.

I fell in love and then out again and for a while I stopped going with boys entirely; it just didn't seem worth while, but I realize now that that is no spirit with which to meet life.

A few years ago I didn't quite know what to think about the stories of low relationships I heard—particularly one story about one certain girl who was a friend of mine and a man I knew. I didn't want to shut my eyes to any truths, but I didn't want to lose confidence in the integrity of people who ought, in my opinion, certainly to possess integrity.

I've been in hell for the past month. It's a love affair. I got a girl into trouble. We haven't known what to do. Night after night I've lain awake going over the five possibilities. There were just five. I had to make the decision; the girl was too paralyzed with fright to help. First we could marry. But there was no sense in marrying unless I took her away some place where we could be happy. My family are Catholics; hers are Protestants. They have vehemently opposed our marriage right from the time we met. She's in college and has never had much experience with the world. I'm in my senior year and have hardly earned a penny all my life. If I did marry her and take her off some place, what under the sun could I do to support her and the baby? Jobs aren't easy to find nowadays. Wouldn't she always hate me for getting her into such a mess? Things would be bound to be awfully hard for her. Well, second, there was the possibility of an abortion. But she had a friend who died that way and my whole upbringing made me regard that as a crime. Third, we thought of joint suicides. Fourth, be it said to my shame that she begged me to kill just her—that it wasn't necessary for me to die, too. Fifth, we could just wait. But that was an impossible course of action. . . . God, I don't know why we were let off. There was a miscarriage. Now all we have to worry about is *when* to marry. Of course, we intend to, but we can choose our time a little more carefully now.

I've had a pretty disturbing experience. One evening a few years ago I was out walking and was approached by another man. You may think me naive, but I'd never heard of such a thing as homosexuality. I got to know this man—he seemed quite nice— and we got into a rather unusual kind of friendship. This went on for several weeks until some of the fellows put me wise. Their kidding was not the least of the whole experience. I pulled out all right, but it wasn't a happy kind of experience, I can tell you.

I've fallen in love with a woman a little older, who happens to be married to a man whom I like and admire very much. At first I assured myself it was purely emotional and I needn't worry, but I'm not very happy about it all right now. I suppose it will come out all right. I suppose what it is doing to me is the most profound influence I've had in my life.

The kinds of questions young people are concerned about seem to fall into four large divisions:

How can I tell when I'm really in love? What are the components of love? What is the difference between love and temporary attraction?

What are the avenues that lead one to true love? What are the blind alleys? Shall I pet? If so, when, and to what extent? How can one relate the physical expression of love to true love most successfully?

What consideration should decide the question of which is preferable—long engagement or early marriage? How can the decisive problem of "money enough to live on" be met? Can and will the parents of both young people continue to subsidize them after marriage? Is it right for them to do so? Can each of the young people assume the responsibility of working in addition to going to school if that would make marriage possible? Should one of them work while the other completes an education? Should they both work after marriage? How can they, as they are waiting to be married, most wisely handle the question of the physical expression of their love for each other? To what extent should they discuss other questions about which an understanding should be reached if they are to live happily together?

How mature is the conception of marriage that each young person holds? Do both persons bring to marriage personal qualities that are some guarantee that they "have what it takes" to succeed in a marriage relationship? Should the two young people work jointly on household questions? Should they keep a budget? If both work, how can they, in addition, most wisely manage their home? How explicitly should they discuss, before marriage, such questions as their sexual relations?   What about the question of having children?

There Are Many Kinds of Love

As contacts with the opposite sex begin to have significance for individuals, as they realize that some people mean more to them than others, they attempt to define for themselves the quality of the various relationships that have become an important part of their lives.   They seek to discriminate between the passing attraction, the joy of companionship and of discovering common interests, and the deeper feeling that forecasts a more lasting relationship. When young people ask, "How do I know whether I am really in love?" they generally imply such questions as: How is this relationship any different from others?   How can I distinguish between love and physical attraction? Do I love this person or am I only accustomed to him? What are the components of love?   Have I any assurance that my present feeling will last?

Mature love implies freedom for each individual; it necessitates unselfishness.   As you trust another person enough to love him—or her—enough to place your life in his hands, as you give him the power to hurt you, you lose yourself in your concern about someone else.   You are simultaneously freed of yourself when you voluntarily tie up your life with that of another.   This does not mean that you weakly place yourself in someone else's power.   The only genuine power that another person can have over you is that power which is developed in you because of a growing feeling that you must be worth while, since that person loves you.   Mature love can teach you unselfishness; it can make you more understanding of people, more sensitive to the beauty as well as to the defects and ugliness of life.

An individual who is not mature emotionally continues, however, to see all reference to love as merely a means of satisfying his or her personal desires. He or she may be attracted to one individual after another, but no one relationship differs essentially from any other, because basically, such a person remains selfish. He cannot love another individual; actually he loves only himself. He may be a calculating person who marries, not for love, but for money or for social prestige; his dearest wish may be to have his marriage labeled "successful" by parents and friends; or marriage may mean only that a complicated life may be made easier because of financial security or of acceptance by a certain social group. Such persons are "gold diggers," out for all they can get from the opposite sex, and not likely to make permanently congenial husbands or wives.

There are still girls who look upon men as legitimate meal tickets—if and when caught and tamed. These girls are the heiresses of an idea that flowered in a certain class of American society in the nineteenth and early twentieth centuries. Each fancies herself as the reason why some "good" man will keep his nose to the grindstone; she wishes to live gently and without undue effort; she would even wear a few jewels with good effect if the meal ticket turned out to be a rich one. But when the desire to be supported is the dominant reason a girl marries, the marriage starts out with one big count against it. If a girl wonders whether she can stick it out with a man if the next depression hits them hard, the man has a right to ask whether the relationship is on a sufficiently sound basis to ensure a successful marriage.

Another form of selfishness is portrayed in the individual who wants a wife or husband only to replace a mother, a father, or a friend, who has pampered and spoiled him. He or she may emotionally shy away from marriage because he cannot bear to leave the comfort of his own home, his mother's devoted attention, his father's affection and protection. If, in spite of himself, such a person becomes interested in a member of the opposite sex, it may be only because he wants someone to continue to take care of him as completely as his parents have done, possibly someone to support him, even do his thinking for him. If such an individual does marry, often his mate becomes merely another person who adores him, caters to his whims, gives him things, is devotion itself. At first a husband or wife may do these things, but it is very hard to continue faithfully to care for an individual who cares for no one but himself. Success in marriage requires give and take from both partners.

Possibly an individual may not want to marry because he wants his freedom. He or she would rather be able to spend money, buy a car, or travel. Such an individual cannot be emotionally mature and generous enough to know what love is. He cannot appreciate the joy of giving and sharing. For him, having and spending are more important.

Another hindrance to the development of a happy love and marriage relationship is cowardice which makes it impossible for a person to love deeply and sincerely. This may be a form of selfishness. The individual may be haunted by any one of a number of disturbing thoughts. He may have within himself the feeling that he is not the kind of person he ought to be. He may fear that people do not like him; he may not feel successful in his relationships with the opposite sex. This lack of self-confidence may be so deep that he has neither realized it nor acknowledged it; but, like a dark secret or a subtle shame, it has always held him back, has kept him from giving the best of himself to others. He has failed to make contributions that he could make to other people; he has spent his energy almost entirely in thoughts of himself, in an agony of embarrassment because he thought he had nothing to give. Few people ever have a chance to know the real self that this sort of person keeps hidden away. This real self never has a chance to grow as it should.

When a person clings to the idea that he cannot do things, when he thinks that effort is futile, the next step naturally follows. He feels inadequate. Then he loses friends because he thinks that he does not deserve to have them. The only cure for such cowardice is self-confidence. It is gained by learning to meet and mix with people, by facing difficulties, and by developing innate abilities.

Often an individual may confuse these considerations. The man may say that he does not want to give up his freedom or that he does not have the money to marry when what he really means is that he cannot bear to leave his mother. Or he may say that his job is the all-important factor in his life, that he needs nothing else, whereas if he faced the problem honestly he might find that he is not yet ready to love anyone as much as himself—or that he fears that no one would really care for him.

A woman may say that she wants a career instead of marriage or that she could not lower her standard of living for a man, when really she still idealizes her father, thinks of him as being perfect, and is unsuccessfully seeking a man like him. If she finds such a man, she will treat him like her father. She will not be able to think of herself as a woman in relation to him as a friend or as a husband.

Mature, lasting love cannot be built on selfishness, no matter what form it may take. One is not really "in love" until his love reaches out to others, until it bestows on him the strength and the courage to give his best that the lives of others may be made as beautiful for them as his has become for him. As one recognizes this quality in a relationship, it begins to be set apart from all other relationships. One begins to think in terms of loving another person so deeply that he will be able to stay in love with him or her for the rest of his life. He begins to want to have children and to wish to bring them up in the right kind of home, one in which they will know the security of love.

The question, "Is this love?" can be answered only by examining the sum of many qualities in the relationship. The strength of the love depends on the degree of emotional maturity of the person who feels it.   Physical attraction is important; a relationship that is to be permanent needs certainly to include the attraction of one individual for another.   But one can feel physical attraction for many members of the opposite sex.   Real love is not exclusively or even primarily physical.   No lasting relationship can be built on physical attraction alone.   In marriage the two people need to live in a multiple relationship with each other.   In order to be happy together, they must be able to share many aspects of life.   Therefore, each of us needs to defer his or her choice of a mate until he or she is grown up emotionally.   Should a person expect to change himself a great deal between eighteen and thirty, for example, then he would be unwise to choose for a mate an individual who suits him at an earlier stage of development.   The two might be suited to live together during adolescence, but could they live together for a lifetime?   Nothing is more tragic than to have one partner outgrow the other.

Suppose that you do feel that you are really "in love." How do you know that you may not later feel the same way about some other person?   It is true that we may throughout our lives feel attracted to many individuals—either consecutively or at the same time.   Whether or not we respond to someone may depend on how much we are in need of companionship at the moment, how rested or tired, how free or how occupied our minds are with other concerns. The particular individual or the individuals to whom we feel attracted at any given time may depend upon the range of our choice at the moment; witness the number of campus and shipboard romances.

The only way to have any confidence that the light of one's life will not suffer an early black-out is to ask oneself, "Have I known enough members of the other sex to be certain that I have developed a basis for intelligent choice?" The younger an individual is, the more likely it is that he is influenced by the fiction that one "falls in love."   Therefore what he mistakes for love may be predominantly a satisfaction in being attractive to someone, or it may be a desire to possess the person who has attracted him or her. Or an individual may not feel at ease with other members of the opposite sex and may, therefore, prefer to remain with someone who gives him security. One should not consider himself in love, however, merely because he feels comfortable and secure with a particular person.

You may argue to yourself that if you do not marry this person, you may never marry—no one as attractive may again be available. Be sure you are not clinging fearfully to the first individual who likes you, who makes you feel worth while. On the other hand, you may fear that, if you know too many members of the opposite sex, you may not know how to choose; you may prefer to hold to someone who seems satisfying rather than to precipitate the struggle that would be involved in making comparisons and new contacts. However, it is not fair to yourself nor to the other person involved to attempt a final judgment prematurely. You need to know well a sufficient number of members of the opposite sex to have a basis for comparison.

There is another rather common feeling you may mistake for love. You may be clinging to one individual because you happen to have been "caught on the rebound." This person may have been the first attractive one whom you met immediately after an unfortunate experience with a member of the opposite sex. You may not want to be hurt again, and since this person offers security, you accept it.

When you believe that you have found the person "meant for you," and you want to assure yourself that "this will last," you need to be able to face honestly and squarely these questions: Will I be as eager ten years from now to live with this person? Will I be equally happy and willing to accept then the consequences of the decision to bind our lives together? Does he—or she—seem to be the sort of person who will "wear well"?

The personal characteristics of each of the partners must be such as to make possible the building of an entire life pattern together. Can the two of you manage a home together? Can you get satisfying cooperation on a standard of living even when it is different from the one to which you have been accustomed? Can you cooperate on making a budget and on money management, on planning for and rearing children, on the status of the woman and her interests outside the home, on religion or the values in life that each of you is seeking? Do both of you have constructive attitudes toward sex and toward the working out of a happy mutual relationship?

It is sometimes true that opposite or supplementary characteristics may contribute to a happy life adjustment, but there must also be sufficient in common between two people to make a day-by-day relationship possible. For example, a practical, matter-of-fact husband may have difficulty in living with an artistic, beauty-loving wife, and she, in turn, may feel that he appreciates only money and fails to understand aesthetic or spiritual values. A tense, active husband may soon despair of a shy, inarticulate wife. If one partner is too much the intellectual superior of the other or if one enjoys social contacts and is popular in social gatherings in which the other feels uncomfortable, there may be difficulty in working out an adjustment.

On the other hand, if the two young people have common interests centered in so narrow a sphere that competition between them is a constant threat, their relationship may also be endangered. For example, two young people who excel in the same sport or who, though married, work in the same profession, need to take care that professional jealousy and competition does not develop.

If two people are to be together constantly, they need some basis of conversation. They need to find many things that they can do together—work and play. They must find ways in which they can spend their leisure time together. Do they have sufficient leisure-time skills in common, or does one, for example, enjoy outdoor life and the other prefer only sedentary activities? Can each multiply the interests of the other? Do they have friends in common? This is especially important if a person is marrying someone outside of his social group, religion, or nationality, since both husband and wife as a result may be snubbed or ostracized by their own groups. A relationship must be strong if it is to survive constant association.

Are both young people emotionally mature enough for marriage? For example, can they talk out difficulties frankly and rationally? Can they make decisions cooperatively, or must one always give in while the other gets his way? Are both mature enough to face disappointment, disillusionment, or heavy responsibilities? Can each person survive financial setbacks with faith in the other intact?

Two people need to know each other long enough and well enough to be able to face honestly the implications of the many questions just raised. If during a long acquaintance, each person becomes "accustomed" to the other in the sense of adjusting gradually, then becoming accustomed to each other is all to the good. If, however, an individual has shut everyone else out of his life to find out something about someone who seemed promising, then he must honestly ask himself whether he is not seeing excellent qualities in that person merely because he wants so much to find them there or hopes perhaps that his influence can develop them.

People cannot be changed unless they want to be changed. None of us wants to become hypercritical of people, but we must be realistic in our estimates of others and of ourselves if we are to estimate accurately the possibilities of our living happily with a particular person. We should be certain that we have given others sufficient consideration, so that after we have married we do not keep, at the back of our minds, a doubt whether we might have made a better choice or whether some day we might see someone who seems superior. If we are honest with ourselves, we recognize that the latter is a possibility. However, if, by the time we meet another individual with whom we might have been happy, we have already achieved a vital, satisfying relationship with the person whom we first chose, then the second individual becomes merely another of the group of friends whom we find interesting. There is no intimate place for him or her to occupy. The pattern of our married life has already been set.

We may conclude that there is no one right person for any of us, for love in all its aspects does not come upon us suddenly. In order to become complete, love must develop slowly; it is, as one young person said, something that we "must work on." If a person knows that he is attracted to someone; if he has intelligently estimated the possibilities for him and the person of his choice in making of marriage a constantly growing partnership; if he is willing to abide by the consequences of his decision to join his life with that of this other person; if he can enter marriage physically, mentally, and emotionally fit; if he understands the obligations of marriage as well as its joys; if he is honestly attempting to be emotionally mature; if he feels that there is mutual loyalty and real comradeship between him and his loved one; if he feels that he has found a partner with whom he can achieve the completion of himself; then the most that can be said in reassurance is, "You have all the certainty that anyone can ever know." We can do nothing more than proceed, in every decision, on the best and most honest judgment that we can make on the basis of all the facts available to us at the time.

We must, even when we have found the one person who seems to be able to fill our lives, guard against too exclusive an affection. Love must be more than selfish concern about one person in the world; this kind of relationship is immature and dangerous. What if that one individual should go out of our lives? We cannot pour the whole meaning and purpose of our lives into our affection for one person. We must not forget, as Bertrand Russell has written, that if we are to "surmount all misfortunes by the emergence after each blow of an interest in life and the world," we cannot narrow down our life "so much as to make one loss fatal. To be defeated by one loss, or even by several, is not something to be admired as a proof of sensibility, but something to be deplored as a failure in vitality."[1]

Even though we may at some time lose the person whom we love or even though we may have to admit that we have taken our love to the wrong person, we still need not blame love. We need to find a person who can take us and whose love we can take; we grow immeasurably, both as we feel ourselves beloved and as we give our love. To love without a return other than that which comes from the very experience of loving can teach us a sensitiveness to the feelings of others, an understanding of their griefs and sorrows. Whatever happens in life, we shall be stronger, better people if we have loved and been loved, if we have participated in the give and take of living.

With this philosophy about love, we are masters of the days that are past. We need not fear the future. Life has given us love; it may give us tragedy with that love. But if we are willing to face this fact, our grief at parting turns, not into bitterness, but into beauty, as we remember the joy of meeting, as we build into our lives the very genuine contribution which that love has made to our growth. Thus life teaches us what it means really to love. Even to lose the person we love may be a part of this growth. With this as our conception of and expectation from love, life cannot break us, for such love endures beyond tragedy; it survives even death.

Avenues to True Love versus Blind Alleys

Of the many components involved in the relationship between a man and a woman, there is one that can enhance immeasurably or detract seriously from the values that we seek in life. This component is sex. Many young people

---

[1] Russell, Bertrand, *Conquest of Happiness*, p. 230, Liveright Publishing Corporation, New York, 1930.

are confused about the relationship of sex and love. They complain that adults give them no help on this point. Adults may feel that they have settled the problem when they have advised that young people either should control their sex urges or forget them in exercise or in some other form of sublimation. One of the things that young people desire is definite information about the nature of and the manifestations of sex so that they can decide intelligently when and in what ways they will use them. They want to understand the limitation of the purely physical expression of sex, so that they may be able to answer their own questions—questions such as: "Where will this urge get me?" "At what points will I be disillusioned?" "How can I make sex contribute to my life instead of trying eternally to avoid its getting me into trouble?" What important facts do young people need to know?

Young people need to know that there is no one pattern of behavior that evolves from the sex urge. Studies of the ways in which men and women in other civilizations behave dispose effectively of the idea that there is any single or right pattern of sex behavior. The wide range of types of sex expression shows that the customs and institutions of a particular group of people, rather than race or any other single circumstance, are the most powerful factors in determining sex behavior. In some societies, anthropologists have found that there is no sex promiscuity whatsoever. Where this is true, young people are taught that their sex organs are given to them for the reproduction of the race and that they must be kept with reverential care for that function alone. In some societies, women are dominant and aggressive sexually, and men develop what we, in our society, would call a feminine temperament. The degree of adaptability of human beings to whatever sex customs are approved by their society seems to be limitless. This fact leads us to the conclusion that the sex patterns adopted by any individual will, in general, be in accordance with the habits and customs of his group.

As we discuss the problems that young people living in our society say they have, we are actually discussing problems as they are related to the unique complex of customs, of accepted modes of behavior, and of taboos of society in this country at this time. Of course, these differ somewhat in various communities. Rural sections in Wyoming, Negro communities in Alabama, "foreign" districts in New York City, and Chicago's North Shore suburbs will all expect what may look like somewhat different kinds of behavior. However, running through the whole of American culture, there is enough agreement and common understanding so that movies, books, and lectures are transferable from section to section without special explanation.

Young people in our present-day society are, for instance, constantly exposed to the attractions of the opposite sex. How can they express the interest that they feel in each other? Holding hands, kissing, and hugging have always been done to a greater or lesser extent—and by the very best people, too. When dancing (which provides for young people a chance to show interest in each other) is forbidden, games and teasing are substituted. But what happens when sex tension develops, as it very naturally does? Society warns young people to restrain their normal impulses and carefully to gloss over their feelings. However, attempts at total repression are fruitless. Sex demands are too insistent; if one form of expressing them is forbidden, individuals will find other means of releasing their tensions, ways that may be of more questionable value or even harmful.

At present in our society, relationships between the two sexes are complicated by the postponement of marriage considerably beyond the period when young people are biologically ready for it or by its denial altogether. Naturally, when progress toward the achievement of a wholesome sex adjustment has somehow become blocked, those individuals who are less patient, those whose sex urges are very strong, and those who do not have strong inhibiting ideals usually manage to find some other way out.

This "some other way" may take the form of masturbation, homosexuality, excessive petting, conscious sublimation, or promiscuity. Sex tension is developed biologically, but the physiological tension in the genital region can be temporarily released by any of these forms of sexual experience. An individual who has not yet been successful in working out a relationship with a member of the opposite sex that involves all the elements that everyone deeply craves—mutual affection, sincere regard, sympathy, understanding, loyalty, and companionship—may clutch at one symbol of these other experiences, naively hoping that if he can somehow capture the symbol he will gain the intangibles that he so desperately wants.

Full satisfaction and release of the personality, however, does not come through a sex experience that has only a limited physical character, just as, for most people, a satisfactory meal does not mean one in which only the stomach is involved. The various substitutes for a wholesome sex adjustment that young people try prove eventually to be disillusioning and unsatisfactory, not because they are not momentarily exciting or pleasurable but because they are inadequate and unsatisfying to the person as a human being. A sex experience is truly satisfying only when it is a genuine love experience, one that is more than physical, one that includes, in addition, many qualities that are spiritual and aesthetic.

One of the commonest substitute forms of sex expression is masturbation, where the individual has a sex experience with himself or herself. Some studies have shown that most people at some time or other in their lives practice masturbation. They drift into it themselves or are taught it by others. Formerly dire consequences were predicted for the individual who indulged in it. We now know that such warnings were exaggerated.

A serious objection to masturbation is that it is an immature expression of the sex urge and that in the late teens it contributes to self-centeredness at a time in an individual's development when he most needs to be turning his attention away from himself to others. Although it may be the best adjustment that a person is able to make at the time, still it is a symptom of thwarted or immature sex adjustment. It is a poor preparation for the marriage relationship, where one's thoughts should be centered on another person rather than on one's self. However, as an individual is helped to make positive and happy adjustments to the opposite sex, thus gaining emotional release and making more mature sex adjustments, the habit tends to disappear.

Another common form of unsatisfactory sex adjustment is a homosexual relationship. Homosexuality, as the term is most commonly used by physicians and psychologists, does not necessarily imply any physical involvement. It usually signifies merely an intense and relatively exclusive friendship with a member of the same sex. Furthermore, such a relationship is not properly considered homosexual in character unless those involved in the intense and exclusive attachment have reached an age where they might be expected to be ready to broaden their affectional interests to include those of the opposite sex. Psychologists say that this broadening and refocusing of affectional interest should have taken place by the time either a boy or girl is twenty years old.

In his early teens, it is perfectly normal for a person to feel most at home with other members of his own sex. Then, as growth takes place, the normal person transfers his keenest interest to members of the opposite sex. However, for the individual who feels awkward, reticent, or embarrassed in relationships with the opposite sex, it is often easier to continue to choose a member of the same sex as the object of his deepest affections.

Homosexuality may be a defense against the opposite sex, not a desire for one's own sex. If an individual is, for some reason, prevented from making a heterosexual adjustment, he may find a member of the same sex who complements his characteristics—a feminine woman with a masculine woman, a feminine man with a masculine man.

Sometimes individuals who have lived in homes or in schools where they have grown up almost exclusively with members of their own sex do not know how to adventure in learning to become really acquainted with members of the other sex.   A person may also have been frightened or have had an unhappy experience with a member of the opposite sex; or he may have been warned by his parents against members of the opposite sex and may, as a consequence, have focused his affections upon someone reassuringly like himself.   Homosexual attachments are by no means always sexual in their origin.   They often have roots in feelings of inadequacy or loneliness.   Every person needs to love and be loved.

Usually homosexual attachments disappear in the development of the normal happy association with members of the opposite sex.   Only when, by late adolescence, relationships with one's own sex are continued with some intensity and none made with the opposite sex is there cause for concern that a homosexual pattern may be developing.

Those who mature normally have no reason to feel shocked by individuals who have, for some reason, remained at a more immature level of social development.   The former can often help the latter to substitute a more adult heterosexual adjustment.   This can best be done by including them repeatedly in fairly small, informal social affairs such as picnics, parties, and dances, where they will have an opportunity to enjoy the company of members of the opposite sex.   Thus they can be encouraged to come out of their blind alleys into the broad avenue of normal heterosexual development.

Some individuals have thought that they can partially compensate for not having become a participant in a happy marriage relationship by indulging in sexual intercourse outside of marriage.   This may take place with anyone who can be persuaded or paid to be a partner, or it may be

with someone who offers also some measure of affection and
sympathy and companionship, so that there may be a
temporary illusion that the symbolic experience is not
entirely counterfeit. Sexual intercourse does temporarily
relieve the physical symptoms of sex tension, but it usually
at the same time contributes to other sorts of tensions
that may be basically more complicating to personality.

When a man resorts to sex experience involving only
physical sensation, he often subsequently finds himself in
danger of relapsing into cynicism, disillusionment, or even
despair. From an obvious point of view he has secured
release from physical tension; but from a subtler psychological, and just as insistent, point of view he has spent some
of himself in a futile attempt to find the sense of deep
human companionship and mutual devotion that his whole
being demands, less blatantly but just as compellingly.
Without knowing just why, he may feel cheated after each
such experience. He may react to this feeling by becoming
contemptuous of women because they have not given him
what he really wants. Or he may try to protect himself
from this feeling of having been cheated by bragging to
other men of his vast experience, much in the same way as
one wants to believe that anything for which he has paid
too much was a bargain at the price.

A woman's sex tensions are not localized physically to the
extent that a man's are. Because her sex feelings are more
generalized, she does not so readily think of them as separate
from her deeper emotional needs. Nor does a woman,
therefore, as easily as does a man, believe it to be possible
to solve the physical tensions of sex without regard to the
other important elements of the relationship of which her
sex feelings are only a part. If a woman does, however,
attempt to make the separation and to have sexual intercourse in a relationship that does not involve mutual love
and complete loyalty, she violates an integrity or wholeness
of her being that it is very important to her, as a person,
to maintain. Counselors see many instances where the

consequences have been serious to happiness and well-being.

Himes, who has recently summarized all the most significant studies having to do with achievement of happy marriage, concludes:

> Many will disagree with this statement, but I do not believe that the average young person can live a promiscuous life without damage to the personality. . . . A person cannot live intimately with many people without somehow cheapening the conception of intimacy. As Bromley and Britten rightly say, "Selectivity and not promiscuity in sex life encourages development of the personality on higher levels."[1]

Without consideration for what it may mean to the personality development of a man or a woman to have sexual intercourse outside of marriage, society—the society of present-day America—sets very definite taboos on violations of chastity. Most young people wish at some time or other to discuss theoretically whether or not society is quite so strict in this respect as they have been brought up to believe. We all know of certain social circles where sexual intercourse outside of marriage is not violently condemned and where indulgences of many sorts are overlooked or condoned.

A few novels about present-day America depict with great sympathy characters, supposedly fine, who have sexual intercourse outside of marriage. Even a superficial study of motion pictures, drama, and literature, however, will bring overwhelming conviction that sexual intercourse outside of marriage is associated fairly consistently in our culture with tragedy. Society almost violently disapproves it, and the penalties that society exacts for violations, especially from women, are severe.

Petting is another form of sex experience about which young people have many questions. Petting has had such blanket condemnation by some intelligent adults that it is

[1] HIMES, NORMAN E., *Your Marriage*, p. 42, Farrar & Rinehart, Inc., New York, 1940.

sometimes thought to have only negative aspects. Its critics are inclined to overlook the fact that petting can be the expression of a genuine emotion and that all of us need to learn how better to give expression to those emotions that are, for us, important and fine. No one of us has skills adequate to the depth of affection to which we need sometimes to give expression.

On the other hand, skill in the expression of love is not acquired by concentrating on technique alone when the feeling that would make it sincere does not exist. Nor, in spite of those who argue to the contrary, can the genuine feeling which we all crave be developed by running through the gamut of techniques of physical expression. If petting does not have anything to do with love, if it is not the physical manifestation of real feeling, then it becomes cheap and mechanical—a process in which one merely superficially goes through a set of motions—something again, that threatens a person's integrity because he seems to say something that he does not really mean.

Petting certainly is not a new invention. It existed as long ago as "bundling," then came to be known as "sparking," "spooning," or "necking." The particular label employed at any given time is not important. The primary fact in a consideration of it should be: Is it being used as a means of sex excitation only? If mutual love or regard does not enter into the experience at all, if the physiological aspects are completely ascendant, then the supreme techniques of love-making are being used for mere physical excitation.

Real love does not develop by such a process; it does not rest on a physical, biological basis alone. Love, as discussed earlier, is much more than that. If an individual puts all the emphasis on petting, he is apt to learn little more about his partner than the way in which he—or she—reacts to a physical stimulation under certain circumstances. He never knows whether he and the other person are suited to each other in any way except the physical. For example, dancing is an effective way of getting acquainted. Yet *really* to know another person, you need to know much more than that he—or she—is a "heavenly" dancer. True happiness may blossom from a physical attraction, but it must be based on something much more real and lasting.

It might be well to investigate the nature of the sex urge and to examine its various manifestations. Two basic urges direct our behavior, that for self-preservation and that for race preservation. The first is easy to recognize. We eat and drink to nourish ourselves. We live in houses; we wear clothes; we do everything possible to avoid accidents, disease, and aggression by other human beings. These activities are necessary in order to remain alive. This basic need for self-preservation is embroidered with an elaborate system of cookery, table manners, and decorations, the functions of hospitality and entertainment. The need for protection has made us build homes and cities, establish transportation systems, and an entire social order.

What of the urge for race preservation? It differs from the urge for self-preservation in that its fulfillment requires two persons and begets a third, for the race can be continued only through the partnership of a man and a woman. When civilization was less complex, marriage was consummated soon after young people reached physical maturity.

However, early in the history of man, rules and customs grew up around marriage. The young man had to prove that he was strong and brave, that he could protect and support a woman. The young woman had to make herself attractive to the man, skillful in the ways of homemaking, clever in the treatment and use of materials the man brought home. After a man and woman had satisfactorily demonstrated that they were suited to each other and wanted to belong to each other, they were married. Thus customs of courtship and marriage arose. Then, gradually, as civilization progressed, a part of this drive found its expression in art, literature, and music.

This urge develops gradually throughout the life of an individual. Contrary to a somewhat prevalent belief, it does not suddenly come into being during adolescence. This is as false an impression as to think that we suddenly awake one day to find ourselves with a complete set of social graces or table manners. Let us trace its development. A small child is chiefly interested in himself. His main interests early in life are to have his stomach kept full and the rest of his body comfortable. Gradually, a child's interests expand, and affection extends to his mother and to other members of the family who share in his care and entertainment. Little by little, a child's affections grow to include his playmates. Through most of his elementary-school years, he shows a preference for the company of members of his own sex; in the junior-high-school and high-school years, he normally becomes more and more interested in members of the opposite sex. Finally, of all those whom he comes to know, there is someone who seems to him to be very special. They talk together whenever the opportunity affords, they enjoy each other's company, and look forward to future meetings. As they meet more frequently or decide that they are "in love," there is the pleasure of anticipation and of memory connected with their meetings. They spontaneously express this pleasure by a touch of the hand, arms around each other. When physical intimacies, such as kissing and embracing occur, these stimulate or start off a set of physical sensations. This is basically the stirring up of sex desire, the beginning of naturally succeeding acts whose ultimate goal is sexual intercourse.

This is the way our bodies and feelings work. Petting stimulates in both partners strong desires that may become hard to control. Control may be more difficult for one than for the other. Some people feel more quickly than others a drive for full sex satisfaction. Prolonged petting may precipitate with anyone a wish for immediate gratification of a strong drive, even though the person may know that yielding to that drive may result in unhappy consequences. Therefore, in men-women relationships, just as with everything else that has great potential value and great potential danger, we should bring into play knowledge, judgment, and self-control. It is certainly worth while to learn how to handle powerful forces of any sort safely and constructively—whether these forces exist in high-powered automobiles, airplanes, or in the love of a man and a woman for each other.

Hardly anyone would deliberately choose to pet in a perfunctory manner, as one girl said she felt she had to do, merely to "keep a friendship." Most of us prefer to treat those whom we "date" as human beings whose friendships are valuable rather than as people who need to be guarded against or taken advantage of. If we would learn to treat people in this way, we need to learn to express, in other ways than by petting, the joy that we find in companionship and friendship. We need to perfect many of the subtle techniques of social relationships that are difficult to analyze but are the signals by which others advance or retreat, extend further invitations, recognize blocks or the necessity to detour.

We need to learn, specifically, how to let another person know, without being too obvious, that "being with you is heaven"; we need to know how, without being rude, to refuse another's invitation, how to get out of taking a drink, how to avoid having to kiss or be kissed. We need to learn how to do these things graciously, without hurting, humiliating, or belittling the other person, and without feeling that we have lost status in our group because we refuse to do as "the gang does." It is well to remember that individuals who feel secure in their status, who know that they are liked by their contemporaries of both sexes, are less likely to be the ones who feel driven to do that which is "expected" of them.

It is true that some young people merely drift into petting because they feel that it is the "thing to do." To what extent is it actually the "expected" or "accepted" thing?

It is almost impossible to discover the true state of affairs in regard to current practices in petting and premarital sex relations. Many studies have purported to do this, but the startling conclusions in regard to the widespread extent of premarital relations that some investigators say they have found have been challenged by other investigators fully as competent. Some of the latter point out that if an individual consulted feels that it is considered smart in his group to have "had experience" he will say that he has—and vice versa. In studies that try to get at such intimate information, the use of the most scientific methods known may not reveal actual conditions. Certainly one must be cautious in assuming that any individual or any group really knows what is happening in any one town or school.

A recent study of youth, one in which a great many people have confidence, states that numerous investigations have shown a relaxation of taboos against intimacy before marriage. These investigations have shown that there is more demonstration of affection between boys and girls, less soul struggle on the part of the timid.[1]

What a given individual decides about petting seems to be affected by the number of individuals with whom he has dates. Many young people say that they prefer to go out with one person steadily and to get to know that individual really well before they make up their minds about switching to someone else, rather than to try to keep several or a large number of friends of the opposite sex simultaneously. All studies indicate, however, that as soon as two individuals begin to "go steady," they must face the question of physical expression of the affection that is drawing them together.

Young people may be confused when making decisions about petting because they have heard that individuals must "go all the way" in order to know whether they are suited to each other physically. Such an impression is false. Anyone can tell early in a friendship whether some-

[1] RAINEY, *op. cit.*, p. 140.

one else is physically attractive to him or her. If he does not respond to another individual, to the sight of that person, to a touch of the hand, to a smile, then no amount of deliberate sex stimulation is going to change the basic feelings. If, on the other hand, there is a strong physical attraction, an individual may be assured, unless he is one of those rare persons who is physiologically abnormal, that sexual adjustment will be among the simplest aspects to work out in the total relationship together.

Paul Popenoe has this to say about methods for ensuring sexual adjustment.

Sexual adjustment is something to be attained, not predetermined. The conditions of attainment are not likely to be present in premarital experiments, which are unrealistic and encounter many obstacles.

What should people do to make sure they will have successful sexual adjustment in marriage?

They should possess normal emotional makeup and attitudes. They should possess knowledge and understanding. This calls for a realistic sex education—now becoming widely available through scientific sources—not one based on erotic fancies turned out by pathological novelists. They should have a psychology of permanence—a recognition on the part of each that this relationship is part of a life long sharing, without reservations. With such a foundation, no one need worry about attaining satisfactory adjustment in marriage.[1]

Exceptions to the statement that young people can trust themselves to know those who attract them may be individuals who have been so unfortunately conditioned that they are blocked in reacting to a member of the opposite sex or those few who find themselves strongly and indiscriminately attracted to almost every member of the opposite sex.

Some people now in their late teens and early twenties have grown up with an attitude of fear toward the opposite

[1] POPENOE, PAUL, "So You're in Love?" *Your Life*, November, 1940.

sex. The parents of other young people have taught them
to be so reserved that they are painfully shy and embarrassed. Because of cheap "kidding" about sex or about
"dates," still others have become very self-conscious.
Some have been unconsciously influenced in a negative way
in their attitudes toward members of the opposite sex.

For these individuals there is merit in going out with one
member of the opposite sex until they feel secure in this
relationship, then of going out often with many different
members of the opposite sex so that gradually they learn to
react normally to them. Then, little by little, the fear of
them may be broken down. After a person has discovered
how innocuous and really delightful many individuals of
the opposite sex are, when he—or she—can admit how much
he really enjoys them, he too can make choices easily
among those who attract him and those whom he wishes to
know better.

A few young people are called oversexed because they
seem to be attracted to every member of the opposite sex
whom they meet. They are at the opposite extreme from
the inhibited individuals who can respond to no member of
the opposite sex. Such individuals must be particularly
careful not to depend upon physical attraction alone to
guide them, lest it lead to ultimate disillusionment. They
must consciously school themselves to seek for the other
factors that must be present if enduring love is to develop.

We learn to love by loving, but the expression of our love
must be characterized by sincerity. To go through the
gamut of physical expression which supposedly symbolizes
real feeling when the feeling does not accompany it results
inevitably in a most unsatisfying experience, in disillusionment, and in the feeling that "there's nothing in all this."

In whatever way we express love, it must be genuine.
Chastity may be a high form of emotional sincerity.
Young people who frankly and honestly face the problem
involved in a physical expression of their feeling are most
wise. There are, after all, only a few ways of expressing

affection. Spoken and written words, music—all art, in fact—provide important forms of expression. However, the person who gets along most successfully in his relationships with others does not make extreme and unfounded statements about his feelings toward them, does not expose himself to ridicule by writing sentimental or intensely emotional poetry to everyone whom he may like or admire. Similarly, each of us does well to cultivate discrimination in all physical expressions of our feelings. A smile or pleasant words may be more appropriate than a kiss. The cordial handclasp of one person may mean more than another's cheaply bestowed embrace. The finest human relationships are always characterized by discrimination and sensitivity. Truly, we need to develop both discrimination and true sincerity of expression if we would be most able to increase the happiness of those we love.

The argument that men, or women, expect physical expression breaks down at just this point. Any friendship that is to be either valuable or lasting must be a mutual relationship, not the dominance of one over the other—one demanding, the other giving. If two individuals have decided that they enjoy each other, that they have much to contribute one to the other, then it is up to each to do his best to preserve what is real in that relationship. Certainly there is no honesty in participating in a physical relationship because "everyone does," because one fears he will have no opportunity to continue a friendship if he does not, because he can think of nothing else to do, or because he thinks that it is the "smart," sophisticated thing to do. A person is not fair, or even decent, to the person with whom he is having such an experience, if he is a partner in it for these reasons only.

Emotional pretense also leads to emotional insensitivity. An individual who habitually demands physical expression without love becomes cruel because he is thinking only of himself. What he does to the other person becomes constantly less important to him. He may not even know whether that person is responding in any except a physical way; he is too concerned with forcing the person to "give in" to him. He may, as a consequence, never know that physical expression that is truly another's sincere expression of affection.

Such a person's life may be rather tragic. His insistence on physical expression is not always due to sex desire, nor does it always give him sex satisfaction. For example, such a person may not be highly sexed; he may actually be uncertain of his sex potency. He may fear the building of too strong a relationship with some one individual. Therefore he is driven to try to "conquer" many. Adler might explain it by saying that the individual needs the feeling of power, of control, and of security that he gains from having someone yield to him sexually. A man may thus try to "even up" the score that he had with a dominating mother, or a woman the score with her father, by inflicting on a member of the opposite sex his or her will to dominate.

This explanation, in some cases, is sufficient. However, such an attitude can also be symbolic of something far deeper. The individual who, without regard to the other person, selfishly insists upon physical expression may be desperately seeking the security of love. He may never have known what it was really like to be loved for himself. Constantly faced with this bitter reality, he is trying in every way to convince himself that he really counts, that he, as an individual, is worth while. Naturally, never having had the experience of knowing real love, he may tend to identify sex expression with love; therefore, he craves this type of expression. If one understands such a person and senses the depth of his or her need for experience with real love and security, such an individual may be the hardest of all for another to refuse, especially if the person who understands is essentially mature and generous.

Yet one cannot really help such an individual. He or she may be brilliant intellectually or may seem to be successful. Yet this lack of a basic security, of certainty that he is wanted and loved for himself, keeps him from believing in himself as a person.   This doubt, in turn, keeps him from believing that someone else really cares for him.   He cannot keep from doubting even that individual who yields to him, honestly loves him, and wants to help him.   His need is too great, his hurt too deep to be eradicated even by another's most earnest efforts to meet his demands.   He has to learn slowly what it means to love and to be loved.   He needs a long-continued experience of security to make him feel that he is an adequate person.

Since no one can, in this kind of temporary relationship, give another person the basic security that he or she needs, it is often necessary for a person to create his own security. He can do so by facing and acknowledging his deepest hurts, then by being willing to be hurt again as he relives those bitter experiences in an attempt to free himself from them or to build on them toward a recognition of what he, freed from them, can be.   But this means suffering.   It may demand a courage approximating that of facing death. Apparently, few individuals possess such courage.   But, as Donn Byrne says in *Blind Raftery*, "Those who have never died in life are pleasant shallow people, soulless as seals," for the alternative to willingness to suffer is remaining shallow.

With the changing attitudes toward the physical expression of love that were cited earlier, many young people face the question of sexual intercourse as well as of petting. They may have discovered that if sex experimentation by means of "heavy petting" is carried on without being brought to a climax, both individuals concerned are left tense, unsatisfied, nervous, and unhappy.   If the climax is reached by means of mutual caressing alone, that is poor preparation for marriage where new techniques and a new point of view must be learned, where one must be engrossed in thoughtfulness of the other, not concerned only about one's own physical reactions.   There are some young people therefore, who argue that "going all the way" is fairer and better for both of them.

Young people, in making a decision in regard to "going all the way," must be realistic. Choices are open to them only at the places where they can take the consequences of their choices. They must be honest with themselves in considering what may be the consequences of any decision that they will make. They must realize, for example, that they are "bucking the rules" of society should they decide to "go all the way."

Some young people feel that they can safely "buck the rules" because they will not be discovered; they have all the information necessary to keep them from getting into trouble. Unfortunately, their confidence is ill-founded. It is impossible for them to be certain that the information that they have is reliable. There is abundant evidence in the figures of illegitimacy and abortions—which have increased a great deal in the last twenty years—that thousands of people have mistakenly thought themselves safe. Any physician could have told them that nothing guaranteeing safety has yet been developed or discovered.[1] The various preparations and devices widely distributed and advertised may be effective a certain percentage of the time, but none is 100 per cent effective. Some are harmful. Young people need, furthermore, to be certain, before they can "safely" have sexual intercourse, that each of them has had a physical examination and that each is free from contagious diseases.

Having faced possible consequences and having argued that since they love each other so much, society does not have the right to deny them this physical expression of their love, should young people wish to go ahead, then they may realize for the first time what the glory of married love could be. But at the same time, they may find that they have thrown away their chance at real happiness in love. Sup-

---

[1] The American Birth Control League, 515 Madison Ave., New York, N. Y., maintains files of physicians and birth-control clinics where birth-control advice may be secured by married people. However, in some states, it is illegal to distribute any birth-control information.

pose that the two do marry.   Some individuals who have
had intercourse before marriage feel that they have cheated
themselves.   They sometimes find it difficult to know the
pleasure of a normal, happy sexual adjustment in marriage
because the conditions under which, before marriage, they
have had their first sex experiences were hostile to a happy
carefree relationship.   They may have had to meet hurriedly
and secretly, perhaps in uncongenial surroundings when
both were uncomfortable, apprehensive of discovery, fearful
because of their distrust of the effectiveness of the contra-
ceptives being used, anything but thoughtful of each other's
adjustment and happiness.   Unconscious feelings of guilt
may also become involved.   Even though one has convinced oneself intellectually that "it is all right," yet
emotionally one is affected over and over by the inexorable
pressures of society.

It may happen, in addition, that neither of the partners is
entirely happy after their marriage because each, knowing
that the other is the sort of person who has "taken a
chance" once, wonders whether the marriage partner might
not do so again with someone else.   On the other hand, if
one has seen one's lover exercise good judgment and self-
control consistently, even under conditions that provide
severe temptation, one's confidence in his or her integrity
and character is unshakably established.   The development of such a basic confidence many young people consider
far more important than the immediate satisfaction of a
strong drive.

Himes, after summarizing the various evidence that can
be mustered at this point, concludes:

The advice of nearly all counsellors is that while petting and
greater intimacy are undoubtedly normal and to be expected, it
is, on the whole, wiser to marry soon than to resort to premarital
sexual relations.   There is no denying the fact that the mores, at
least at present, oppose premarital sexual relations; that birth
control methods are by no means 100 per cent perfect, and that
consequently some pregnancies will certainly result; that pre-

marital sexual relations do not guarantee that a woman is not frigid; that the circumstances and conditions under which sexual intercourse is enjoyed are not conducive to the full satisfaction that one normally experiences in marriage.[1]

Young people can protect and show consideration for each other by planning their activities so that they are tension releasing instead of sex stimulating. During the cycles when sex tension is particularly strong, young people need to understand why they are restless, to be patient with themselves and with each other, and to avoid over-exposing themselves to sex stimuli. If young people will plan together activities in which their whole selves are involved—their brains in directing the activity, their emotions in enjoying it, and their muscles in taking part in it— then they will find themselves, after such experiences, happy together, satisfied, and relaxed. Possible activities are dancing, swimming, hiking, tennis, and other games.

There are those who advocate frank, explicit discussion of sex relations before marriage. They feel that complete understanding on the part of each partner about the facts and attitudes that are important to the other is essential to a happy sexual adjustment. This would be an unassailable position if it were really possible to reach complete under-standing, to discover feelings and emotional reactions, by means of words. However, in the realm of art, skill, and emotions, words at best are but vaguely related to the experiences that they are meant to suggest. For two people who had had little experience in aesthetic dancing to sit down solemnly ahead of time to discuss in detail a dance routine would be ridiculous.

Anne Lindbergh vividly expresses the limitations of words when she says:

To write or to speak is inevitably to lie a little. It is an attempt to clothe an intangible in a tangible form; to compress an immeasurable into a mold. And in the act of compression, how Truth is

[1] HIMES, *op. cit.*, p. 104.

mangled and torn! The writer is the eternal Procrustes who must fit his unhappy guests, his ideas, to his set bed of words. And in the process, it is inevitable that the ideas have their legs chopped off, or pulled out of joint, in order to fit the rigid frame.[1]

It is necessary, of course, that young people possess the essential physiological facts and that they understand the interrelationship of their psychological "sets" and their attitudes about sex with their emotional reactions; but, given such an understanding, human relationships that relate closely to the feelings are actually better left unverbalized in all but a few of their very simple outlines.[2]   Do you remember the story of the centipede who stumbled and fell all over himself when he attempted to describe just how he walked?   Because the whole realm of sex has to do with the most delicate and complex of human relations, most young people find that the actual adjustments in this area are relatively untouched by verbal discussion.   Understanding and appreciation of one's own feelings and of those of one's partner are progressively developed in experiences together, as one's capacity for tenderness and understanding grows.

Although there are many blind alleys into which one can stumble while trying to find true love, still true love always has been and always will be one of life's supreme rewards for those wise enough and fortunate enough to find it. Both men and women as they come of age need the stimulation of the opposite sex, through companionship, ideas, and points of view.   They need to build relationships that are real.   Such relationships can be looked back upon with satisfaction because they have contributed to mutual growth, increased self-confidence, a knowledge of people

[1] LINDBERGH, ANNE, *Wave of the Future*, p. 6, 7, Harcourt, Brace and Company, Inc., New York, 1940.

[2] For information regarding physiological facts and the various factors associated with happiness in marriage, see the works of the following authors, listed in the bibliography: Burgess and Cottrell, Elliott and Bone, Himes, and Terman.

and an ability to create happy human relationships. Inevitably, a time should come when both parties to this kind of relationship will grow to feel that the other is very "extra special" in a new and unique, wonderful way. Each wishes to express this feeling. We all need to show affection. We grow hard and cold and selfish if we do not express, in some way, our feelings for those we love. As soon as this feeling has been sufficiently tested—and confirmed—the two will decide to become engaged.

When this ecstatic moment comes, the two begin to get a first, faint notion of the happiness that may be theirs if they can remain together and continue through life to deepen and strengthen their relationship in marriage. The engagement period is the time when the two young people can prepare further for their life together. The success of their marriage relationship is going to depend not so much on their having all the answers to every problem as on the maturity of the two parties to the marriage, on the kind of personality traits they have developed, on the quality and strength of their love for each other, and on their determination to work out, just as cooperatively and wisely as possible, all the many large and small problems that will develop.

Early Marriage or Long Engagement

Every young couple who become engaged must weigh the advantages and disadvantages of an early marriage against a long engagement. In considering an early marriage, economic problems usually are paramount. When either young person has not finished his education, the problem is still further complicated. Of course, if it is possible for young people to do it, it is often wise for both the husband and wife to continue in school. The woman needs cultural education and vocational competence as much as the man, for she, as well as the man, will want to use every resource possible in the building of a happy and useful life.

If completing educational plans that have been begun is the specific problem, the decision should be made in the light of realistic answers to these questions: Can and will the parents of both young persons continue to subsidize them after marriage? Is this a wise procedure? Can each of the young people assume the responsibility of working in addition to going to school, if that would make marriage possible? Should one of the young people—generally it is the wife—work to support the other while he completes his vocational preparation? What are some of the other "money complications" of young married couples?

Needless to say, many parents would find it utterly impossible to subsidize their grown-up children. Nor should parents be expected to do so if the immediate sacrifice would be too great, or if funds planned for use during the parent's old age must be used up, leaving the parents dependent upon their children or upon the state. In contrast with their parents, young people still have before them the opportunity of building a life, even though their doing it together in marriage may need to be delayed a few years.

If parents do subsidize young people, several considerations will determine the contribution that the subsidy can make to their net welfare. Are parents using the subsidy as a method of keeping the young people under control, dependent in their actions upon the parents' decisions? How free from all kinds of restrictions is the subsidy? Young people should realize that they are asking their parents to be paragons of sympathy and virtue when they ask them to continue financial support, but to keep hands off the running of their lives. A few parents—but only a few—really are such paragons. They realize how important it is for young married people to run their own lives, to make their own decisions, and to take the consequences of their actions—whether fortunate or otherwise.

It is possible, if parents cannot subsidize young people financially, that they might do special things for them, help them out in stated ways that they and the young people have decided upon together. For example, parents might temporarily allow a young couple to fix up one or two rooms in the parents' home and live there rent free, or they might allow them to share a vegetable garden with the family. Such arrangements have frequently been worked out satisfactorily as temporary expedients until the young people could get on their feet and establish themselves independently from their parents.

On the other hand, is accepting a subsidy an immature reaction on the part of the young couple? Will they expect parents to keep on supporting them indefinitely? Are they using their subsidy to live beyond their means or to have luxuries that their parents are denying to themselves in order to give the young people the subsidy? Is the young couple planning in such a way as to be able to get along independently as soon as possible?

Parents sometimes withhold a subsidy if young people are marrying against their wishes. Again, young people may be hesitant to discuss with parents the possibility of a subsidy if they fear that their parents do not approve of their marriage, or that the parents will be hurt if they marry. It is generally true, however, that young people and parents alike would prefer to have the situation frankly discussed so that there are no misunderstandings about the situation. All are happier for having discussed the problem, even though the discussion does not eventuate in one viewpoint for all concerned.

Certainly, discussion of the situation is vastly preferable to a secret marriage. Many young people who marry secretly find that their relationship cannot stand secrecy long. The complications that arise in trying to keep a marriage secret mar their happiness in being married.

When young people discuss their marriage with their parents, often they discover that it is not the desirability of marriage that the parents question. Rather, they wish some assurance that the young person is certain that he has found an individual with whom he can spend his life happily, and that he has faced the situation realistically and still wishes to be married immediately. The parents are concerned about the many factors in the situation that may jeopardize the relationship, such as the lack of economic security. In these days when statistics show that young people's wages are low and their chances of retaining their jobs uncertain, parents are loath to be enthusiastic about a marriage that may, in a short time, result in much unhappiness because of economic strain.

Parents who oppose early marriage often are not opposing the young person's living his own life; they are only attempting to protect him from the consequences of a choice that he may later consider a poor one. If parents can be assured that the son or daughter is ready to face reality squarely and can happily abide by the consequences of his or her choice, their attitude may change.

Another solution to the problem of early marriage may be for the woman to work to support the man while he is finishing his vocational preparation.[1] In this case, young people will want to consider the implications of such questions as: What effect will this adjustment have on the two young persons themselves? Will the community make life difficult for the young man? Will the young woman feel robbed of a standard of living that she could have had if she were not paying for her husband's education? If he is away from her at school, does he use the money that she sends him to take out other women? Is the young man willing to hold a job as well as to go to school in order to help to support himself, or is he becoming accustomed to being supported by his wife?

COMPLICATIONS BECAUSE OF MONEY

The money that one partner alone can earn is often insufficient for the maintenance of a home. Often both

[1] SHALLCROSS, RUTH, "Should Married Women Work?" *Public Affairs Pamphlet* 49, Public Affairs Committee, Inc., New York, 1940.

husband and wife must undertake to hold jobs that bring in some monetary return. This business of both young people's holding jobs has its special complications.

Sometimes a man's pride demands that he be the sole support of the household. But he may be earning only enough money to support himself. A young man with these ideals may forget that if he decided to postpone marriage until his income increased, the young woman would still have to support herself until he could marry her; and if the choice were left to her, she might prefer to be married and to continue working as long as necessary rather than to remain apart from him while she awaited the increase in his income.

As a matter of fact, most women have always made some contribution to the support of the home. The economic value of the pioneer woman, for example, cannot be over-estimated. Her job was the equivalent of institutional manager. The woman's helping to support the home is not a new development; only the receipt of a pay check, the method by which she now supplies the support, has changed.

Many women are asking, as a matter of fact, whether it may not be unwise for them, at marriage, to abandon their professions or jobs. There are many examples of older women, left widowed, perhaps with a family to support, who regret the vocational ground they have lost during several years' separation from their business or profession. Statistics show that more and more women, from necessity or choice, are working in professions or jobs after marriage. If the woman's work contributes either necessary income or psychic values to the marriage, it may not be wise to erect artificial difficulties to restrain her from making this contribution.

Husband and wife should decide together on a plan for the use of everything that each earns. Neither should expect to hold out any part of his or her salary from a joint plan for using all for their mutual advantage. After the plan has thus been made, neither husband nor wife will have any need to ask the other for money. Each is free to use their joint resources carefully in accord with the agreed plan.

Actually planning a budget, in all its details, then spending according to it and keeping account of all expenditures is one of the most important safeguards of the harmony of the home. Young people who drift along spending their money without any definite aims in mind and without much idea where they have spent it, often find themselves quarreling about the fact that the supply of money is exhausted; they are suspicious of one another and each accuses the other of carelessness or extravagance. They may also find themselves with no money available in an emergency.

It is important for young people to realize the extent to which the power of decision or even the domination of the will of one partner over the other may be tied to the economic contribution of each and to economic dependence. Sometimes both husband and wife have jobs, but the wife happens to earn more than the husband. This is a situation that may be difficult for a woman to handle wisely—and difficult for the husband to accept gracefully. In most instances, as the economic world is constituted, this turns out to be only a temporary state of affairs, but while it lasts it is worth while for both partners to exercise all their wisdom to avoid any complications in their relationship to each other that may arise out of this fact. Again, if both pool their resources, without attention to whose check is the larger, draw up a plan for the total amount, and then spend and save according to that plan, unfortunate emotional feelings can be avoided.

It is detrimental to the personality development of most people to feel themselves inescapably and indefinitely at the mercy of someone who resents, even subconsciously, contributing whatever he or she can to their mutual welfare. We have all seen cases of a wife's so undermining her husband's feeling of self-respect by the grudging way in which she shared her earnings with him that eventually the wife has found herself married to a man who has lost most of his ability to stand up to the world.

After all, if one acquires any asset in life, he or she usually wishes to try to conserve it, not to depreciate it, or to permit it to deteriorate. A husband or wife is usually the greatest potential asset that life can provide—not often nor primarily in a financial sense, but most frequently and most importantly in all the other values that make our lives worth while. To keep one's partner at his or her very best, to contribute to his feeling that the world can never totter completely because the one he loves best is permanently and solidly behind him is not only the thing that provides the most glorious sense of satisfaction for both partners in a marriage but is also the only intelligent course for a somewhat selfish and shortsighted partner to pursue if he or she wishes to preserve his or her own surest happiness and security in life.

If both husband and wife are to be wage earners, the young couple needs to do some careful thinking to determine how the home responsibilities are to be distributed. There are husbands who feel, when they have worked all day, that they are entitled to come home and sit, regardless of the fact that their wives may be equally tired from a trying day. There are even husbands who feel, in spite of the fact that their wives also are working outside the home, that housework is exclusively woman's work. They do not assist with it, and would consider it an insult to be asked to assist.

On the other hand, many wives not working outside the home do not shoulder their share of home responsibility as they should; they make little effort to become competent in household skills and do not learn enough about cooking, for example, to be able to prepare a really good meal unassisted. They seem to make it a point always to have a list of jobs for their husbands to do around the house, so that the husbands can never feel free of household chores even though they may be working almost to the limit of their endurance on jobs outside the home.

Many men enjoy doing what they can in the home and often find great satisfaction in discovering that there are some things that they can do better than their wives: for example, some men always broil the steak or prepare the salad dressing for a meal. In fact, so many men have become interested in sharing household responsibilities that there has been a constantly increasing demand in adult schools and in social agencies for classes for men in buying, cooking, budgeting, homemaking, even in child care and training.

Again, young people who are wise will discuss together every phase of homemaking for which responsibility must be assumed if the home is to run smoothly when both young people hold jobs outside it. They will divide that responsibility in such a way that each knows definitely what his and her contribution is to be toward the daily tasks that must be performed. If home responsibilities are divided equitably, if each knows his and her tasks, then the petty quarrels that sometimes arise, especially when both young people are tired, over who is to do which task, will be less likely to occur.

An equitable division of labor between young married people of today depends not so much on what was traditionally supposed to be men's work or women's work as it does upon whether both the husband and the wife work outside the home, upon how great is the physical strength of each, and upon the procedure that will best ensure the maximum values of life for each member.

Working out the best possible solution to the question of each partner's meeting his or her social and professional obligations is another challenge to the young married couple when both of them are working outside the home. It is generally taken for granted that the young man will have certain professional obligations: work that sometimes keeps him busy past the hour when he usually goes home, meetings that sometimes take place at night or during a week end, banquets and social functions at which he must be present. Of the young woman, similar professional duties are often required. Both partners need to be thoughtful of each other as they plan to fit these obligations into their daily routine; for example, to inform each other of an obligation sufficiently prior to it so that the other may arrange his or her time and plans accordingly.

Social obligations can be both shared and enjoyed separately. Each partner will wish to have the other meet and know his or her friends. They will both want to entertain and be entertained together. Both will want, after marriage, to keep in touch to some extent with friends of both sexes who were known and enjoyed before marriage. Each will wish to grant the other the privilege of continuing membership in his or her own social organizations. Friendships with members of the opposite sex will tend to become fewer unless these friends are accepted also as friends of one's husband or wife. To some extent, although not so much, this will also be true of friends of one's own sex. After marriage there is a tendency to find most of one's social life with other married couples with whom both husband and wife are congenial.

Living Happily Ever After

In much of our romantic literature we are told that the hero and hereoine "were married and lived happily ever after." The reader breathes a sigh of relief that all trials and unhappiness and frustrations are at long last over. He thinks of the couple as safe in each other's arms with life for them now stretching blissfully ahead.

High schools and colleges seem to have taken their cue from romantic literature, for most of them assume that, with little effort on their part to provide information about how to "live happily ever after," and with little or no guidance, young people will nevertheless be able to attain this coveted goal. There is, fortunately, an increasingly realistic appreciation of the fact that the "rosy fade-out" is actually only the beginning of the most important venture a person ever makes. After the rice has washed into the gutter and the wedding silver begins to tarnish, the most serious and soul-trying, as well as the most thrilling, part of one's life begins. It has previously been stated that some high schools and colleges are beginning to offer formally organized courses on marriage. An increasing number of school and college counselors, ministers, priests, and physicians are studying to qualify themselves so that they can help individuals who are determined to create in their marriages the greatest possible personal happiness and social good.

Those who have more than a shallow appreciation of what marriage is have no doubt that it is an arrangement that provides the basis for almost everything that is good in life: someone to love and to love increasingly as one's capacity for love grows; someone to whom to give one's unquestioned loyalty and support; someone with whom to feel secure; someone to learn more and more thoroughly, a beloved personality to explore and enjoy and appreciate; someone for whom to do things and to make sacrifices and for whom to exceed and transcend oneself. It also, of course, provides one with a partner who generously and flatteringly appreciates one's own qualities, who wishes to be understanding and congenial and helpful; someone with whom jointly to discover the most important objectives of life and with whom to work for the realization of those objectives. Marriage means a home, not only physical shelter but the place around which plans and activities and experiences revolve. It means children—that most indescribable experience of being the means of bringing new life into the world. It means keen delight in seeing one's children grow fine and strong, and it means deeper insight and self-discipline when development grows awry. It means continuously and freely sharing one's joys and one's anxieties about one's children with another person who is as joyful and as anxious as oneself.

In spite of the fact that marriage can provide almost everything that is best in life, there are no guarantees

offered at the time of marriage that these things will
be automatically forthcoming. Marriage is a favorable
arrangement within which to work for these blessings, but
work for them one must.

Some people undoubtedly pick their husbands or wives
on the basis of what they themselves will gain thereby in
the way of financial security, prestige, sex gratification,
or good housekeeping. They conceive themselves in a
passive role, as people to whom their partners bring certain
advantages. Even when divorce does not result from such
marriages, life becomes hollow. The man who seemed to
have a good job may lose it. Prestige proves fickle. Sex
gratification realized becomes a less compelling motive.
And those who continue to live in a marriage that has lost
its meaning are beaten and hurt and bitter about their lot.

A much surer basis for choice of a marriage partner is
to consider whether the individual is the kind of person
with whom one can work toward the priceless privileges
that marriage at its best can offer. Divorces result much
less often when the choice is so made.

In planning how to live happily ever after, certainly
planning should go beyond the early adjustments of married
life. Both young people should determine, no matter how
neatly early adjustments may be worked out, not to stick
at any immature level, like a worn-out victrola record that
goes round and round in the same old groove. Both the
husband and wife should look ahead, determine courageously on a long-view plan that will ensure for their lives
increasing human rewards rather than dwindling ones.
They should work out a scheme of living and a calendar of
events that will lead them on into more and more satisfying
living.

Young people may effect quite happily the many adjustments that are necessary in the early stages of married life.
Yet, because of the very fact that the adjustments are
worked out satisfactorily, there may develop, on the part of
one or both partners, a fear of upsetting these arrangements

in any way. The couple may drift on and on, content for some years with the arrangements that they have been able to work out, and without serious thought for some of life's deepest values. For a baby to interrupt their pleasant arrangements may come to seem a terrible threat. The natural desire for children to love and to care for and to enjoy may be stifled in personalities that are, by that very fact, held back from ever coming to full fruition. For two young people to live as pleasantly and effortlessly as possible in the present may be to store up inescapable bitterness for the future when the choice between a comfortable but barren twosome and a full, exciting family life is no longer possible.

During the past decades, certain circles within American society have, to some extent, lost the appreciation of babies and children, both as adorable beings in themselves and as vital human resources. To the extent that this has occurred, something virile and sound and wholesome has gone out of individual personality and out of American life.

One's basic idea about marriage and what it is for is of tremendous importance in determining the quality that a marriage relationship will have. No marriage can rise much above the level of the personal qualities of the partners involved. In the last analysis, it is dependent on the degree of emotional maturity of each partner; on the capacity that each has developed for generosity and whole-hearted affection; on the willingness of each to exert himself tirelessly in the best interests of both. It depends on the integrity of both and their determination to deal honestly with each other. It depends, too, on the skill that each has developed in knowing how to be patient as well as delightful and interesting to the other.

The dynamic for living cannot be brought into a situation from the outside. It is inherent in facing the situation that confronts you. If you can understand someone else without submerging yourself in that person, if you can reserve judgment, if you can supplement yourself by learning from someone else who can do things that you cannot do, if you have a real respect for the inner life of the person with whom you live, the kind of awe and expectancy that makes you honestly try to understand what life is attempting to express through that person, then you have the ingredients for building a lasting and increasingly satisfying and beautiful relationship. Nor need you fear the selfishness that goes into making yourself mean something to that individual.

CHAPTER V

EFFECTIVE VOCATIONAL ACTIVITY

All of us want and need to be socially useful. Since usefulness is often thought of in terms of vocations, the work that we do to earn a living is very important, especially when we are dependent upon ourselves to earn the money needed to balance our personal budgets. In addition, work contributes to the fullest realization of personality because it gives a feeling of achievement, of making a success of life, of gaining some security, of being of worth to others and to the world.

However, personal happiness as well as social usefulness is dependent upon other activities in addition to vocations. Living completely satisfying lives involves many things, such as building up physical, mental, and emotional efficiency; studying and giving expression to aesthetic values; contributing to the home life of some group; developing civic as well as social relationships. All these activities are valuable in helping us to develop poise, companionability, and the ability to hold to established patterns of behavior no matter what uncertainties arise in daily living. Besides learning to do something that will bring economic rewards, each of us must learn to contribute to society other values than economic ones.

We soon find that there are many different kinds of pay other than money. Even during a period when a large number of people do not find the opportunity to produce goods—and earn money—no one needs to feel inferior. We can recognize that there are many services to perform, that all kinds of effort may be valuable, that it is false to presume that any one kind of work necessarily contributes any more real value to society than any other.

As we become more social-minded, we tend more and more to measure successful living in terms other than the ability to earn money alone. No one would accept as his list of the most valuable members of society in any country those with the highest incomes. In fact, history demonstrates that those who have made the most valuable contributions to society have seldom received monetary rewards in proportion to the value of the services rendered.

Necessity for Careful Vocational Planning

Important as other factors are in rounding out our lives, a vocation must for most of us be the center around which we fit our other interests. For example, the amount of money a person has to spend is determined by his vocation. The amount of time and energy he has left after his vocational activities are completed depends upon the nature of his work. Since our work takes approximately a third of every working day and sets limitations on the other things that we do, it behooves each of us to choose our work wisely.

In recent years young people have often found that a satisfactory vocational adjustment is difficult to make. A national study of youth[1] indicates that within a recent eight-year period young people between the ages of sixteen and twenty-four have constituted one-third of all unemployed in the United States. This condition cannot be considered to represent voluntary idleness; the Maryland study,[2] for example, showed that 48 per cent of those questioned were actively seeking work.

Young people are handicapped in finding jobs in that they frequently have nothing to offer employers except their willingness to work. They are in competition with appli-

[1] RAINEY, HOMER P., and others, *How Fare American Youth?* p. 34, D. Appleton-Century Company, Inc., New York, 1937.

[2] BELL, HOWARD M., *Youth Tell Their Story*, p. 151, American Council on Education, Washington, D. C., 1938.

cants who have both training and experience. Sometimes young people do not even know how to locate employment opportunities. Although society may have been lax in its efforts to train youth to take its place in the vocational world, young people cannot wait for the desirable social reforms to be made for them. There are things that they can and must do for themselves in order to become happily adjusted in our complicated vocational world.

In thinking about making a living, it is important to consider more than one occupation. Of course each person must limit himself to the lines of work for which he has some native endowment, but the idea is outmoded that there is only one job in which each person can be a success, and that it is the responsibility of each of us to discover that one job. On the contrary, vocations can be grouped according to the kinds of abilities required, such as mechanical ability, social adaptability, and physical strength. The average person can expect to be reasonably successful in any of the occupations in the group or groups for which his qualifications fit him.

Every young person should attempt to discover on as scientific a basis as possible what kind of ability he has and what specific occupations offer the best chances for the use of his ability. Furthermore, he should investigate the extent to which society needs the kind of vocation in which he is interested. For example, only 6.7 per cent of everyone employed is identified with a profession,[1] yet in the study of Maryland youth, 36.4 per cent of those questioned said that they would take professional training if it were possible for them to get it.[2] They were either disregarding or were unaware of the fact that only 3.8 per cent of the young people in that state held professional positions. Such a lack of knowledge about social and economic conditions can lead only to frustration for those who prepare for positions that do not exist.

[1] RAINEY, *op. cit.*, p. 27.
[2] BELL, *op. cit.*, p. 131.

Making a Vocational Survey

Census figures for specific communities and also for all 48 states show that there have been a great many occupational changes in the last 20 years. Some occupations have disappeared entirely. New and unexpected ones are developing all the time. Almost every field of work has undergone some changes because of the introduction of new mechanical devices. In the types of work that have been in existence for some time the young person must, of course, compete with trained and experienced workers. Young people who keep themselves informed of changing needs and take advantage of opportunities for training in new fields will improve their chances of employment.[1]

A group of young people working through a school or other community agency can gain a great deal of information that will be valuable in helping them to prepare intelligently for vocations. The most effective procedure is to conduct a survey of the community in order to discover vocational possibilities and to become acquainted with prospective employers. The help of local business and professional organizations, of the local or even the state or national Chamber of Commerce, and of individual businessmen can often be enlisted and will ensure the accuracy of the information secured. The American Youth Commission has prepared a handbook setting forth the essential steps in starting, planning, and carrying out local fact-finding investigations of the status, needs, and aspirations of the community young people. This handbook should prove helpful in carrying out such a survey as we suggest.[2]

[1] The Division of Occupational Information and Guidance Service of the Office of Education of the Federal Security Agency in Washington, D. C., has established a department of occupational information which keeps a current account of the broad shifts in vocational opportunities throughout the country.

[2] CHAMBERS, M. M., and HOWARD M. BELL, *How to Make a Community Youth Survey*, American Council on Education, Washington,

The kind and degree of cooperation gained by a group of young people from employers will vary. In most communities, businessmen are willing to talk to a group of young people who want specific information, if the young people have definite questions prepared and are able to discuss them intelligently. Some employers prefer to interview a small group that has specific questions to ask and that will take the information back to a larger group. Usually businessmen consider it worth while to let young people know what a prospective employer expects and seeks in an employee.

Employment managers have been found willing to demonstrate an interview with an applicant for a position. Thus it is possible to learn what is expected of a person applying for a position; and, therefore, how best to prepare for such an interview. Businessmen are often willing to explain the various types of jobs open and to conduct young people through their places of business. Watching someone actually working at a job may clear up many questions in the mind of the future worker.

Some businessmen have cooperated in a community survey to the extent of estimating the number and types of positions that they will have available in the next few years. Then schools and other agencies preparing young people for jobs have some definite information on which to base their advice concerning the kind of training to be undertaken. Communities often welcome the help of young people in organizing this type of community planning. After such a plan is under way, it requires the cooperation of everyone concerned to make it successful.

Efforts to secure vocational information need not be confined to the local community. Statewide occupational surveys are available in some states. These may furnish valuable data.

D. C., 1939. (This pamphlet costs 25 cents and may be obtained from the American Council on Education, 744 Jackson Place, Washington, D. C.)

Another useful publication of the American Youth Commission is a pamphlet[1] written for community leaders, parents, and youth, which suggests what should and can be done to improve vocational opportunity, education, health, and recreation for the community's youth.

In some occupations, the advantages of applying for a position in a community where one is known may be outweighed by the larger number of positions open in another community. The nature of the occupation determines how far-reaching the survey should be so that one will know whether he should be prepared to leave his home community —or even his own state—in order to have the best possible opportunity in the vocation of his choice.

The securing of a good vocational opportunity may involve making the adjustment from small-town to city life, from a warm to a cold climate, even from one country to another. There is pioneering work in certain vocations to be done in countries other than our own. A young person, instead of limiting himself to a certain community or locality as he makes plans for his lifework, should investigate thoroughly all possible locations and phases of work in the occupation in which he is interested. In this way he may find that his chosen vocation presents real opportunities that people with less foresight have not discovered.

The number of jobs available and where they are to be found geographically are by no means all the questions for which a survey should furnish the answers. Each occupation involves different factors to be investigated. For example, are there important facts that one should know about the organization and operation of labor unions? What are the health hazards? Is there legislation protecting or restricting the workers? Are opportunities in the occupation likely to change, to disappear entirely, or to be expanded within the next few years?

[1] CHAMBERS, M. M., *The Community and Its Young People*, American Council on Education, Washington, D. C., 1940. (This pamphlet costs 15 cents.)

CHOOSING THE BEST SOURCE OF TRAINING

As a young person considers the question of which occupations shall be given detailed study, he must also consider where training for these occupations is offered. Some of the possibilities are: a trade or technical school, a secondary school or college, a business school, or on the job itself. Young people sometimes need to remind themselves that a liberal arts course in a college or a secondary school academic course does not furnish them with skills or with technical knowledge. These courses are designed to give cultural background, to help young people to become familiar with the best that the world has developed in the way of appreciations, beauty, and science. Society needs to have its hard-won culture carefully transmitted. Those young people who need to complete their vocational training in as short a time as possible may be wiser to enter a business or technical school.

This country provides some of the best technical education in the world in its technical schools, universities, and business colleges. However, a young person should seek accurate and unprejudiced advice about the particular institution best suited to his needs. He needs to choose one that will best advance him toward his ambition— not to succumb to the school that uses the most aggressive advertising and promotion schemes for obtaining students.

If an individual chooses to enter a business or industry and receive training directly on the job, he should study the opportunities offered by a particular firm much as he would investigate a school. He will want to know if the firm is large enough to give him the experience he needs. He should know its stability, its standing in the community, the reliability of its business practices, its chance for expansion and his for advancement, the respect that a recommendation from it will command. The first three or four years of work may be considered from the standpoint of apprenticeship value, and many immediate disadvantages of the job may be discounted accordingly.

ANALYZING YOURSELF

When a misfit in a particular position is condemned for being generally incompetent—or just lazy—the criticism is often misplaced. Probably the vocation was chosen on an impulsive or entirely opportunistic basis rather than on a rational and carefully thought-through basis. The person may have seen a motion picture about aviation, read an exciting book about exploration, or been intrigued by the crisp white uniform of a nurse, then decided to be an aviator, explorer, or nurse. Perhaps the family tradition may have ordered the unhappy person into a ready-made pattern, into a vocation where he did not belong. Or he may have taken a certain job in order to work near his friends. None of these methods of choosing one's lifework makes for the best kind of vocational adjustment.

Young people need to know what qualifications are necessary for success in different types of occupations. Each case has many individual aspects. Everyone needs to discover for himself, in as honest and intelligent a fashion as possible, whether he possesses the qualifications required for the vocation in which he is most interested, whether he is fitted for it as well as interested in it. Everyone should try to answer these questions: Do I have the abilities, aptitudes, and interests that will make for happiness and satisfaction in my chosen occupation? Have I the resources to gain the requisite training?

All of us were born with different native capacities. In respect to a particular job, we need to ask ourselves: What are the demands as to stature, physical vitality, soundness of heart and lungs, skill of hand, eye, or ear, sensitivity of touch or smell, speed of reactions, degree of muscular coordination, patience, endurance, or intelligence? And how do I measure up? For example, airline hostesses must comply with definite requirements as to stature and weight;

a good radio mechanic or watchmaker needs a skillful hand; a railway engineer and an airplane pilot must have excellent vision and fast reaction time.

Training can do no more than develop potentialities and help individuals use their abilities to greater advantage. Nature determines our potentialities. It sets the limits to their development; but it does not determine how we shall use whatever capacity we possess.

There can be no question about the wisdom of getting facts about oneself, facing those facts squarely, and doing something about them. Reaching a satisfactory conclusion about the facts obtained may prove to be a perplexing problem, as many adults will tell you, but it is worth the effort to try. Gradually one is able to decide, within a fairly narrow range, the occupations for which he seems to be fitted.

How can facts about oneself be secured? The academic subjects young people find most interesting are worth noting, and also the extracurricular activities chosen. Other helpful sources of data are experiences with summer or part-time work undertaken to test oneself in a particular job; informal talks with people who are engaged in various occupations; intelligence and aptitude tests.

Using Tests

Various kinds of tests are available. Tests of mental ability can furnish facts about ability to see relationships, reasoning capacity, the sense of spatial and abstract relationships, the ability to reconstruct complicated structures in memory. The abilities needed in most vocations are, however, much too complicated to be analyzed entirely by objective tests. Another fact to bear in mind is that retesting is important if the results of a given test are to be considered as stable factors in predicting success.

The aptitude tests available help us to evaluate our probable degree of success in a vocation by comparing our own qualities and qualifications with those of others who have been successful in our chosen field. These tests are valuable as a guide insofar as they save us from investing money and time in preparation for a position that for some reason we think we would like but for which we actually do not have aptitude. The following statement by Bingham furnishes a summary of the case for and against aptitude tests:

Understanding of the vocational significance of test scores does not rest on mathematics alone; nor on general psychology. Close familiarity with the occupations and their requirements is also indispensable. It is, to be sure, not always safe to assume from one's observations of workers and one's familiarity with certain tests that an aptitude measured by a test and an aptitude apparently demanded by an occupation are really identical. They may be similar in name only. There is, with reference to a great majority of the occupations, a deplorable lack of data regarding the measured characteristics and minimal abilities of people successfully pursuing them, and a correspondingly strong temptation to make assumptions regarding essential aptitudes which later experience may not justify. Even when measurements are available, there is a further danger in assuming uncritically that any one ability or aptitude is really essential in an occupation, since it is possible that the lack of it can be compensated for by exceptional excellence in other aptitudes. When interpreting test results, ingenuity and fertility of insight as well as an understanding of psychological statistics is indeed to be desired, and richly informed common sense must hold the reins.[1]

Other types of tests than aptitude tests are available. Interest tests can give clues as to whether a person could live happily with people engaged in working in a particular occupation. They may indicate whether a person has the capacity for response and sympathy with people necessary to win cooperation and gain confidence, whether the person is the outgoing type who likes people, enjoys associating with them, and is sensitive to them, or whether he prefers to

[1] BINGHAM, WALTER V., *Aptitudes and Aptitude Testing*, p. 264, Harper & Brothers, New York, 1937.

work alone on some interesting problem, instrument, or
machine.   Other tests called adjustment inventories indicate a person's degree of mental and emotional health.
They point out emotional instability or excitability which,
if not corrected, might be a handicap in doing certain kinds
of work effectively.

Making a Decision

Before young people can make any permanent vocational
adjustments, however, they need to know much more about
themselves than tests can reveal.   Some of the important
considerations are suggested by the following questions
which might be used as a personal quiz: What do my tastes
and attitudes indicate about the degree of adjustment
possible for me in a given vocation?   What do I most want
out of life?   Do I measure my success in terms of money or
in terms of usefulness to society?   Is my self-respect bound
up with my ability to make money?   Do I make a distinc-
tion between economic success and social usefulness?   How
much income do I need to be happy?   How much appreciation of my work and social approval do I need?

Realistic answers to these questions will help in making a
final decision.   For example, a person should not plan to
work in solitude if his greatest spur to achievement comes
from contact with and approval of others.   Again, the
person to whom recognition and social approval are of great
importance must estimate the attitude of others toward his
choice—will they greet it with wholehearted approval,
resignation, or supercilious contempt?

A young person needs to explore all these questions as
completely as possible in addition to gaining a wide variety
of information about the vocation chosen.   He needs to
talk to people engaged in it, to find out their attitudes
toward their jobs, to know the satisfactions and disadvantages inherent in the jobs.   If possible, a person should
know what it feels like actually to do the job he is interested
in: to run a lathe, to cook, to operate a threshing machine,

to take a car apart, to teach a group of children something. One can best judge the depth of his enthusiasm for a job by finding out for himself what it involves. It is often helpful to talk with people who have tried the job and either failed at it or rejected it for something that seemed better to them.

Young people need to discuss objectively all angles of their vocational problems with some unprejudiced person, preferably a skilled vocational counselor. The United States Office of Education of the Federal Security Agency will send upon request a very useful little pamphlet entitled "Where Is Vocational Counsel Offered?" This pamphlet gives a list of free state vocational guidance and employment services.

Having collected every fact that might be pertinent, there are still two important steps in deciding on a vocation—to weigh and arrange all the facts so that they give as true a total picture as possible, and to come to a decision. The effects of this final decision may last far longer than association with one's immediate friends and advisers; therefore, it should be made by the person most concerned—oneself. Pleasing one's family or counselor or best friend may bring satisfaction at the moment, but it is often followed by sad if not tragic consequences.

ATTITUDES TOWARD WORK

In our concern about being well equipped in skills and aptitudes, we sometimes neglect to consider our attitudes toward work. It has often been said by employers that young people do not know what it means to work hard, that they do not have the ability to remain calm when work and contacts with co-workers are not going smoothly, that they have poor work habits and little determination to stick to a job regardless of how hard it is.

It may be that young people have heard so much about the growing problem of leisure that they think of a job merely as something that fills up the hours between sleeping and leisure time.   Perhaps they have yet to discover that the business and professional people who are doing the most effective and successful work are often those who work the hardest, who put in such long hours that an evening at home free from meetings or from preparation for the next day's work is a luxury.

The application required in different kinds of jobs varies greatly.   At one end of the scale there is the routine job that requires one's attention during working hours and then can be forgotten.   At the other end of the scale is the work that absorbs most of the time and energy of the person engaged in it.   Young people will find that success has its price in energy expended as well as in other demands. For example, it is often necessary to choose between learning to work with a difficult person and disrupting the morale of an entire organization.   A choice sometimes must be made between staying after hours to do a task well and leaving one's desk the minute the closing bell rings.

General versus Specialized Training

In the last decade the rapid changes in vocations and the widespread unemployment have pointed out the necessity of everyone's being prepared for a possible change in his vocational activities, regardless of his age.   Having wide interests has been found to be helpful.   Each interest is a possible start in preparing for a new vocation in case a person needs to change his plans because no jobs are available in his chosen field.

Another way in which some people hope to avoid unemployment is by becoming so expert, so specialized in one particular field, that their services will surely be sought. This solution to the problem can be applied most surely in occupations that require specialized technical training or in trades demanding a high degree of skill.

Certainly individuals who know only the vocational possibilities in the professions should explore those in the fields of skilled and semiskilled labor, while individuals who have been exposed only to various kinds of manual work may eventually discover that their forte is in the professions. These discoveries can be made only if there is a genuine interchange of experiences and ideas among all groups of workers. Young people will be wise to avail themselves of every opportunity that makes this possible. Such broad knowledge can do a great deal to make one's future more secure.

Wide interests founded on knowledge afford the most valid basis for vocational choices. Tests, after all, can be no more than short cuts to self-knowledge. The cultivation of several interests can make an individual more useful in any one of a number of jobs because of his versatility and skill. If a person is equally able to work in several fields, he is less likely to experience prolonged unemployment or frustration. For example, a person interested in industrial designing might become an automobile mechanic until he has the money necessary for further training; one interested in becoming a registered nurse might first take care of children; one interested in rural sociology might work on a farm.

On the other hand, some people allow themselves to be handicapped by their own versatility. Unusually intelligent children often show many interests and abilities at an early age. It was formerly thought that great intelligence displayed itself in one dominating direction. Now much evidence has been gathered that shows that the most intelligent people in our population can usually do many things well. But this high general ability has not always proved to be an asset. Counselors are frequently approached by extremely capable and intelligent individuals who have reached the age of twenty-five or even thirty without having any definite accomplishments to their credit. This type of person often displays an unfortunate resistance to any particular job. When he tries to fix his eye upon one objective, all the other possibilities glitter so attractively that he is distracted. By trying to embrace many objectives simultaneously, he fails to progress toward any goal. In trying to develop all his possibilities, he disperses his time and energy over too many fields and consequently loses confidence in his ability to achieve anything.

There is evidence to suggest that a gifted young person should choose in his early twenties to focus his efforts on one or two of the many goals possible for him. Even though he does this arbitrarily, he will find that he can organize all his efforts much more effectively than if he had no goal and that he will be much more likely to reach eventually several of the objectives that are important to him.

Some well-informed counselors feel, however, that although it is well for the most intelligent young men and women to have worked out some hierarchy of vocational aims early in their twenties, there is also a good deal to be said in favor of prolonging the period of preparation, since gifted young people have much to give to society. Our present professional preparation does tend to postpone vocational activity, especially for those students who take graduate work immediately following the receiving of a bachelor's degree. Long ago the philosopher Plato, in his *Republic*, advocated educating the most gifted until they were thirty years old, so that they might be well prepared to give to the state the maximum benefits of their gifts.

Is Disillusionment Necessary?

In the workaday world, there are many unexciting but necessary tasks to be done. With increased specialization in industry, the number of routine tasks has increased. Young people are sometimes discouraged when they discover this fact. Yet someone must fill these jobs. Good working conditions, fair wages, security, and opportunities to use one's leisure time in ways that are profitable and inexpensive make some routine jobs more attractive. If viewed in contrast to no work at all, even the less attractive jobs seem desirable.

Young people, however, find it difficult to view jobs from this realistic viewpoint. Numerous studies show that all during their high school and college years, as young people mature, their vocational choices shift a great deal. Even as they leave school, many still cling to the vocational ideal, gathered from romances or from the tradition of our early history, that for every young person there are worlds to conquer and fame for the asking. This romantic, unreal attitude must meet actuality sooner or later. It is not to be wondered that young people who leave school expecting to set the world on fire, or to find Prince Charming waiting on a white charger, often feel despondently doomed to mediocrity when their first jobs fall short of expectations.

On looking back, many adults find that some of their most disappointing experiences came when they were faced with the need for earning money and found that they could not carry out their vocational aspirations. The best preparation for meeting this situation is to be more realistic during the period when one is preparing for a vocation. Much as one may want to engage in a certain vocation, it is futile to prepare for it if it is overcrowded or if it is passing out of existence because of changes in the world of occupations. The vocational survey suggested earlier will prove helpful in bringing out the facts. The United States census report on occupations is well worth studying. Besides giving an idea of the jobs that are overcrowded, it suggests a wide variety of interesting and necessary jobs that are not commonly known to exist.

When a person realizes that there is little chance of doing the work that he has set his heart on, he will prepare with less mental conflict for a job that is more likely to materialize. In recent years many young people have been forced by economic necessity to seek work that does not fulfill their vocational ambitions. Many young women, for example, have found themselves forced to become household assistants. A fortunate few have found that this type of work under favorable conditions offers satisfactions and advantages that they had never heard discussed. Others have found that the only advantage if offered them under the circumstances which they had to accept was freedom from starvation and freezing until they could find something else to do which more nearly met their needs.

A young man, two years out of college, decided to seek a household position in a wealthy home which employed male help, because it would give him about four hours free during the day and evening when he could work at his writing. In addition, he was able to save most of his wages. The arrangement proved to be very satisfactory to him. Fortunately, it is a national ideal in our country that no occupation need cut one off from a better job when and if the opportunity arises.

Young people need to develop a philosophy that will help them to meet uncertainty. They dare not tie their estimate of themselves or their self-confidence to their ability to make money. Happiness cannot be interpreted as meaning economic security only. We have overemphasized money-making and often have failed to look for other satisfactions in life. The nature of an individual's development—what he is making of himself, the life pattern that he is developing —should be his paramount consideration in estimating himself.

The way in which one meets joy and success, or danger and frustration, the manner in which he endures failure, pain, or disappointment, the ability that he shows progressively to interpret the meaning of his experience in evolving goals for which he will give all—these are what really determine one's integrity as a person and his value to society. Day-by-day experiences are open to him which can influence his behavior away from patterns that characterize infancy toward those that represent responsible adjusted childhood.

Young people cannot always blame themselves for their inability to find employment. Many young people are caught in social conditions too complicated and too difficult for them to meet alone or without the aid of society. The problems of each individual are a direct reflection of the problems of the society in which he lives and has grown up.

PERSONAL EXPERIENCES IN SELF-SUPPORT

The experience of actually working at a job has brought forth varied reactions, as the statements given below show. Most of the young people quoted are commenting on their first experiences in earning money.

Experience in earning money has made me more conscientious than I used to be. When you're trying to please someone else, you have to try hard. Then, too, seeing how hard it is to earn money has made me appreciate far more than I ever used to the advantages I have and my own nice home.

It's done something to me to know that I can earn money if I need to. It's increased my feeling of self-respect, in a way, and made me feel lots more secure than I did before.

My experience at earning money has taught me that I must find something I really want very much to do and then stick at that instead of just working for money.

As a camp counselor I've come to have much greater understanding of and sympathy for other people. I've had to learn to control my own emotions too.

It's increased my feeling of independence and of self-control. And it's helped me overcome an undesirable amount of self-consciousness that I used to have.

It jacked me up on a bad habit I had of not being punctual. It provided me with mighty good discipline in other ways, too. One has a sense of at last being up against reality.

I think that anyone who has gone out and tried, applying at job after job, to get something to do. can't have helped but learn a lot.

It helped through giving me an idea of how the other half lives. My sphere had always been pretty limited until I got a job as a file clerk.

It brought me into contact with so many different kinds of people. I found it immensely stimulating.

Working has taught me not only the value of money but the value of everything—especially time.

Working in a florist shop during the summers and a little bit during the year has brought me into contact with people different from those that one meets at school. I have come to have a cherished feeling of independence because of the fact that I can work and help support myself.

I've done clerical work for College Board and clerked. I am sure this experience has broadened me and given me a taste of life I would not have gotten in any other way.

I've worked ever since I was ten years old. I love to work. It brings broad experiences you don't get otherwise. I've held lots of different kinds of jobs. I've learned that you have to be good in whatever you undertake. It certainly bears out everything my father has told me.

Working as an orderly in a big hospital inevitably brings a lot of experiences. The first thing was the fact that the organization of a hospital is so kind of militaristic and the nurses and doctors hardly thought of me as a human being. Then, too, seeing sickness and death, as I have, has made me think rather soberly of life in general.

One of the things I learned is just how rotten people can be about money. I'd always kind of taken money for granted, but it seems that it is rather hard to get and people will do almost anything for it.

I know from the little experience I've had at working that I'd rather work at an interesting job all my life for $3,000 a year than at an uninteresting one for twice that.

Men Have Special Vocational Problems

Women seem to get a good deal of special consideration because their vocational problems are recognized as especially complicated. Men also have vocational problems that fall upon them with a special weight simply because they are men. The special weight comes because pressures are applied indiscriminatingly by society without regard for important human values in individual cases.

One of the pressures that weighs most heavily upon men is the idea that a man can have little personal worth except as he has and holds a job. Most men also have difficulty in disassociating their worth as persons from the amount of money they are able to earn.

Another factor that colors the vocational adjustment as well as the personal happiness of many men is the fact that society tends increasingly to attach prestige values to each job, and a man tends to be assigned rigidly a certain position in relation to his fellows merely by virtue of the kind of work he does without much consideration for how well he performs that work or the kind of personal qualities he possesses. The pressure from this fact persuades some men who would find contentment and fulfillment in working with animals or with machinery, for example, to accept instead constricting lives in a city, bent over desks, and eternally dressed up in white collars.

On many individual men these relentless social pressures operate oppressively and destructively. Many years ago, Thoreau escaped from these social pressures by deliberately creating for himself a simple way of life that enabled him to escape from the money economy of his social group. His way of life included opportunities to learn and enjoy nature and aesthetics in a way that gave his life deep meaning. Today one finds groups and clear-sighted individuals trying in many ways to escape these distorting social pressures, reaching back to a simplicity of living that they feel deepens the meaning of life for them and makes possible the discovery of themselves as persons.

VOCATIONAL ADJUSTMENTS PECULIAR TO WOMEN

Women do not feel these particular pressures in the same way nor to the same extent as do men. They have their own special vocational problems as women, but they are not dependent to nearly the same degree as men for a realization and appreciation of themselves as persons on the fact that they do or do not have a job. Nor are their personal qualities eclipsed to the same extent by the amount of money they do or do not earn. Prestige values of particular jobs are also less rigid for women. Many women feel that they are fortunate because, as women, they have a number of keyboards on which to play in an attempt to find the harmonies most satisfying for their own lives and the lives of others.

The very breadth of possibilities, however, presents its problems. For it means that women must decide how to distribute their attention and energies so that they may be best prepared for the double career that they may wish to adopt, either consecutively or simultaneously. Every woman has, as she grows up, to get ready to meet most satisfactorily the demands that society makes upon her: to prepare to be a good mother and homemaker but not to sit around in idleness merely waiting to get married; and, after marriage, to work out an adjustment so that she continues to make her full contribution to the world, or, if she does not marry, to be prepared to compete adequately in the vocational world with those who have been devoting themselves to vocational purposes with no reservations and a single purpose.

The great majority of girls think the ideal solution to the vocational problem would be to work for a while and then to marry and stop work. But this, they admit, tends to make work seem somewhat less important since they always have in mind that it may be temporary.

Vocational Problems of Married Women

As mentioned in Chap. IV, many girls find that marriage does not necessarily mean that it is possible for them to quit their jobs. A very common case is that of the young man and woman who are very much in love but cannot set up a home on the man's salary. Many couples decide that they prefer to marry even though the wife must work until the husband's salary is sufficient to support two people.

Many other reasons for the wife's working may arise. The parents of either the husband or wife may become dependent. When the children are growing up, it may seem wise for the mother to work to help pay for their education. During periods of widespread unemployment, it has often proved easier for the wife to obtain a job than for the husband to replace the one he has lost.

Surveys made by the Department of Labor[1] have shown that more than half the women working do so for one or more of these reasons. The often-mentioned criticism that married women work because they wish to purchase luxuries has not been proved to be a fact. Women have always helped to support the home in one way or another. However, it is only recently that a choice has been possible between a contribution through household management and housework on the one hand and through a pay check on the other. Society has not yet entirely adjusted to this new state of affairs.

Although one reads of consistent efforts on the part of various groups to decide arbitrarily the problems that exist in this area, they cannot be dismissed by decreeing that the activities of all women should be limited to the home. As has been suggested, the wife's income is in many cases necessary to help to maintain an acceptable standard of

[1] See the following publications of the Women's Bureau of the U. S. Department of Labor: *Employed Women and Family Support*, 1939; *Gainful Employment of Married Women*, 1936; and the *Supplement to Gainful Employment of Married Women*, 1939.

living.   Even when there is no financial necessity for the
wife to work, there is another important consideration.
Women, as well as men, need to feel that they are socially
useful.   Many married women have much to contribute to
society in addition to being good homemakers.   The principal difficulty arises when there are not enough jobs outside of homes for all who want them.

When the income of the family is large enough that there
is no economic need for the wife to work, volunteer work
in one of the many community activities can offer her real
responsibility and genuine satisfaction.   If a woman is not
to have some opportunity to develop interests and responsibilities outside her home, she may tend to build her life too
closely around her children.   She may not allow them the
independence they should have, because feeling necessary
somewhere is a fundamental requirement in all of us.
Women as well as men need to find some vocational satisfaction, some accomplishment outside the home that gives
a feeling of complete usefulness and.makes it as possible
for the woman to grow in her role in life as it is for the man
to grow in his job.

Formerly when the family was a more self-centered unit,
all a woman's energies were needed to organize and direct
the home.   In many communities, this situation is changed.
In the larger cities, families live in apartments instead of in
individual houses surrounded by yards.   Household tasks
have been simplified by mechanical devices.   Many of
these tasks have been taken out of the house; for example,
laundry work and the canning and preserving of fruits and
vegetables.   Many social and recreational activities now
involve groups of people of the same age who gather outside
the home.   This change presents a problem that did not
exist when all members of a family from the youngest children to the grandparents spent their leisure time together
at home.   In many families today, women not only miss
the satisfaction of making a substantial contribution to the
home, but also find that the many activities outside the

home make the problem of budgeting the income difficult.

When the mother of a family works outside the home, any one of a number of special problems may arise. There are often so many things such as cooking, dishwashing, and darning to be done, that the mother's time when she is at home is completely taken up with these. In order to leave some time for recreational contact with the children, it may be desirable for both husband and wife to share many of the household responsibilities. The time the woman should give to her home and to her work outside the home will vary in different stages of the children's growth. This problem should be reexamined periodically with open-mindedness and insight by both the husband and the wife.

Should Married Women Work Outside the Home?

Many young women have said, in surveys, that they would be glad to remain at home if their husbands' salaries were adequate to support the home. When one considers facts revealed by the Maryland study, that the average man with a wife and one child was earning $17.06 working 49.2 hours per week,[1] one can understand why many women look outside the home for an opportunity to increase the income of the family.

As a result of depression conditions and the consequent unemployment of men, there has grown up a great deal of feeling against married women having employment outside their homes. It has been suggested that restrictions be set up to prohibit married women from working unless they need to. This idea could quickly be carried to absurd lengths, and its possible complications are easily seen. If employment were determined on the basis of financial need, sons and daughters of wealthy fathers would be denied the opportunity to work. In fact, wealthy men themselves might be dismissed as soon as they had acquired enough money for a comfortable living. Or jobs might be refused

[1] Bell, *op. cit.*, p. 234.

them. They might also be refused to sisters and brothers in a family in which one man was already earning enough money to support the others. Society might soon deprive itself of the services of many of its most useful citizens, if everyone were to be given employment on the basis of financial need alone.

The women who work outside their homes do not seem to be taking men's jobs. Reports of the Women's Bureau of the Department of Labor show a concentration of women in a few occupations. For example, about one-third of the women working are household assistants. A comparatively small per cent of women, about one-twentieth of all those employed, hold positions requiring considerable skill, such as professional work, stenography, or bookkeeping. The 1937 unemployment registration showed that of the unemployed men more than one-third were laborers and 18 per cent were skilled artisans. The jobs held by women are, in general, not ones that unemployed men are trained to fill. The problem of unemployment as far as men are concerned would not be solved if married women were forbidden to work outside their own homes.

JOB HUNTING

It is becoming increasingly true that most individuals have some experience with being unemployed. Many young people who do not have jobs have been found to be apathetic, indifferent to the future, defeated, believing that the community has no use for the abilities and skills that they have to offer.[1] Others become dissolved in self-pity at the possibility of not finding jobs after they have completed their training. Their apprehension prevents them from preparing intelligently to meet the problem of securing employment and attacking it with the expectancy of finding a solution. No one would question the fact that employment is often difficult to secure, especially for the inexperienced person.

[1] BELL, *op. cit.*, p. 151.

The fact remains that there are jobs to be had.   In some fields there are not sufficient applicants to fill the positions that are open.   Young people need to be explorers instead of followers of well-beaten trails.   They need to prepare for and develop new fields of work.   They have a great deal in common with the young people of a few generations ago who went out into a vast unknown to settle the western part of our country.

During the past year a number of newspapers and periodicals have run series of articles telling about some of the young people who, since 1930, and with little or no capital, have opened up new fields and made names for themselves. In this country we are rapidly improving our agencies for keeping track of current and prospective work possibilities so that young people can make their vocational plans more realistically in terms of the distribution of work opportunities.   The United States Office of Education, already mentioned, and Science Research Associates[1] are two agencies that provide information on vocational opportunities.

Making Temporary Adjustments

No one wants to plan for unemployment any more than he wants to make plans for an illness.   However, it is better to consider ways in which to make use of one's time if he is unemployed than to let it slip by while skills are being forgotten and personality development stagnates. Imagine yourself confronted with this problem.   Ask yourself these questions about making use of your time.

Will I build up my mental and physical health, or will I excuse myself because I seem to have no incentive for

[1] Science Research Associates has set up a Vocational Advisory System through which it provides, according to its statement, "accurate and up-to-date occupational materials prepared in periodical form for individual and group use.   Through a steady stream of reports from field correspondents and by consulting scores of research bulletins and publications every week, they [the educators, economists, and sociologists on the staff] keep constantly abreast of the country's changing occupational trends."

doing so? Will I become ingenious in using my time in worth-while and satisfying recreations and hobbies? Will I provide myself, as much as I can, with opportunities to retain my present skills or with further training in my chosen vocation? Or will I yield to the fatalistic "Why bother?" Will I merely condemn the society that at present does not need me or will I use this time to prepare for the future, to grow into a wise adult? Will I use all possible opportunities to learn to know, to appreciate, and to get along with other people? Will I try to gain happiness and security somewhere apart from money?

Some skills are lost by disuse more easily than others. For example, the ability to take shorthand rapidly is one that requires unbroken practice. In order to maintain this skill, an unemployed stenographer may decide to offer her services to a charitable agency in the community. She will have the satisfaction of knowing that she is conserving her skill at its greatest efficiency, and that she is also making a worth-while contribution to society.

Those who are employed in jobs in which they are dissatisfied, as well as those unemployed, will want to investigate the possibilities for developing avocations or recreational activities that afford real relaxation and satisfaction of achievement. An avocation should be chosen by the same careful process by which one chooses a vocation; and only as one submits to the discipline of an avocation can one achieve a sense of accomplishment from it. Avocations that are practiced continuously until a certain skill is attained can do a great deal to offset the frustration that many young people feel in unemployment or in unsatisfactory occupations. In their avocations they can gain prestige by the exercise of abilities that they possess but cannot utilize in occupations.

Because a growing number of people fail to achieve security, recognition, and a sense of achievement through an occupation, avocations and different forms of recreation are becoming increasingly important. Recreation allows for legitimate release from restraints and inhibitions. It is useful to the degree that one actually participates in it. Being an onlooker does not bring the same result.

One study, based on a survey of young people throughout the country, concluded that the need for recreation was on a par with that for employment, education, and better health facilities.[1] Young people throughout the country asked for recreation almost as often as they asked for employment. It was revealed that now they spend their time in reading, in individual sports, or in doing nothing. They suggested replacing competitive athletics in schools with sports such as swimming, cycling, and tennis which develop recreational skills that can be used after school days are over. These young people also asked for an opportunity for more group social activities.

HELPING TO IMPROVE VOCATIONAL POSSIBILITIES

That young people can help in the solving of vocational and social problems confronting them may be a new idea to some, but it is by no means an unpractical one. By organizing groups in schools, churches, or social agencies in the community, young people can prepare to present the needs of youth to the various schools and service organizations of the community. In this way, young people can effectively take hold of the problem of vocational adjustment, one of the severest problems confronting them. This activity furnishes satisfaction in itself, because it is a real contribution to others. The public opinion aroused can help also to build a community more sensitive to the problems of some of its members.

It is true that young people are confronted by heartbreaking suffering, by profoundly baffling problems. It is evident from studies that many of the unemployed are restless, discontented, resentful. Yet rather than yield to despair or to blind rebellion, young people can use this

[1] RAINEY, *op. cit.*, p. 77.

experience to gain insight into social problems that may prove to involve many more people than themselves.

Most young people have learned through their social studies in high school that our society is somewhat confused. Perhaps it has been discouraging to find that ready-made answers to the problems were not furnished. However, in a democracy the answers are left for each individual to make for himself. Perhaps this way of life has some defects, but most of us would not willingly give it up for any other.

One fact is encouraging. Many young people have formed opinions about ways in which to bring about much-needed changes. It is imperative that all of us, both young and old, examine contemporary life critically and become increasingly willing to locate and explore the problems that our country is facing. Knowing the factors that gave rise to these problems is also important. No one is too young to make it a habit to think about social problems. Human beings have the intellectual equipment to make possible social planning as well as individual planning. Perhaps we must always depend upon youth to solve the problems of tomorrow.

Since many of our problems are extremely complicated, it is necessary to consider carefully how they can best be attacked. For youth, one of the most serious problems is the fact that in the sixteen- to twenty-four-year-old group, the sixteen-year-olds have the greatest difficulty finding jobs. The Maryland study showed an increase in the rate of employment each year straight through the sixteen- to twenty-four-year-old period.[1] The average age for securing a job was a few months over seventeen years.[2]

If this gap were closed by raising the school-leaving age to seventeen or eighteen years, we would approach the equalization of educational opportunity which we try to maintain in this country. We would also increase the earning power of young people. Most of them would have

[1] BELL, *op. cit.*, p. 104.
[2] *Ibid.*, p. 121.

finished high school. One study indicates that the youth with a high-school education earn 50 per cent more than those who leave school before the eighth grade is completed.[1]

About 3 million of the 20 million unemployed in this country are young people out of school and out of work.[2]

The Maryland study showed that although only 19.4 per cent of the sixteen- to twenty-four-year-old group were in school, only slightly more than 4 in 10 of those out of school had jobs.[3] These facts make it obvious that it is very much worth while for young people to try to make their community and state conscious of the implications of leaving school too early.

Another possible point of attack on the problem of vocational opportunities is through agitation for vocational clinics. These would give young people specific guidance to help them intelligently to discover their own aptitudes, interests, and abilities, so that when they apply for a position, they will know what they have to offer. In some 65 cities where this idea has been tried,[4] it has been found that placement offices are most effective when operated jointly with the school where the young person is known. His adjustment to a job can be to some degree foretold by school counselors and teachers. Public agencies are not effective unless young people take the initiative in going to them for help. School agencies, on the other hand, can help young people daily in making wise decisions.

Another important fact disclosed in the study of Maryland[5] was that the median wage of the sixteen- to twenty-four-year-old group was $12.96 a week, with a range from $7.20 to $21.50. Hours of work varied from 40 to 50 a week. It was found that $21.50[6] a week was the peak

[1] *Ibid.*, p. 121.
[2] *Ibid.*, p. 106.
[3] *Ibid.*, pp. 105, 137.
[4] RAINEY, *op. cit.*, p. 38.
[5] BELL, *op. cit.*, p. 108.
[6] *Ibid.*, p. 113.

attained by young people under twenty-four in managerial and professional positions. Obviously, a great deal of thought needs to be given to the problem of the wage scale for the young worker.

Through the use of the ballot and through their own and other organizations, young people can work for the maintainance of an adequate wage and for an increase in the number of jobs. If a five-day week and six-hour day are secured by legislation in order to give employment to more people, young people can do their part to see that these changes come without a corresponding reduction in wages.

There are many other possible points of attack. Young people can become interested in a nationwide system of employment agencies, one in which each state registers its unemployed and, with the help of the national government, provides unemployment insurance for them. They can work for adequate relief. They can give serious thought to legislation by means of which the local and national governments undertake new creative activities, such as clearing slums, which will be of value to society and also utilize the energies of people eager to work. In other words, young people can work in many definite ways to increase the degree to which human values will have precedence over property values.

CHAPTER VI

EDUCATING YOURSELF

If we have been alert to things going on around us, most of us have, by the time we have become adults, discovered that our knowledge and experience is still meager. We feel impelled to broaden our horizons to include some of the things that we have only glimpsed.

Formal education through a college or university is undoubtedly one of the quickest ways of increasing one's knowledge and opening up avenues of endeavor for the years that follow. However, getting an education is by no means entirely a matter of going or not going to school or college. We can all think of many people who have never attended college whose command of knowledge is truly imposing, whose skills are highly developed, and whose relationships with other people are productive of happiness and deep satisfactions for all concerned. On the other hand, we all know college graduates whose knowledge is limited and superficial, whose specific skills or talents remain unused and sometimes undeveloped, whose attitudes are selfish, undemocratic, snobbish, or even antisocial, and whose relationships with other people are characterized by misunderstanding and bitterness. We know that the development of attitudes and standards in accord with the best that the world knows is not dependent upon college attendance.

As a matter of fact, regardless of the number of years of formal education we have, we cannot assume that our pursuit of knowledge can or should stop. Most of the people who have made outstanding contributions to the world have seemed to follow at least the first line of the old adage:

Learn as if to live forever;
Live as if to die tomorrow.

"WE ARE NOT ALONE"

Getting an education, in school or out, is a problem of utilizing most wisely and intelligently whatever educational resources are available. These may consist of college or trade schools; technical school, professional school, or business college; night school; CCC; or an apprenticeship in business or industry. Or they may consist of using the opportunities afforded by the public library, newspapers, churches, community forums, public lectures, and radio programs.

The college and university have no monopoly on education, although colleges unquestionably offer a wealth of educational opportunities to the young person who can and will take advantage of them. The specific advantages offered by institutions of higher learning are discussed in another chapter. The following discussion is concerned with other possibilities that are open to young people who for one reason or another are not in residence in a college or university.

Many of the suggested activities may be pursued with equal benefit by college graduates and those who have not been able to finish high school. Keeping alert and informed in our complicated world is a problem for all of us.

Young people who long for opportunities for furthering their education are not alone in their yearnings. To most of us it will probably be surprising to learn that only 19 per cent of the sixteen- to twenty-four-year-old group in the United States were in school in 1930.[1] In a recent year in the state of Maryland the number of young people who had left school was as follows: more than one-third of the sixteen-

[1] BELL, HOWARD M., *Youth Tell Their Story*, p. 51, American Council on Education, Washington, D. C., 1938.

year-olds, more than one-half of the seventeen-year-olds, and more than three-fourths of the eighteen-year-olds.[1] The same report showed that out of every 20 sixteen- to twenty-four-year-old young people in Maryland now permanently out of school, 8 had never gone beyond the eighth grade, whereas the median-grade attainment of all youth in Maryland was approximately the completion of the ninth grade.[2]

In 1930, there were over 20 million persons between the ages of fifteen and twenty-four in the United States. This is the largest number in this age group ever recorded by the census, the number having nearly tripled during the last 60 years. At every age level between sixteen and twenty-four, there are slightly over 2 million youth. In this age group there are practically the same number of women as men. Women from the age of fifteen to twenty-four represent 9.25 per cent of the total population; men of the same group compose 9 per cent. In all ages taken together, however, there are 102.5 men for every 100 women.

As might be expected, the percentage of married youth is lower than the percentage of married members in the general population. Of every 100 young men between fifteen and twenty-four years of age, 85 are single and 15 are married. Young women between the ages of fifteen and twenty-four include, for every 100 individuals, 66 single, 32 married, 1 widowed, and 1 divorced. This is a striking difference between the marital status of the sexes. Thirty-two out of every 100 young women and only 15 out of every 100 young men are married. American youth of sixteen to twenty-four includes 3 million housewives, 4 million young people in school, 8 million employed, and 5 million unemployed.[3]

---

[1] *Ibid.*, p. 55.

[2] *Ibid.*, p. 56.

[3] "Youth Education Today," pp. 29–31, *Sixteenth Yearbook,* American Association of School Administrators, Washington, D. C., 1938.

What is the explanation of this low average educational achievement? Is it because, as some authorities have stated, young people are not interested in taking advantage of educational opportunities offered them? Facts do not support this hypothesis. When young people in Maryland were asked why they had left school, 54 per cent gave economic reasons. Only 24.6 per cent stated that they lacked interest in school. Four out of 10 young people stated that they would have preferred to remain in school, but that they either could not afford it or that their families needed their services at home or needed the money which they could earn.[1]

The occupation of a young person's father is the greatest factor in determining the length of time that a young person can remain in school. The size of the family, race, and sex are also significant. In one state, a report showed that 7 out of 8 young people whose fathers were farm laborers and 2 out of 3 whose fathers were unskilled laborers failed to go beyond the eighth grade, while only 1 out of 13 whose fathers were in the professions failed to do so. The median grade attained by boys was 9.4 and by girls, 11. The median grade attained by white youth was 10.8, by Negro youth, 7.5.[2] A young person from a family of nine had one-third the chance of an only child to go beyond elementary school.

The inequality of opportunity to go to school is evident from the facts just stated. Increasingly, however, the people of our country are recognizing that if democracy is to survive, educational opportunity must become more nearly equalized. Therefore, more and more states are passing laws compelling young people to stay in school until they are seventeen or eighteen years of age, the time when, we have pointed out in another chapter, they are most likely to find jobs.

Statistics indicating the difficulties young people have in finding jobs point to the necessity for each individual to

[1] BELL, *op. cit.*, pp. 64, 66.
[2] *Ibid.*, pp. 58, 60, 63, 92–93.

educate himself to the greatest possible extent. The Maryland study showed that only about one-third of the young people who had left school were employed in full-time jobs.[1] In New York City in 1935, more than 330,000 young people were seeking work. These unemployed young people were almost half the entire body of gainful workers under 25 years of age.[2] Equally as serious as the inability to find employment is the fact that low-grade attainment limits a worker to low-wage occupations.

The facts stated indicate a crying need for adult education. In Maryland, for example, only 1 young person out of 11 was receiving part-time education. Of the young people who were asked if they would attend adult-education classes if they were available, 60 per cent replied in the affirmative.[3] No doubt if surveys were made in other states, the results would be comparable.

Opportunities for adult education are, however, being increased. In a recent year, adult education was said to involve 20 million people, or about one-sixth of the total population.[4] During the same year, the demand for WPA classes and for forums sponsored by the National Office of Education was constantly growing. Classes in CCC and other residence work camps, apprenticeship programs in industry, and internships in business concerns were all providing valuable experience as educational authorities worked with the sponsors of the activities so that the work program could become truly an educational one.

There can be no doubt that in these days of swift and constant advances in every branch of knowledge, of ever-changing economic and social conditions, the social, vocational, and general competence of each individual depends upon his planning for himself a continuous program of

[1] *Ibid.*, p. 55.

[2] McGILL, NETTIE PAULINE, and ELLEN NATHALIE MATTHEWS, *The Youth of New York City,* p. 57, The Macmillan Company, New York, 1940.

[3] BELL, *op. cit.*, pp. 68–70.

[4] RAINEY, HOMER P., and Others, *How Fare American Youth?* p. 51, D. Appleton-Century Company, Inc., New York, 1937.

education. If he does not do so, he is likely' to find that much of the information acquired during his formal schooling has been outdated. He will also discover that to continue to be a productive worker, he needs vocational retraining; and to be a happy and effective citizen, he needs to keep abreast of social change. Every ambitious young person might well canvass his community: first, to discover what opportunities for further education it offers, opportunities for cultural as well as vocational education; and second, to work intelligently on the problem of expanding these opportunities or of adapting them to the needs of the community.

Many groups and organizations are working on the problem of substitutes for college. The *Journal of the National Education Association*[1] recently submitted the following list of substitutes:

To remain with parents and to help about the home, business, or farm.

To conserve the accumulated savings of parents to care for their sunset years.

To join a CCC camp or to enlist in the United States Army or Navy.

To marry and make a home for someone.

To work and save money looking toward the establishment of a home and family.

To build up a rich personal library and to carry out a course of reading.

To travel or work in different sections of the country or in other countries.

To get established in some good job or to learn some useful trade.

To get located and started in some small enterprise of your own.

VOCATIONAL AND EDUCATIONAL GUIDANCE

Young people, both in and out of school, are wise to take advantage of whatever resources for educational and vocational guidance are open to them. Adequate vocational

[1] Vol. 28, No. 3 (March, 1939), p. 88.

guidance usually consists of the provision of vocational information, counseling on individual problems of adjustment, and placement service. These services are rendered by public school systems, state employment services, and by social agencies.

Because of the varied interests and abilities of the ever-growing number of boys and girls in public high schools and because of the variety of courses offered them, it has become increasingly important for schools to provide vocational orientation as well as educational and personal guidance so that young people may be helped to solve their many problems. However, all public schools have not yet been able to provide an adequate program of guidance. A national study of young people showed that only 16 out of 100 young people had been able to secure vocational guidance in schools.[1]

In New York City, only 4.7 per cent of the young people interviewed by the National Youth Administration stated that they had received vocational guidance in either school or college.[2] The Maryland study showed that of the young people who had received vocational guidance, 93.3 per cent had received it in school and the remaining 6.7 per cent had received it from employment agencies. A majority of these young people reported that they had found the service helpful.

Some towns and cities have developed agencies that supplement the work of the schools. Vocational guidance programs are sometimes operated in connection with the adult education project of a community. The New York City program has been described as follows:

The Guidance Service is a division of the WPA Adult Education Program of the Board of Education. It is a free service to students of Adult Education classes and is conducted to help individuals solve educational, vocational, avocational, and personality problems.

[1] BELL, *op. cit.*, p. 78.
[2] LINDSAY, MARY ROGERS, *Youth Gets Its Chance*, National Youth Administration for New York City [mimeographed], 1938.

Counselors in Adult Education Centers try to supply definite answers to definite questions concerning educational, vocational, and avocational opportunities.

In special Adjustment Centers, clients discuss their problems with counselors who are qualified by training and experience to advise mature persons, so that they may be enabled through their own efforts and abilities to make progressively better adjustments within themselves and to their environment. The case worker studies the family and social relationships as revealed by the client in the interview and as far as possible endeavors to get an estimate of the client's physical condition, referring to the proper agencies those who need special physical examination and treatment. Group psychometric tests for intelligence, achievement, aptitudes, interests, and personality are administered and interpreted by experienced psychologists. Individual tests are given in accordance with the needs of each client.

The Guidance Service also offers information about schools to fit individual needs. Students are helped to register in suitable schools or courses. Through regular follow-up their progress is checked periodically. Consideration is given to aptitudes and interests, occupational opportunities are pointed out, and training and retraining in all available schools of the city are suggested.

While this service is not primarily a job-finding agency, it considers the intelligent fitting of the right work opportunity to the right person an integral part of its guidance plans. Suitable jobs are found and filled through a cooperative arrangement with the New York State Employment Service.

Counseling services have also been developed primarily for young people, for example, those services operated by local social agencies such as settlement houses, the YMCA, the YWCA, and churches. Young people would do well to canvass thoroughly their own locality to see whether some social agency offers a service comparable to the Junior Consultation Service in New York City. This service was established

. . . as a joint undertaking by the Junior Division of the State Employment Service and the Vocational Service for Juniors,

---

[1] McGILL AND MATTHEWS, *op. cit.*, pp. 113–114.

a voluntary social agency. The sponsorship is now shared also by the National Youth Administration for New York City. The organization furnishes a counseling service for young people between 16 and 25 years of age and gives constructive help in working out their vocational plans. Through the Vocational Service for Juniors, a scholarship fund is available for the aid of young people who need help in carrying through these plans. Counselors work in close cooperation with established educational, health, and recreational agencies under both public and private auspices.

. . . the Vocational Service for Juniors . . . incorporated in its present form in 1920, has made a practice of conducting demonstration programs with the object of convincing some appropriate public agency that the program should be accepted and made available to all youth. Its school counseling demonstration some years ago led to the appointment of the specially trained counselors in the public school system, and its junior employment demonstration resulted in the creation of the Junior Division of the State Employment Service. In 1934 . . . it established the Junior Consultation Service in cooperation with the State Employment Service . . . it still maintains an Employment Training Information Service giving information to applicants of any age about suitable non-profit employment agencies in the city and about possible vocational training. It conducts a psychological department giving tests as a basis for educational and vocational guidance.[1]

Obviously it would be a good thing for young people to cooperate with all local efforts to expand or to adapt vocational, educational, and personal guidance facilities available in the community. They might study the two plans in operation in New York City and urge their communities to follow these examples. Both the young people and the community will profit by any plan whereby an ever-increasing number of young people receive the help of vocational clinics in discovering their own abilities and aptitudes, in learning about the technical requirements of specific jobs, in securing accurate knowledge of available opportunities for employment in a given field, in preparing

[1] McGILL and MATTHEWS, *op. cit.*, pp. 114–115.

most wisely for the kind of work they have chosen, and in knowing themselves—their own problems, aptitudes, and abilities.

EDUCATIONAL INSTITUTIONS IN ONE'S COMMUNITY

In large cities an almost unlimited variety of adult education opportunities are available. City colleges and universities may give free extension courses or provide opportunities to residents of the city through part-time classes to secure both general and professional education. In both towns and cities, public school systems may conduct evening classes in both elementary and high schools; vocational schools may provide day and evening courses for workers in industry as well as special terminal courses for workers who wish training in some particular vocational skill. Vocational schools may offer training for as diversified vocations as: aviation trades, textile trades, printing trades, automotive trades, needle trades, building and metal trades, electrical work, dressmaking, millinery, advertising, costume design, costume illustration, home nursing, and child care. A directory of Federally aided all-day trade and industrial education programs has recently been issued. This directory lists the trades taught in 1,053 all-day public trade schools throughout the country.[1]

Recently vocational schools in many communities have been utilized in the country's defense program to give two types of free short courses: (1) preemployment refresher courses for workers with previous experience; (2) supplementary courses for employed workers needing to learn additional skills. The courses most frequently offered include blueprint reading, lathe work, milling machine, chipping and filing, parachute making, welding, riveting, toolmaking, auto mechanics, aviation mechanics, patternmaking, drafting, electricity, radio, aviation, sheet metal,

[1] Copies are available on request. Ask for, by number, *Miscellaneous* 2375, from the U. S. Office of Education, Federal Security Agency, Washington, D. C.

foundry practice, machine shop practice. The courses run for 6 to 12 weeks.

The following description of vocational courses now being offered to advance the defense program appeared in the "March of Education":

Preemployment refresher courses run six or eight hours per day, supplementary courses two to four hours per night two or three times a week. A student may take more than one course at a time. Some take a preparatory refresher course and follow up with supplementary courses after they have secured jobs.[1]

In order to ensure that the courses given in a particular community will be those in which employment can be secured, advisory committees consisting of representatives of labor and employers are working with educational authorities in 1,300 local communities. They assist in making local surveys of the supply of labor in relation to the needs of industry and they help to determine the most satisfactory policies for operating vocational training programs in their respective communities.[2] Information about these courses in your community may be secured from local vocational schools and boards of education.

For young men and women who have had some engineering training, opportunities for further education are now being opened because of the fact that defense industries need engineers with specialized knowledge. The Federal Security Agency reports that:

Shortages of engineering skill have appeared in the following classifications: naval architects, ship draftsmen, marine engineers, engineers skilled in airplane structures, airplane power plants, and airplane instruments, machine tool designers, and engineers to supervise and speed up production in the industries essential to the national defense program.[3]

[1] *March of Education*, No. 21 (September, 1940), p. 4, U. S. Office of Education of the Federal Security Agency, Washington, D. C.

[2] *Ibid.*, p. 5.

[3] *Ibid.*, p. 9.

To help eliminate these "bottlenecks," plans are being considered by Congress to appropriate money to engineering colleges to defray the costs of giving specialized short courses. Young people who can qualify would find it of profit to themselves to inquire at engineering colleges about this program.

Many engineering schools are supplementing their undergraduate and graduate engineering programs of study by intensive courses varying in duration from one to six months. Such short-term courses are generally

. . . available to engineers who have had the equivalent of at least three years of a recognized standard engineering college course but who lack specialized knowledge. Thus a civil engineer, through a four months' intensive course, may be prepared to design airplane structures. A mechanical engineer, through an intensive course of about the same length, may be qualified for airplane engine design.[1]

In many cities and towns, adult education facilities have been expanded by the Works Progress Administration, operating often under the supervision of the State Department of Education. The WPA is interested in furnishing employment as teachers to unemployed professional workers; the Department of Education is interested in providing opportunities for adults further to educate themselves. Classes are generally free, are given at convenient hours during the day and evening, are open to all adult city residents, and comprise opportunities to study in many fields. The subjects offered often include a wide variety of cultural courses, vocational courses, handicrafts, and health courses.

Forums and informal groups of various kinds are often organized. Every young person would do well to find out from his local board of education what educational facilities are available to him through the local public school systems.

Adult education is becoming an established custom. In many communities, both large and small, the equipment

[1] *Ibid.*, p. 9.

and facilities of the schools are regularly taken over, at stated times during the week, by adults interested in a variety of subjects. These adult schools are generally organized in response to a need for such education expressed by an organized group of community members. In a community where the needs of young people are not being adequately taken care of, a group of them might present their needs to representatives of the school administration and to interested organizations in the hope of working out a more adequate program. The following description of the development of one of the many successful adult education programs in our country may prove useful to young people who wish to know specifically how such a program can be developed.

In a certain community of about 19,000 people, the Parent Education committee of an elementary school Parent-Teacher Association[1] invited the school superintendent, and the principals of the senior high school and the junior high schools, to a meeting at which they discussed their plans for parent education in their organization. Those plans were so extensive that the administrators suggested appealing to the Board of Education for the use of the township high school, since that was the largest school plant in the township. It was further suggested that the program be opened to all residents of the township. The committee decided that before taking such a step they needed more information about methods by means of which so large an undertaking could be developed. They also decided to recruit the cooperation of other community organizations.

A meeting was called to which representative members of the community were invited: presidents of men's and women's clubs, of parent-teacher associations, of churches, and of other organizations. Representatives of adjoining school districts where adult schools were successfully functioning were invited to discuss the origin and nature of their

[1] Cheltenham Township, Pennsylvania.

projects. A well-known member of the community was asked to preside at the meeting.

Those present at the meeting were sufficiently impressed with the possibilities inherent in an adult education program to elect officers and a planning committee. The meeting described took place in late spring. Throughout the summer the committee worked. They secured permission from the Board of Education to use the school plant; they hired teachers, wrote and released publicity, and planned a curriculum. In regard to courses to be taught, they welcomed suggestions from individuals and organizations in the community. They advertised in local newspapers and used community organizations to distribute their publicity.

Registration reached 800 during the first semester, 1,400 during the second semester, and 1,700 during the fall of the second year of the project. The class fees are small, generally averaging $2 per course per semester, yet the school pays its own way. It pays the Board of Education $50 per night to operate the school plant; it pays its teachers; and, in the first year and a half it set aside $150 for scholarships. This money is given to the local social service agency to be distributed, so that no one connected with the adult school knows who is in school on a scholarship. A representative of the agency is a member of the Board of Trustees. In addition to the active members of the board, who determine the policies of the school, the school superintendent, the high-school principal, and the principals of the two junior high schools are ex-officio members. The curriculum committee is chosen from this board. What has been done in one community by a small but determined group can probably be repeated in countless other communities with equal success if plans are made in a fashion equally as intelligent.

In many communities the NYA and CCC have, for young people out of work, combined financial aid with a measure of education, stimulation, and vocational training under supervision. In CCC camps not only have young people's aptitudes for certain vocations been discovered as a result of vocational activities in the educational program, but their cultural interests have been widened by participation in music, drama, and arts and crafts groups.

The NYA has furnished young people valuable training in various occupations. They have been trained as kindergarten assistants, typists, stenographers, recreation workers, landscape gardeners, automobile mechanics, electricians, and plumbers. Through radio workshops in some cities, young people have had experience in script writing, announcing, entertaining, sound effects, production, and engineering. Other cities have organized household training units, in such work as beauty culture, photography, machine-shop work, furniture refinishing, woodwork, power sewing-machine work, welding, and enameling. Young people who wish to gain information about the NYA and CCC programs in their communities can secure it from the local social agencies, the Board of Education, or the local NYA office.

The Passamoquoddy Village Work Experience Plan[1] has served many young people throughout the country. The plan includes study, counseling, and testing for every participant. Work experience may be obtained in such subjects as aviation, radio, carpentry, drafting, and pipe trades. Such experience contributes to education in the broadest sense; the development of specific skills overcomes the handicap of lack of job experience and increases vocational consciousness.

Free lectures are an excellent but neglected means of keeping oneself informed in certain fields. By watching newspapers and public bulletin boards it is possible to learn of many lectures of an educational nature. For example, a Rotary Club recently sponsored a course for voters which was open to the public. Most colleges and universities schedule some lectures that are free and open to the public.

[1] Eastport, Me.

Helpful lists of organizations with leisure-time services for youth can be found in "*Youth Education Today*"[1] and in *Youth-serving Organizations*,[2] an American Youth Commission report. These books are available in many public libraries.

OTHER EDUCATIONAL POSSIBILITIES

The offerings of state-supported schools should also be investigated by young people desiring to broaden their education. Often it is possible to take an extension course, a short summer or winter course, or even a one-year or two-year course at little cost. These courses are often, but not always, limited to high-school graduates.

The variety of courses offered is evident from a cursory examination of a handbook published by one state.[3] It offers courses in commercial floriculture, nursery landscape service, air conditioning and refrigeration, radio, power distribution, electrical construction service, farm mechanics, the dairy industry, agricultural production and management, growing and marketing of fruits and vegetables, child study, homemaking, institutional management, building construction and architectural drawing, automobile repairing, watch and clock repairing, poultry production, forest-ranger work, training for the merchant marine, ceramics, and veterinary surgery. Information about the location and curricula of state-supported institutions can be secured from the State Department of Education located in the capital of each state.

Extension courses are available through many universities and colleges. Since the instruction is carried on by

[1] Pp. 310–324, *Sixteenth Yearbook*, American Association of School Administrators, Washington, D. C., 1938.

[2] CHAMBERS, M. M., *Youth-serving Organizations: National Nongovernmental Associations*, American Council on Education, Washington, D. C., 1937.

[3] Special Educational Opportunities Offered in State-supported Institutions," *Handbook* 44, N. Y. State Department of Education, Albany, N. Y., September, 1940.

mail, this work can be taken by anyone, regardless of where he lives. Even sailors in the United States Navy are enrolled. Their lessons are delayed somewhat, of course, because the papers cannot be mailed until the ship puts into port. Schools vary greatly in their offerings. A good way to learn the names of institutions giving courses in which one is interested is to write to the National University Extension Association, at Bloomington, Ind.

Many state agricultural schools will send representatives to rural communities which invite them. This service enables a group to receive firsthand information regarding some of its problems. A contact can be made directly with one's own state agricultural school.

In addition to educational facilities offered by institutions of higher learning, there are a great many schools that give training in special fields. One has merely to turn to the educational advertisements in a current magazine to find a list of schools that would seem to meet practically every need. Many of the courses offered can be studied by correspondence.

Some of the schools maintain a high degree of excellence; others turn pupils out after short courses with little or nothing to show for the money spent. Some schools make extravagant claims of being able to guarantee positions in the fields of work for which the school purposes to prepare them. Seldom can an examination of their records uphold the guarantee of a position.

Newspaper and magazine advertisements furnish a good way to learn of the available schools, but a person who intends to enroll should try to get information about a school other than that printed in advertising material or stated by a high-pressure salesman making a neighborhood canvass. Getting accurate information is often difficult; one precaution is to look with suspicion upon extravagant claims.

Sometimes it is possible for young people to extend their vocational knowledge while they are employed. There is a trend towards cooperation of schools and colleges with industry and labor in an apprenticeship system. This arrangement has, in some industries, proved more satisfactory than having the schools train for specific trade skills. In such a case, the school's responsibility has been to provide a broad general basis of knowledge on which to build specialized training as it is needed. Some of the country's best-known universities and technical schools operate a joint work-school plan.

During the depression, apprenticeships declined. Recently a shortage of skilled workers has existed in some occupations partly because not enough young people have had opportunities to learn the trades, partly because older workers have, through prolonged unemployment, lost their skill. Therefore, in 1934 the national government established a Federal Commission on apprenticeship training in the NRA. In 1935 the commission was taken over by the NYA and is now a part of the Department of Labor. It cooperates with state and local committees to develop apprenticeship standards which can be adapted to community needs. Often apprenticeship classes are maintained by local boards of education in cooperation with this commission and with employers. Important information might be secured by investigating the work of this commission in your community.

Specific professions and trade unions are concerned with the need of educational programs for younger members. An older member of a group active along this line may be able to help a young person to take advantage of these opportunities. In fact, the progress of a young person in his chosen profession may be determined by his attendance at the professional educational institution provided for him—for example, the American Banking Institute.

Cultural and Recreational Activities

Many young people continue their education by participating in a variety of cultural activities. Through these they learn to use leisure constructively, often meet congenial friends, and are provided with an opportunity for self-expression. They must exert themselves physically or mentally, and must certainly be psychologically aware of association with others in a common enterprise. Shared activities may include some form of social life, study and appreciation of the world's cultural heritage in music, drama, literature, or fine arts, and games or outdoor exercise.

Although the facilities for a broad educational program may be lacking in many communities, young people often are unaware of opportunities that do exist. Usually a wide variety of cultural and recreational programs will be found to be available through some of the organizations listed here: voluntary social service agencies, settlements, YMCA, YWCA, church groups, museums, libraries, the local recreation department, the board of education, community centers, parent-teacher associations, and local service clubs.

Adult schools have already been mentioned. In their offerings a wide variety of cultural pursuits are generally included. In addition, schools, social agencies, churches, and community clubs may operate as community centers and sponsor a more informal type of education, or club work, which may include singing, dancing, dramatics, crafts, learning to play a musical instrument, to paint, to draw, to write, or to participate in some other cultural activity. Museum and library staffs often open their buildings in the evening, both for free popular lectures in various specialized fields and for hobby classes in the arts. They may also sponsor free illustrated lectures, gallery talks, study hours, or special exhibits.

The Federal Theater and Federal Music Projects have made these cultural activities available to everyone. The Federal Theater presented well-known plays to thousands of individuals during its long runs. Subsidized music at popular prices has long been a feature of community life in many towns and cities. Open-air concerts, song festivals, and the like are often given, in summer in the parks, and in winter in the churches, museums, or social agencies. The Federal Music Project has greatly accelerated the popularization of community music, band and other types of concerts, and song festivals.

The park systems of many towns, cities, and states now include bathing beaches, free swimming lessons, baseball diamonds, handball and tennis courts, golf links, lakes for boating and fishing, facilities for a variety of winter sports, bridle paths, and an extensive program including concerts, dances, festivals, song contests, dramatic productions, handicraft classes, and exhibits. Parks also make possible motoring, hiking, bicycling, nature study, and camping.

Many state parks now have clearly marked trails and overnight accommodations for hikers; the social service agencies or clubs of a community are usually eager to sponsor bird or botany walks, camping and woodcraft programs, or winter sports. National parks furnish ranger-naturalists, government employees who accompany hikers and explain the beauties of nature peculiar to a particular national park, maintain scientific museums, and give lectures, often illustrated, designed to acquaint travelers with the most interesting facts about a park.

In some communities, play streets have been established. They are closed to traffic at stated times and utilized for daytime recreational activities. In addition, they are used when the young people living on the block sponsor block parties. These usually take place in the vicinity of some social agency that works with a committee of people living in the block to plan the party. Traffic is shut off the block on the evening of the party. Entertainment is provided for all ages: dances, folk songs and music of their fatherlands for the adults; relay races, various kinds of games, and dancing for young people. The block party may be used not only to provide some social life for people in overcrowded sections of the city, but also to acquaint various nationalities, living in close proximity, with each other's culture.

Two comparatively recent developments which young people would find it rewarding to investigate are the Youth Hostel Association and day-camp programs. In many communities, the public school system or the social agencies have established a day-camp program whose objective is to give young people an opportunity to spend time out-of-doors in the woods and to promote interest in and knowledge of nature, camping, and allied activities. During the day and over week ends in the summer small groups of young people are taken to near-by state or city parks.

The Youth Hostel Association[1] arranges inexpensive tours for young people in our own country as well as in some foreign countries. The organization maintains supervised hostels throughout the country where members can stop for 25 cents a night. Entertainment is provided in the evening and information service is available. The hostels are placed so as to be convenient for hikers and cyclists. By using these accommodations, young people can satisfy a desire to extend education by travel experiences. The out-of-doors is an inexhaustible source of education that will richly repay whatever efforts young people make to use facilities at their disposal.

MAKING USE OF EVERY POSSIBILITY

Social agencies, churches, and community clubs may sponsor civic as well as cultural activities. Because these organizations are primarily interested in the welfare of the community, young people can usually count on them for cooperation in any reasonable request for the extension of educational facilities in the community. Certainly an

[1] American Youth Hostels, Inc., with national headquarters at Northfield, Mass., publishes annually a handbook containing a list of hostels. Membership for young people under twenty-one costs $1; for those over twenty-one, $2.

intelligent young person must be interested in social and economic problems, must regard politics and questions of national policy as his personal concern, and must be aware of civic and political issues.   Education for citizenship may be secured by attending lectures and public forums; through attendance at group meetings where current events are discussed and interpreted by someone with adequate knowledge and understanding of the underlying economic, international, and government problems; or by becoming a member of organizations in which there are political and civic duties to be shared.

Reading as a means of educating oneself is a possibility no one can afford to neglect.   A thorough and thoughtful reading of good newspapers should be a daily habit.   An extensive and critical reading of good magazines is also a "must."   If a person cannot afford to buy magazines, they can be read in public libraries or perhaps in the reading rooms of social agencies, schools, or young people's clubs. There are many kinds—trade magazines, magazines dealing with public affairs or summarizing news, fiction and nonfiction magazines, magazines centering around the home, and magazines catering to special interests and hobbies.

Reading lists on a variety of subjects are furnished by many local libraries and also by the American Library Association.[1]

Developing a hobby or taking private lessons in a subject that interests one is to be heartily commended if it can possibly be included in one's educational program.   Intelligent and selective listening to radio programs is one excellent means of self-education.

Businessmen, chambers of commerce, factory owners, city service clubs such as Lions and Rotary, parent-teacher organizations, and women's clubs might assist young

[1] Write to the American Library Association, 520 North Michigan Avenue, Chicago, Ill., for information about the lists that are available. Lists for a large number of vocations and avocations have been compiled.

people in organizing a program of education if they present to such groups definite suggestions for the type of education needed. Such suggestions carry a good deal of weight if they are based upon an actual survey made in the community and show clearly needs and desires. Churches and social agencies are usually willing to offer their facilities and their cooperation in working out such a program. They are also usually willing to help young people to organize in groups that will work toward the establishment of a community educational program.

Such activity on the part of young people would do more than anything else to eliminate the situation that now exists in many towns and cities where there is a set of distinct educational institutions, public and private schools, business colleges, and special schools, each with its own vested interests, each lacking coordination with the others. The result of such a campaign would tend to be a total educational program that would provide much more satisfactorily for the needs and interests of the whole community.

In making such a survey,[1] young people should be careful not to concentrate on vocational training to the exclusion of all other educational opportunities. An individual who is to get the most out of life and be the most valuable to society must be an intelligent citizen as well as a good worker; he must have individual integrity, a real concern for the welfare of the group, and the ability to deal wisely with the facts of contemporary life. He must be able to take responsibility for the control and direction of our democratic society, to display social intelligence, to help to create standards by which the behavior of a group is controlled, and to have a sensitivity to aesthetic values, as well as a growing appreciation of spiritual values.

In other words, a person should, ideally, plan his educational opportunities in such a way that he is prepared for

[1] CHAMBERS, M. M., and HOWARD M. BELL, *How to Make a Community Youth Survey*, American Council on Education, Washington, D. C., 1939.

intelligent participation in those experiences of life that are shared by all people. Therefore, his education should revolve around a discussion and evaluation of all phases of life. He should become acquainted with our cultural heritage of language, literature, philosophy, science, habits, and customs. He should develop and explore as wide a range of interests as possible. Then he will be more likely to plan his future according to a realistic estimate of himself, his abilities, and the needs and opportunities of his environment. A liberal education that provides such an understanding of our culture should also furnish a background for vocational activity. Thus the young person may prepare himself to take his place as an individual, a citizen, and a worker in the life of his community.

Chapter VII

GETTING THE MOST OUT OF COLLEGE

Many young people who enter college are confused by the conflicting points of view from which they are exhorted to get the most out of this opportunity. Ambitious parents may wish them to be social successes or outstanding scholars or to acquire a "culture" background. High-school commencement speakers may exhort them to become good citizens. The students themselves may be most concerned about making the football team or becoming members of a particular fraternity.

Educators are not agreed as to what students should get out of college. Two opposite viewpoints are both deeply entrenched and there are many variations of each of them. One point of view is expressed by President Hutchins, of the University of Chicago, when he says, "The object of general education is the training of the mind."

The other school of thought asserts that individuals are not disembodied intellects, that for satisfactory living in the world today a trained intelligence is not enough. Thinking is only a part of living. The individual must be concerned with the education of his whole self, not with his intellectual training only. He must strive for social adjustment, physical fitness, aesthetic, emotional, moral, and religious development as well as for intellectual superiority.

Choosing the College

The fundamental viewpoint of the institution should, of course, be considered in choosing a college; but many other factors should also be taken into account. Some colleges are coeducational; others limit their enrollments to men only or to women only. Some have a religious orientation, others pride themselves on their secularization. The programs of some are definitely colored by vocational considerations. Others try to avoid what they feel to be narrow pecuniary interests, and devote themselves largely to abstract, as contrasted with applied, thinking.

The various departments in any one institution differ in the quality of the work they offer students. There is an increasing tendency for each college to capitalize on its strongest departments and to permit neighboring institutions, where strong, to supplement its weaker departments.

An individual's book-learning ability is an important consideration. A person who excels in this quality and has good high-school marks is much less limited in his choice of a college. In many colleges he could get along with trifling exertion—if that appeals to him—or, with good work habits, he could excel. In a few colleges the average I. Q. is around 140 and a student who tests lower than this score has difficulty in meeting the school's scholastic standards. For satisfactory development, most students prefer to work in groups in which their ability is at least average for the group.

There are colleges where a student with mediocre or even poor scholastic ability can count on getting along if he possesses good athletic ability or a good social background, or even simply money, good looks, and charming manners. There are a few institutions that call themselves colleges where the possession of tuition money alone seems to satisfy every important requirement.

The wise young person will investigate carefully such matters as these before he finally enrolls in a college. Otherwise he may find himself in an uncongenial environment. He may be forced to admit that he has chosen a college for some reason no more important than that "it was one of the places near home" or that it had a good football team. Perhaps he took literally some convincing advertising and asked no further questions.[1]

The amount of money a student will be able to spend may be an all-important factor in his choice of a college, although restricted finances need not prevent anyone from attending some college since expenses vary so widely. There are colleges where a student has a hard time getting by on less than $1,200 a year; there are others where $500 provides amply for all his needs.

What college to go to may depend to some extent on geographical factors. The growth of junior colleges in the past decade has been phenomenal. Young people have continued to live at home and attend a junior college conveniently located. When a student considers a college away from his own community, he must decide which of two possibilities is of more value to him, that of being away from home and becoming oriented to a new environment or that of attending a college near his home so that his friendships and contacts will be near his home.

Sometimes wanting to go to a college located in a city or wanting to go to a college that is not in a city determines what the final decision will be.

Any one or several of the following factors may weigh heavily in the final decision: a big versus a small institution; the success with which a college prepares for further specialized training; the advantages to health which location may offer; the beauty of the buildings and surroundings; the social status that attendance at a certain institution

[1] For information about colleges and universities consult such references as the following:

American Universities and Colleges, American Council on Education, Washington, D. C., 1940.

EELS, WALTER C. (comp.), *Directory of Junior Colleges*, American Association of Junior Colleges, Washington, D. C., 1940.

DAVIS, WAYNE, *How to Choose a Junior College*, Harper & Brothers, New York, 1939.

LOVEJOY, C. E., *So You're Going to College*, Simon & Schuster, Inc., New York, 1940.

may confer; the number and desirability of fraternities or clubs; where one's best friends are going; the ease with which social contacts with the opposite sex can be made; opportunities to earn money while attending school; the success of the football team; the amount of racial prejudice.

But there is no neat check-list that can be ticked off and added up to give automatically the correct answer to the question of where one should attend college. Although a great many factors need to be investigated, evaluating the data is an individual matter and the answer will depend upon the person involved.

IMPORTANT INFLUENCES IN COLLEGE

Even though one's college has been thoughtfully chosen, the results of an education are not entirely predictable. What an individual learns is conditioned by the way in which he acts and feels, as well as by the facts and opinions he hears or reads. Young people in colleges have been asked to discuss the influences that have been important to them during their college years. They have given telling answers to these questions: What experiences and conditions are most likely to give developing young people adjusted, wholesome personalities as well as those attitudes and value concepts which can be the basis for valid choices of behavior in each situation which they meet? What do individuals need in the way of people, things, experiences, activities, and relationships which will help them to attain functional effectiveness and to be happy in our society—in other words, to get the most out of life, as well as out of college?

The experiences that college students have mentioned as important to them involve: relationships with deans, with other administrative officials, and with members of the faculty; the stimulation of courses and voluntary reading; extracurricular activities; life in fraternities and sororities; the necessity of supporting oneself partially or wholly; and the influence of churches.

Verbatim reports from a few students give some idea of the influence of each of these factors.

PRESIDENTS AND DEANS

According to student testimony there are among administrators some personalities who contribute appreciably to what one gets out of college. Young people soon learn that they need someone to talk to—"to help me think things out," as one individual stated. The following statements indicate ways in which presidents and deans have helped and inspired students.

The president has certainly made me think a lot about the issues for which he stands. Yes, I should say he had influenced my development for the better.

I admire my president's poise and fairness and power very much. I really think it has passed the point of simple approval on my part to one of real motivation for me.

I have always liked the president. He was one of the first men I met at college. I was struck then, as I have been again and again, by his straightforwardness, his fairness, and the way he always keeps his good sportsmanship.

I've had a good deal of contact with the president. He has shown me the disadvantages of being a crusader. I admire and respect him. He has shown me, I think, that a person has to see a thing clear through. He has precipitated action, I would say, on decisions I had to make. He's sort of "fitted in" to the general scheme of working out my philosophy.

I have come to believe, partly through the president's influence, that ideals are a good thing to have.

I admire the president to such an extent that it really has influenced me. I hear most of his speeches and have read much of what he has written.

After mid-terms I went all to pieces. I got all "A's" on my mid-terms but I paid dearly for them. The dean did a lot for me. She's a dear. One has the feeling that the dean can always get one out of trouble.

I have had a great many contacts with the dean and thoroughly admire him. He's a fine fellow. If you give him any chance at all to help you, he always will. I sure would like to be like him.

The dean is the one man I admire most on the campus. He's sort of father to us all. We go to see him without being sent for. I was called in once, liked him and what he had to say, got real help from him, and have gone voluntarily ever since. He's a fair guy. You can count on him always to look at both sides.

At the beginning of my second year I almost flunked out. My family wanted me to give up, but the dean told me to stick and so I did and I'm glad now I took her advice.

The dean was one of my teachers during my freshman year and will always be my favorite professor. He's very friendly and always willing to help. He's the best liked person on the campus. He seems to take a personal interest in every student. Somehow, he seems to have seen possibilities in me from my freshman year when I really should have flunked out.

I think she is a little out of touch with life but I think she's admirable. She and I don't agree at all in our ideas about a lot of things, but she seems to be able to get a sort of objective appreciation of my ideas—which are so different from hers. She and I have talked a good deal. I don't think she has made me change my ideas any but in a very real way she has influenced me just the same.

He's the only real gentleman I've ever met. He's wonderful. No one ever has a word to say against the dean. He's done a lot for me personally. I'd say he has been the strongest influence I've had in these four years.

She has influenced me a great deal. She's the best friend a student has in college. She called me in once to have me tell her my troubles. She's the sort of person one can confide in. I don't know how I could have gotten through without her.

I've had various interviews with the dean. At one time he was ready to throw me out of school. He sure had a fiery look in his eye. But in the last interview we had, I think we were on a better basis. A fellow was telling me that he had to go in to see the dean for something and when he was leaving the dean pulled some money out of his pocket and told him he needed an overcoat and to go and get one and pay him back some day when it was convenient. You know, it isn't every chap who could buy a coat for another man like that and get away with it. That money didn't come out of any college fund either.

I have to talk to the dean frequently in an official kind of way, but I drop in and chat with her unofficially very often too. I'd say the dean was among the three or four most important influences I've had since I came to college.

The older fellows always used to say that if you get into trouble, go and tell the dean before someone else does. I've had to do it several times. The first time was after a Christmas vacation during which I had held about as wild a celebration as a fellow could. I decided when I got back to college just what kind of a fool I was and I thought I'd go in and let the dean tell me, too. Anyway, I preferred telling him myself to having him hear it first from someone else. I've gone several times since then, but the stories he has to listen to have gotten a little less sordid.

The dean's a darn fine educator. He threw me out of college twice. It took a lot of talking to get back in but he listened to me and seemed to take a lot of interest. Anyway, I'm expecting to graduate and I think I've got a lot more sense now than I used to have. I ought to know the dean pretty well because of all the trouble I've been in in my time.

I had a talk with her in my freshman year on a pretty serious subject. She got me straightened around. I'd say it was her method of treatment more than the concrete advice she gave me that has stuck. We've had more pleasant contacts since my freshman year.

OTHER ADMINISTRATORS

Other administrative officials whom students sometimes felt it had been worth while to know were: the admissions officer, the registrar, a vocational counselor, and the placement officer, who, as one student said, "helps you find jobs when you're pressed for money."

College medical officers, psychiatrists, and psychologists are sometimes outstanding personalities who can give a student not only necessary professional information but also invaluable help in determining viewpoints and attitudes. One college physician who is apparently outstanding in her influence on students has been described in these ways:

She has certainly influenced me through the advice she has given me and through her sympathetic personality.

She has taught me dynamic health values. I try to practice what she has taught me.

She knows all the girls by their first names. She has made health habits really popular in the whole student body.

She makes one definitely conscious of health as something to work for.

She has exerted a personal kind of influence on me. She's very cheering and restful. She gives one a kind of sense of security.

She's made me realize the ethical and practical value of living a clean, healthy life. In personal contacts with her she makes you feel that you really do count.

She has such a wholesome attitude toward life. She's done a lot for me in freshman hygiene classes and in the individual health examinations I've had.

She has a genius for being very friendly and for winning one's complete confidence.

She made me want to see things in a grown-up manner. There's nothing else really cheerful in college; but she is.

She doesn't moralize. She's broad and unshockable.

I admire her very much. I could tell her anything at all. She's sympathetic and understanding and always ready to talk. She somehow knows how to help when one is depressed. I'd go to her sooner than to anyone else in college.

She makes you feel she'd stand up for you under any circumstances. She can always somehow see the best in you and help you to see possibilities for yourself.

I don't know what I would have done without Dr. —— last year when my mother was ill and then when she committed suicide. Dr. —— took me in hand and pulled me through it from beginning to end. She's marvelous. She's certainly one of the biggest influences in my life.

It is true, of course, that young people are generally very sensitive to the slightest contact with administrators, that a nod or a casual remark of a person high in authority in the college is remembered as highly important, and that an administrator who calls one by one's name is likely to be considered a most unusual person. But a college student would undoubtedly lose many valuable contacts if he were graduated from college without having known well at least one administrative officer.

Faculty Members

Faculty people, because of their special position as administrators or their specialized knowledge in their own fields, can help students to gain an insight into human nature and can be a stimulus to widen curiosity and develop interests in new directions. In some cases students may find it difficult to build up genuine relationships with faculty members, but often faculty members are glad to meet informally and to become better acquainted with their students. They are happy to have students utilize their office hours or other occasions that arise when they can meet for conferences. On some campuses, young people can learn to know faculty members because they often invite students to their homes for teas, Sunday suppers, parties, or "at homes." When young people take advantage of these opportunities, they generally find that they are glad to have made this new contact.

Faculty wives can become interesting friends, who can contribute a great deal to an individual's development if he grows to know them well. Even seemingly casual contacts in faculty homes may be remembered. One man student said that he had been sent by the college employment bureau to a professor's house to polish silver before a party. The professor's wife had come out into the pantry and had talked to him as he worked. He never saw her other than those few hours, but he said she had made a big impression on him through what she said and the kind of person she was. When he marries, he said, he wants to find a girl like her.

There are actually a great many opportunities to meet faculty people in normal, natural situations—as they sponsor activities, as they attend social events of the college or are invited to the houses or dormitories where students live, as they entertain in their own homes, as they accompany their classes on field or camping trips, as they act as advisers, as they hold office hours, or as they teach.

Students can take advantage of these situations and gradually build genuine relationships with faculty members, relationships based upon mutual interests and mutual appreciation. Possibly the student has read an article or book in which the faculty member may be interested. Possibly the student wishes to talk over a personal problem. He may need help on a class assignment, or he may want to congratulate a faculty member upon a recent achievement or honor bestowed on him. Possibly student and teacher may discover that they have a hobby in common. Students may miss stimulating friendships with instructors because they fear that they will be suspected of being "apple polishers." They forget that sincerity is easily recognizable and certain to be appreciated by a faculty member. A relationship built on such a sound basis is a very different thing from an attempt to impress the teacher for the purpose of improving one's grade.

The things that students have to say about the influence of instructors indicate that contacts with them are considered secondary only to those with student friends. The benefits derived from the courses themselves are discussed in the following section. Here are the various ways in which students expressed the feeling that "I wouldn't for worlds have missed knowing him."

He is my idea of what a really cultured man should be like.

He teaches philosophy, but he taught me the poetry of commonplace life.

He teaches Latin. He's the most charming, brilliant, scintillating, and really helpful teacher I've had.

He kept me from quitting in my freshman year. He's been awfully human and taken a real interest in me straight through.

I'd never thought much of fine arts until he made me think maybe there was something to it. He certainly is far from being a sissy. I shall always feel eternally grateful to him for all the joys he has opened up to me.

He taught me values. He's also taught me optimism. I'd like to be like him.

I got into a frightful depression in my sophomore year. That year I took a course with him in philosophy. He was mighty fine to me, giving me a lot of his time. He showed me how to get out of the dumps.

He changed my whole method of looking at college life. I so greatly enjoyed studying his course that I began to study for other courses too. He's really changed the whole course of my life.

He helped me form the habit of thinking in terms of ends. He doesn't advise, he helps evaluate.

She remembers everybody's name and seems to take a real interest in us as individuals. I try to do the things she wants us to do. Another teacher treats each of us like "a case." I forget what she says as fast as I can.

The teachers in the Physical Education Department are so attractive. I've deliberately tried to copy them in dress and manners and attitude toward life.

They're the best dressed department in school. That may seem silly, but it doesn't hurt their influence on us a bit. Some men and women teachers get kind of grubby and flabby-looking.

He is young, doesn't drink, and is admirable in every way. He is definite and pronounced in his views, but he is not bigoted.

I've taken every psychology course he offered. It is mainly by his help during these four years that I have been able to overcome a very bad case of stammering which I developed as a little child.

He is the sort of man you can talk to about anything. You couldn't shock him. He lets you kind of talk yourself right. He doesn't tell you.

There seems to be a good deal of personal rivalry between the coaches. We don't like that kind of thing. It makes us think some of the coaches just use us for their own ends. Two of them are square shooters though, and I've tied up with them.

He drives us terrifically but I kind of like it. That's what life is, to my way of thinking.

He gave me a sense of the unimportance of grades.

We go up to his room and have lengthy bull sessions. I have got a lot out of those talks.

He's awfully sophisticated, but I doped him all out and got to kind of like him.

I admire him very much. He's a real scholar.

He gave me some pretty stiff adverse criticism. I've lived to thank him for it though.

There are two teachers who stand out way above the others as far as my own personal development is concerned. One told me in my freshman year that I wasn't as smart as I had been led to believe I was. I admired her; and I took it from her. I was pretty much of an atheist and materialist when I met her. She let me talk and did a lot of listening and I eventually found I had to alter my ideas. The other teacher directed a mean, insulting remark at me in class one day. I resented it deeply. But later she helped me a great deal to make a transition from a desire for general approval as a conduct control to relationships—the importance of what other people want and need—as my control.

I have come to have a definite sense of responsibility for taking physical exercises. I think this is a recognition of one of the paramount values in life, don't you?

She puts everything up to you to decide. She really makes you grow up.

He always acted so antagonistic and defensive in the classroom. I simply hated him—as did all the rest. But he has been tutoring me for months now for nothing, and since I've really gotten to know him I've found he's pretty firm underneath.

There was a chap who jumped out of a window last year. It's one of the real jars I've had in life. He had influenced a lot of the students. He was in terrible physical pain most of the time, but he's stand up in front of crowds of students and lecture brilliantly. Sometimes you could see the beads of perspiration standing out on his face, and it would be gray with pain. But he'd grin just the same and go right on. We used to crowd into his lecture rooms even if we hadn't been able to register for the courses. There were always some sitting on the floor just to listen to him. We did a lot of thinking when he stepped out of life.

I once fixed a report in physics. But the whole spirit of the course was one of such high standards of scientific procedure that I couldn't stand my own conscience so I told the professor. He was grand about it. I got a real lesson from the experience.

The outstanding fact here is that young people feel that it is decidedly worth while to know their teachers as individuals. Coming to know them personally, to know the kind of people they are, to know what they believe, what kind of lives they live, to talk to them informally, to feel that they are interested in and will help a student with personal as well as study problems, to feel that here is a person who embodies the qualities one would like to possess for oneself—all these factors young people feel are very important to their development.

Every young person is intensely interested during his college years in the picture that he has in his mind of the kind of person he wants to be. He is interested in knowing how to become such a person. Therefore, he studies the examples of teachers who are living admirable lives. A student realizes, however, that listening to a lecture by an individual who has achieved an admirable life is not enough. He must also seek opportunities for informal discussions between himself and that teacher, discussions concerning various aspects and values of life which he cherishes or wishes enhanced and clarified. The young person is wise who takes advantage of opportunities offered him to visit in the homes of his teachers, to observe to some extent just how they organize those lives which to young people seem so admirable.

Courses

Many of the students interviewed said that the ideas, attitudes, skills, and understanding that they had derived from certain courses in college deserved a great deal of credit for their personal development. Every college student might compare his evaluations of his own academic work with such comments as these which follow.

Science has taught me to weigh values. I appreciate situations as they really are more than I once did. I don't waste so much emotion on wishful thinking.

I've majored in psychology. I think it has saved me from a lot of maladjustment, and that I really try to practice making better and better adjustments.

I've gotten a bigger idea of things from studying philosophy. It's developed my ability to argue soundly, too.

The very conflict of ideas in my various courses and the ideas I used to have has made me more tolerant and thoughtful and stronger.

Freshman hygiene more than any other course has helped me. It has given me an ideal of a well-balanced individual.

My study of history and government has given me an interest in world affairs and a sense of real responsibility for party government.

An orientation course in contemporary civilization we all take as freshmen has had more to do with my development than any other course. It started the overthrow of dogmatism.

History and government and freshman orientation changed my attitude from one of jingoism and dogmatism toward one of critical, tolerant, broad-minded thinking.

I studied abnormal psychology while my mother was sick—before she committed suicide. It gave me a more sympathetic understanding of what she was suffering and has given me a basis for handling myself more wisely than mother did herself.

Anthropology has had a big effect on my views with regard to race relations. I think I see that ethics are really involved.

Psychology has made me inclined to excuse other people—perhaps too much for their own good.

I was awfully smug when I came up here. Freshman orientation more than anything else helped knock it out of me.

All my work in English has helped develop a keen perception and appreciation of values.

That professor is an awful fusser, but in his course I learned real appreciation for accurate detail.

All the work I've had in journalism has brought me in contact with life. I love it. It means broad contacts and real experiences.

I'm getting into labor legislation in economics this semester. This course is doing more for me than all my other courses put together.

We had some radical ideas presented in sociology but we also learned something about fundamental thinking.

My study of science has taught me the imperativeness of being perfectly honest with oneself, although one may not always be with others.

Psychology taught me the objective method—to think objectively and do away with so much introspection. Science has made me believe there is no magic or mystery—that most things can be solved. This belief gives me a sense of security which I need. French has made me realize the likeness of all parts of the world—the universality of psychology. Freshman orientation, especially the illumination of the Renaissance, was awfully valuable.

I broke away from my home pretty much this past year. I used to rely almost entirely on mother and my sister. I think it was my study of psychology that determined me to break away. I feel stronger and more self-reliant now than I did, but I have a long way to go yet.

French literature threw my ideas into a terrible turmoil. It has pretty much destroyed my Puritan ideals. Perhaps it is a good thing. I am very conscious of having to build up another system that will be more adequate.

I went to one school for my prep work. There I received very intensive religious training. I began to question whether anything could be quite as cut and dried and definite as they had tried to make it out to me. I came down here and took a lot of religion and philosophy and psychology and I've changed a lot—for the better, I feel. My whole effort now is one of trying to find a new morality and religion which will be adequate. At the present time, religion for me is merely aesthetic and social but I'll keep working at it and see what it turns out to be.

In high school, everything seems so true and certain, but in college everything stimulates thought. I've profited by studying the teachings of the various schools of psychology, for instance. English certainly stimulates one's curiosity. Freshman orientation disrupts some men, but it stimulated me to think things out for myself.

The courses that young people choose and their reactions to their classwork are indications of differences in maturity and interests. Courses contribute important experiences, however, that influence further growth.

To get the most out of college, young people need to take advantage of every opportunity offered to help them make the wisest possible choices of courses. Some of the ways of getting help are suggested by the following questions: Do I read carefully the catalogue describing courses offered? If I am not certain whether the contents of a given course will meet my needs, do I go to the instructor and ask for more detailed information concerning it? Do I seek the advice of my counselor? Do I take advantage of the interpretation of aptitude and other tests which could reveal to me my own ability, interests, strengths, and weaknesses? Do I plan my academic work in line with definite goals—personal, occupational, and cultural?

There are students who wake up on the morning of registration day suddenly realizing that they must sign up for some courses. They go through the catalogue, glancing at all the courses of which they have ever heard anything, then jump at those that are held at the most convenient hours or are reputed to be snap courses. Obviously, such students are failing to take advantage of much that college could do for them.

The farsighted student plans his work in the light of what he wants to do with his life, of the kind of person he wants to be. If he tries to see his personality as an entire pattern and to recognize how each experience interacts with and affects this developing life pattern, he has a vantage point from which to gain an overview of the information, materials, and skills that he needs before he can reach his goal. He is more likely to choose wisely in the light of his own needs.

He is aware of the elements of strength in his personality, puts to the best possible use his desirable and admirable qualities, and sets out to choose experiences or to capitalize on experiences which come to him in order to modify, improve, and correct his undesirable qualities. He is constructively critical of what he reads and learns. He thinks, rather than merely accepting, assimilating, and regurgitating information. He uses the opportunities college offers him in such a way that he will be getting and keeping an education that will function in his life.

Voluntary Reading

In addition to work in their regular courses, many students said they felt that reading which they had done simply because they were interested in it had contributed a great deal to their development. Among the books mentioned specifically were *The Life of Henry Wright*, *Disraeli*, *A President Is Born*, and *Point Counter Point*. Among authors named as having brought memorable additions to college experiences, were Josiah Royce, through his *Philosophy of Loyalty*, William Hyde, through *Five Great Philosophies of Life*, Hugh Walpole, through his book

entitled *Fortitude,* Walter Pater, John Dewey, Marcel
Proust, Virginia Woolf, Lawrence Stern, Shakespeare, and
Sophocles.

A variety of subject matter was mentioned as having
proved helpful. The list includes biography, philosophy,
psychology, social problems, science, drama, all kinds of
poetry, essays on many subjects, articles on higher mathematics, and various kinds of religion including Buddhism,
Mohammedanism, and Confucianism.

One student said that his voluntary reading had helped
him more than any class:

> I've read more books that weren't required than I've read in
> connection with my courses of study.

Other statements indicate a variety of reading interests
on the part of college students.

> The reading I've done in psychology under the direction of a
> psychiatrist friend has been the most important influence I've
> had in college. I've gained an understanding of myself and of
> others and of life. It has helped me to learn to control myself and
> my environment and to reconcile the two.

> I read novels, poetry, and drama constantly. Every once in a
> while one hits upon something that rounds out an idea or modifies
> an attitude.

> I love biography. Don't you think accounts of lives of others
> are very helpful?

> I've acquired the magazine habit. On the whole, I think it's
> a kind of anesthetic, and detrimental; but occasionally it does
> something for me in the way of helping me clarify my ideas.

> I read a lot of fiction. It makes me feel more intelligent with
> regard to present-day thought and manners.

> My reading is limited to philosophy and history. I regret my
> lack of reading in literature but I get so much out of books of a

more serious nature that I read them first.   I don't seem to get the modern novels read.

I find historical novels profitable reading.   They give one perspective and broadened sympathy.

I read a lot of French literature.   I find it an antidote for American exuberance and lack of social living.   It plays a certain role in helping me evaluate my own development.

I've read everything Bertrand Russell has written.   Also the *Nation* and *Forum* are rather important in my thinking during these past four years.

You may think this funny, but I really think S. S. Van Dine has been good for me.

Modern novels in my experience would furnish examples of ways of reacting to negative influences.   They have made me want to avoid being a mess the way most modern characters in books are.

The reading I've done voluntarily—especially in science—has influenced me more than my courses have.

My reading is rather varied.   It includes poetry, particularly the French poets; Plato (he strengthened the theoretical morality I absorbed at home); Aristotle to some extent, although I didn't much like him; and Bertrand Russell (he gave me a lot to think about).

Nobody at home has ever read, although we have a big library which we inherited from an uncle.   I never used to read many books, but just having them around and looking at them made some impression.   My father thinks it's foolish to spend two days reading a book when one can see a movie in two hours.   I used to agree with him, but no more.   I'm getting a lot of fun out of books this past year or two.

Since I came to college I've voluntarily read the Bible through for information and culture and historical values.   We never had a Bible at home.   My family is religious only in a certain sense. Perhaps I have enjoyed and profited by this experience of reading the Bible as literature more than a fellow could have who had always had it on the parlor table and had it quoted at him over and over again as the ultimate authority.

This is an impressive list, both in the type of reading and in the amount of reading done. It suggests that young people who manage their time so that they can read sometimes on their own find that this practice contributes a great deal to their getting the most out of college.

EXTRACURRICULAR ACTIVITIES

A great many of the young people whose experiences are recorded in this book declared that anyone wishing to get the most out of college should take advantage of the opportunity of participating in extracurricular activities. Some felt that these experiences had been more valuable for their personal development than any other single influence in college. A large number of students said that participation in athletics had proved most important. In those colleges having organized student government, the experience of participation in its functioning was highly prized. Taking part in the planning of social functions and activities was considered by students as of great worth for an individual's development. Young people rated high as having influenced their development, activities on publications; in honorary, literary, or debating societies; in departmental clubs; in dramatics; and in the programs of musical or religious organizations.

The following statements suggest ways in which students felt that extracurricular participation had helped them.

I think extracurricular activities give an excellent opportunity to get experience and train for later jobs. They make one strain the sinew a bit. I think they've taught me, too, that a man makes the job and not a job the man.

My biggest extracurricular influence has come through being managing editor of the newspaper. It's been a lot of responsibility and I've had to carry it.

Going as college representative to an intercollegiate conference is one of the biggest responsibilities and privileges I've ever had.

Being on the executive council of the dormitory has made me a little more responsible. It's made me realize that getting away with a thing isn't the best criterion.

I have always been rather shy and unhappy, so when I came to college, I dove right in. The momentum carried me along. I've been wonderfully helped.

I've gotten a more wholesome attitude through working hard at extracurricular jobs. I've come to feel that I was doing my job by helping other people.

I've so thoroughly enjoyed college dramatics and I've done quite a bit in them. They link up with so many other interests and points of view.

Social activities here have done a lot for me. I felt terribly inferior my first two years but I made myself go to the various social functions and now I feel quite like the rest.

I've been in charge of some of our social affairs. It's had an equalizing, stabilizing effect. I think I've gained a lot of poise.

I've worked on the committee to advise freshmen. It certainly makes one wonder about college and its values in general. I'm sure that committee has done more for me than it has for any freshman.

College teas have developed a sense of poise, self-confidence, and self-respect. I used to be terribly shy.

I've been president of the French Club. It's given me some idea of the way people react. It's been rather discouraging but very valuable.

Coming into contact with all kinds of people through student activities has made me more cosmopolitan, more tolerant, and adaptable.

Being president of my hall decided me as to my vocation. Lots of problems of right and wrong were presented, many of which rather staggered me. But I appreciate the opportunity of having had to think about them. I want eventually to become a dean of women.

Through sports I've come really to know and like different kinds of girls. I used to be an awful snob.

Work in activities has taught me tolerance. I've learned that more than one standard of right and wrong are possible and I've learned that I don't always help a situation by trying to impose standards.

I'm getting opportunities in school activities for the first time this year. I'm getting a tremendously big kick out of it. I've gone along for the past three years doing my duty as I saw it and making good grades. But having all this open up all of a sudden gives me a new sort of recognition which is very stimulating, to say the least.

As manager of several major sports I've had to run a training house for forty persons, take them on trips, take care of visiting teams, and take care of many other details. That kind of experience certainly involves everything—including a lot of grief.

Being on a team most of the year keeps me from over-indulging, in social events, for instance. I find that being interested in a sport and wanting to make the team tends to keep me eligible scholastically. I've learned something about kidding myself along and being a good little boy for the sake of the future reward.

Athletic participation certainly enables a man to meet and get really to know other men in a way nothing else does. It certainly has been a medium for influences.

I've made debate my major activity. I've come to feel that I cannot debate for anything of which I absolutely disapprove. At first I didn't care. I'd debate just for the sake of the intellectual gymnastics.

Debating has given me self-confidence and made me want to develop an open mind. It has given me poise.

The Greek Club and a literary society have meant valuable friendships. Singing in the chorus has broadened my outlook on all of life and given me real inspiration.

Being a member of the club which brings students from many different countries together socially has had a great value. It has broadened my ideas and helped me evaluate things more accurately.

When I was a junior I was on the class social committee. I had never realized before what an easy thing it was to cheat on a thing like that. I was in charge of decorations. Why, it seems to be the accepted thing to get a "squeeze" out of a thing like that. I didn't do it, but the boy in charge of the orchestra did. I think that experience strengthened my moral fiber considerably. Then, too, being a member of the senior honorary society certainly gives one close contacts with really big girls—knowing how they feel about things and what they think ought to be done. I'd say I'd really had my most vital experiences in college in extracurricular activities. They give one actual practice in some pretty important matters.

Extracurricular activities rate absolutely first among the influences during college. I've gotten my most thrilling experiences of accomplishment after hard and tedious work in publications. The only time I've really been confronted with a situation where other people were cheating and cheating hard was in the College Show, of which I was manager. That experience gave me some vicarious practice in character qualities and a lot of worry as to what to do about the students whom I knew had stolen.

Activities are more important than classes! Being on Student Council, for instance, has taught me system and how to organize my time and activities. I've just had to do it, you see. It also made me feel a personal responsibility when I had to participate in considering questions of student honor, for example. Going out on trips with men on the teams and being right with them and working with them for two or three weeks at a time certainly makes a dent.

Extracurricular activities are the most powerful influence I've had during these four years. Being a member of the senior honorary group always makes a fellow feel kind of responsible. I know all the other men say they feel it, too. Working in another activity gave me all the opportunity I could have asked for to exercise initiative and take responsibility. It was a dying organization and it meant hard work to save it. In a publications job, I took a defeat because of rotten politics, and then came back and licked them. That certainly did me good. As manager of the paper I learned a lot. That activity absorbed a whole year of hard work but it's the most successful year they've ever had financially. We cleared about $6,300.

I'm so sleepy that I can hardly see straight right this minute because of what I guess you'd call an extracurricular activity. I'm president of my house but I never thought that meant much. They just didn't have anyone else to put in this year. As a matter of fact, that's all I have ever done in the extracurricular line. What was it that made me sleepy? You see, tomorrow is Homecoming and we all have to have our houses decorated. The committee I appointed didn't seem to take hold, so yesterday afternoon I told the fellows we'd all have to pitch in. I discovered we had only about five dollars to do the job on. You'd be surprised how much bunting and rope it takes for a thing like that. We had to run over the five dollars. I feel kind of bad about that because money doesn't come easy to a lot of those fellows who will have to help make up the difference. Well, we decided we'd make a big football player out of bunting and cover the whole front of the house. We had to outline him in rope to give him some substance. Gosh, I never undertook such a thing before in my life. I worked the fellows all night in shifts and we kept it up all day today and this evening until just now. I sure was tempted to cut this appointment with you tonight and sleep instead.

Most students by the time they are seniors seem to have had some experience in extracurricular activities, and 82 per cent of the seniors interviewed felt that such participation had had a definite and important influence on their development. Occasionally a student intimated that the experience had not been particularly meaningful. Students considered leaders in activities glowingly volunteered the information that the benefits which they personally received more than repaid them for their hard work.

The young people who had not participated in activities at all generally seemed regretful. They explained their failure to do so by poor health, the necessity for having to be entirely self-supporting, or the fact that they commuted such long distances that they could not fit extracurricular activities into their schedules. Failure to participate was never explained by too heavy an academic load. This evidence all seems to suggest that it would be wise for every young person who goes to college to investigate the possibility of doing some work in extracurricular activities on his campus if he wishes to make college the happiest and most valuable kind of experience possible.

Membership in a Fraternity or Sorority

Some colleges have sororities and fraternities and some do not. A student who plans to enter a college that has these organizations needs to have an intelligent opinion about them before he arrives on the campus, because he is very likely to have to decide early in his college career not only whether or not he wishes to join one but also which one he wishes to join. The influence of individual groups varies from one campus to another, as does their prestige. Furthermore, the quality of each group seems to rise and wane and rise again in almost rhythmic regularity.

Let us examine some of the testimony of students who gave credit of a high order to their fraternity or sorority. In general, they added the information that, for them, "friends" and "fraternity" were practically synonymous. In other words, most of their friends were within their fraternities, and the chief value of the fraternity was the friendships which it made possible. Samples of their statements are:

Fraternity makes for tolerance. It helped me to get over my extreme sensitiveness. It has been the greatest inspiration I've had in making me go out for activities and keeping up my scholarship.

My sorority has given me most of my close friends. It has given me lots of responsibility and built me up to the point where I could carry it. This has increased my self-confidence. Of course, I try to bring credit to my sorority in every way I can. Its ideals, heard in the ritual at least once a week, can't help but make an impression. Another way in which it has influenced me has been in keeping me from going to questionable places. I couldn't afford to be seen in some of the entertainment places other girls don't mind going to.

During my pledge term, I learned more about living with others than I had ever learned before, because I had always been the only child in our family. The idealism of the sorority also has had its influence.

My sorority brought me out of myself more than anything else ever has. It helped me overcome self-consciousness in social things. I got my first real chance to lead in my sorority. The best friends I have ever made are among my sorority sisters— many of them among the alumnae.

At first I think my fraternity had quite a negative effect on me. But I got my real toe hold in the University through the fraternity; it got me jobs so I could be self-supporting. I found the fellows really would do anything for me, so I began to kind of warm up to them. I'd rate it pretty high now as a good influence.

There have been two rather marked cliques in the sorority since I've been in it. The two groups have had some pretty stiff encounters. I wouldn't give anything for the stimulation and the challenges that I've gotten from those skirmishes within our tight little group.

There is something in group activity that is very valuable.
Then, too, one finds her best friends in her sorority. The discussions we get into are broadening and good for all of us. Being
a sorority mother and having the guidance of some of the younger
girls has helped me a lot. I've been treasurer of the sorority this
past year and, for the first time, have learned something about
being businesslike.

One's fraternity provides fellowship. It tries to drive a fellow
to give his best. The older fellows stimulate the younger ones
and try to show them how to make the most of their opportunities.
Within a fraternity one can get very constructive criticism. Then,
too, there's something about just being a member of the same
group important men on the campus belong to, knowing them
intimately, having a chance to study them, and to get their honest
advice.

Being president for two years has given me a wonderful lot of
experience. Having to uphold the idealism of the other girls,
knowing how the others watched me to see what decisions I made
and how I lived up to what I said I believed, having to be worthy
of their confidences and their friendship—it's all been tremendously
important in my college experience.

I'd rate my sorority second only to extracurricular activities
as a factor in whatever development I've achieved in college.
Most of my good friends have been within my sorority. I've
felt the value of group counsel in various problems I've had to
meet. Being a member of a sorority has afforded me a wonderful opportunity of leadership.

The responsibilities one has as a member of a fraternity; just
getting along with others, having to understand their points of
view and justify one's own; the influence that comes from deep
friendship—these are awfully important.

Being compelled to make judgments of others has made me more
critical of myself—just feeling that I want to do my part to
advance the group as a whole.

My sorority has made me more broad-minded and tolerant. I
used to be very introspective, too, and it's helped me get over

that somewhat. Then, too, one of the older members is pretty much my ideal of what a woman should be. She's been very nice to me and I have studied her and consciously tried to be like her. If it hadn't been for the sorority I probably couldn't have known her so well.

My fraternity has been the biggest influence I've had in college. I've been able to look at the other men and pick out the best elements in each and try to duplicate them in myself. It has developed my tolerance for the points of view of others. I've had to take responsibility for making rather important decisions and have had lots of experience in attempting to influence the group to adopt what I considered the better policies. It's done a lot for me.

As president of a new sorority, I've had plenty of troubles. It's been uphill work. I've had to try to hold the girls together staunchly in the face of pretty big odds. I've found that I've had to exert the strictest kind of control over myself. I haven't dared ever show annoyance. I've become much more considerate and understanding and sympathetic.

My fraternity experience has done a lot for me. It has furnished me with a chance to examine my standards as compared with those of other men. This has made for tolerance; I realize that one can't just impose one's standards on others.

Fraternity was an influence for good study habits. It gave me a campus home that had some of the virtues of a real home.

My fraternity has been a very, very strong influence. We had a lot of strong senior leadership in my freshman year. When that class graduated we were left pretty high and dry because the next class was weak. With the advice and guidance of my father, who was a member, I assumed a good deal of responsibility from my sophomore year on toward building it up again.

I learned something about loyalty through my fraternity.

My fraternity has influenced me because I've worked for the approval of the group, and their standards are, for the most part, pretty high.

The ideals of my fraternity have made me want to try to do the right thing. It's been a very great influence. Most of my friends are in my fraternity.

By no means were all students enthusiastic about what fraternity membership had meant to them:

I was pledged to a sorority in my freshman year but I didn't care for the girls and I felt that being a member of a group like that interfered too much with independence, so I broke my pledge. I think the struggle I went through at the time trying to make up my mind what to do probably was a grand thing for me.

A fraternity depends an awful lot on the kind of seniors and alumni that are influential at the time. There happened to be a bad bunch in control when I was a freshman and sophomore—just during the years when a fraternity exerts the most influence on a fellow. I got to drinking and running around with women in imitation of the older men. Then I got pretty much involved in football and had to cut a lot of it out. I don't think a fraternity means much after the first two years.

There are undoubtedly some good values I've gotten out of my sorority; I've learned more about how to live with people; I've learned more about self-control. But, on the whole, sororities are rather petty and too discriminating about things that don't matter.

I've made many enemies in my fraternity. We've had a Protestant-Catholic conflict in the chapter for four long years; I don't take much stock in that kind of thing. I've practically pulled out of the fraternity.

Well, fraternity has given me a fine dislike for snobbishness—of which it seemed to me some of my dear brothers had too much. I've almost had a nervous breakdown several times during college. I live in a kind of a fog a lot of the time, but by nature I'm a nonconformist and I don't mind admitting that my fraternity rather irks me at times.

I'm a member of a fraternity but it hasn't given me anything of value.   I've found my best friends outside of my fraternity.

Well, I learned how to swear and drink in my fraternity, but I could have learned that elsewhere.   I don't regret having belonged to a fraternity, but I don't give it credit for any of the fine things I've learned in college.

I was pledged in my freshman year but I never got the habit of hanging around the fraternity house.   I had far more interesting friends outside the fraternity, and my own home was much more to my liking than the fraternity house.   I just let the thing drift on and on and they finally asked for my pin.   I have always been glad that I did not go and be initiated.

One boy said that his fraternity had certainly been an important influence during his college years because the experience had been one fight from start to finish.   He despised the smugness of his group, their insistence on stereotypes, their intolerance, their self-righteousness.

One girl said that she didn't like sorority life; that sororities were very narrow; and that her eyes had finally been opened to the real nature of such organizations.

One man told a long and rather involved story of his entire college experience, which had been rather bitter, on the whole.   He felt keenly that people value one for one's money or social position, and he had neither.   He joined a fraternity the first year when he had more money.   His second year he had to be more careful of his expenditures. Because he had a job that took him to another town in the middle of the day, he hadn't wanted to pay for board at his fraternity house.   He and the president didn't get along very well anyway, and because he owed two months' dues and board, his fraternity took his pin away.   This made a deep impression on the man, who appeared to be quite sensitive and to have a good many additional burdens. He hoped some day to be able to pay that bill and get his pin back.   His whole fraternity experience had been a source of bitterness and regret, and had served still further to destroy his self-confidence and sense of security.

This testimony ranges from very enthusiastic endorsement of the fraternity system as a valuable part of college experience to disapproval of the system. The indifferent group includes those who say that fraternity membership has not made enough difference to them to deserve to be considered as influencing their development. Their reasons and the reasons of those who feel that fraternities have actually retarded growth can be very illuminating to young people attempting wisely to decide for themselves about fraternity membership.

Each young person entering a college that has a fraternity system must be prepared to face the problem: Do I wish to join a fraternity? If I do not succeed in joining, will the experience of failure be devastating, or will I be prepared with a definite plan whereby I will meet the situation? If I become a member of a group other than the one I desired, how will I make an adjustment? By what criteria can I determine the group with which I shall probably be happiest? These are questions that every thoughtful individual will wish to answer to his own satisfaction upon entering college. The _Manual of American College Fraternities_[1] may prove helpful in formulating answers.

It is interesting to note that the students quoted, all seniors, scarcely commented on the evils of the methods used by fraternities and sororities in recruiting membership, or on the heartaches of those students to whom membership is denied. This testimony suggests that students interested in fraternitity membership should investigate to discover as accurately as they can the type of influence that all such groups, and in particular the group with which they wish to become affiliated, seem to have upon their members. The influences attested to in the remarks of students range from the very valuable to the detrimental,

[1] BAIRD, W. R., _Manual of American College Fraternities_, George Banta Publishing Company, Menasha, Wis., 1935.

and tend to confirm the theory that groups may have cycles during which their influence on individuals varies considerably. It is important to know all that one can about the type of and the reason for a group's influence on its members if one is to decide wisely whether or not he will become a member of that group.

Experiences in Earning Money

A great many young people have to face the problem of aiding in their own support while they are in college. In a large number of colleges as many as 50 per cent of the students earn money during college months. More men than women attempt to earn their way through college.

How do young people estimate the value of self-support? Most of those interviewed felt that this experience had contributed to their development in very specific and important ways. A very few students, all of whom had had to be entirely self-supporting, felt that the experience had been detrimental. The statements that follow represent both viewpoints.

I've done interesting things rather than things that paid particularly well. For instance, during three summers I've worked as a sailor and seen the world.

I've worked some all four years in my father's coal business. I don't get any money in return for it, but I've learned a lot. For one thing, I am convinced that morality is the best policy in business.

I've made a little less than $300 a year during college. I've enjoyed it. It kind of rubs away the scholastic veil.

I've never had to support myself, but most of the fellows here do work more or less. I've tutored and I've worked out at a country club. It's given me a valuable perspective I couldn't have gotten otherwise.

I didn't do much in the way of self-support my first two years, but these past two years I've turned every check my family has given me into the bank and supported myself entirely. They don't like me to do it so I don't say much about the fact that I am working. I feel lots steadier and more levelheaded to be carrying plenty of ballast. Then, too, it's a mighty nice sensation to have securities of one's very own tucked safely away.

I started in with a debt of $40. I've worked hard all four years and I'm finishing up with all expenses paid, and own a small piece of property which I've been able to buy on the side. Gosh, it does me a lot of good when I think that I've put it over.

I haven't had to work at all but I wanted to. I've worked on construction jobs mostly. I've met some pretty tough fellows and some pretty tough jobs. I've been able to save all I've earned, though. I am sure the whole experience has been very valuable.

I've worked for my meals all four years. It's helped my feeling of self-respect to know I wasn't entirely dependent on dad.

I've contributed quite a lot to my self-support during these years. Sometimes it's been necessary and sometimes it hasn't. I got just about $100 from my family last year toward my total expenses of $1,500. But I made about $1,200 on the stock market, too.

I've worked or borrowed my entire way. A scholarship I've held has helped, too. I'm finishing up with a debt of $1,400, mostly due to a spell of illness. I feel pretty happy about next year because I have a job as recreational director which will pay $100 and maintenance during the summer and $60 a month and maintenance during the year, enabling me to do a certain amount of graduate work in economics, too. College has seemed pretty stiff at times, but I wouldn't have gone through on a feather bed for anything. I've lived through it and I'm the stronger for having stuck it out.

I've worked this semester in a department store at odd hours. It's helped ever so much in overcoming shyness from which I suffered painfully.

I haven't had a cent from home since I entered college. I don't suppose they've given me more than about $50 worth of clothes since I was eleven. It's come pretty easy for me, though. For instance, just imagine this! During this coming vacation I have a job which requires that I dress up every evening and take a young scion of a wealthy family, who is home from his prep school, out to the most exclusive restaurants and then on to the best shows in town. Not only is he a nice kid and not only are my expenses paid, including the price of the best seats available, but I get a salary in addition. It's a good thing most of my jobs haven't been as easy as that or I'd be completely ruined. Why, I'd feel a big share of my life was cut out if I didn't have to work.

I've had only $10 from home all year. Working the way I do has made me appreciate the practical side of life. I have a pretty healthy feeling of independence. I've seen inside of life.

I've worked as a waiter in hotels during the summers, very much against my parents' wishes. It's given me broad associations with different kinds of men. I've been badly shocked, but I've been educated by it, too.

I didn't come to college until I was twenty-five and had had five years of army experience and 10 years of working as a union member. In college, I've gone to classes every day and studied all I could up until 6 o'clock and then worked as a printer from 6 to 2 A.M. every day. It's rather a terrific pace to keep up for a number of years. Believe me, though, when you work so hard for a thing you appreciate it when you've got it.

I was partly self-supporting my freshman and sophomore years and almost entirely the last two years. I don't know—being on your own makes you realize the value of money. In my case, it's given me practice in being kind of scrupulously honest because I knew there wasn't any margin of safety I could fall back on; I've had to face the bare facts and live according to them.

Self-support has both helped and distracted. I've earned the bigger share of the money I've had. It's meant that I had to apportion my time very carefully and practice a lot of self-denial at times.

I have had a job waiting on table all during my college course. It's helped me get over a certain conceited attitude I used to have and that I really didn't want to keep.

I've been 90 per cent self-supporting these past three years. I've worked at the stadium, I've worked as a chauffer, I've waited on table, I've been steward at the fraternity house, I've worked for a cigarette company—I don't remember what all else. I know now that it's simply survival of the fittest and I want to be one of the fit ones. I've come to rely on myself. Working at all kinds of things with all kinds of people gives a fellow a taste of life he can never get in college.

I have earned only my board during college but I'm glad I had to do that. I've waited on table in a girl's dorm. I used to be terribly shy of girls, but being around a whole gang like that three times a day and having them kind of ignore me and yet knowing that they knew I was there and having a date with some of them occasionally has gradually given me lots more confidence in the presence of girls in general.

I've been entirely self-supporting, but I've been able to get the kind of work that would let me organize things so I could participate in activities as well as earn the requisite cash. It's very good discipline and I know the value of money lots better than I once did.

I haven't earned a lot during college, but I've thoroughly enjoyed my work. It takes me into contact with men who amount to something; it's taught me the value of money; it's given me something to build on next year. I feel happier about graduating than some of my fraternity brothers do, for instance.

I've worked—sure—but it isn't hard to be self-supporting when you're an athlete—the jobs come easy. Earning my own money has made me feel self-dependent and I wouldn't want to feel any other way. The way I look at it is this: the more independent you can be in this world, the better off you are.

Having the feeling that I must make the best use of my time because part of it must be spent in earning money helps me concentrate on my studies; it seems to help me in making my schedule more regular.

I've had to borrow $800 altogether. That debt rankles, but it was necessary. I think it's been a good thing for me to have to work as hard as I have. It's not only made me figure my time pretty closely, which I think is a good thing to learn, but it has provided me with contacts which I consider very valuable which I wouldn't have made otherwise.

It's enhanced my appreciation of college, and given me an idea of the value of time, and made me feel that I can stand on my own feet. It takes some fellows several years after they get out of college to be able to earn enough to be entirely independent financially. I'm mighty glad I don't have that uncertainty to face.

I've been entirely self-supporting except for a scholarship I've held the past three years. Self-support has been of considerable value for me, but if I had it to do over again I think I'd stay out and work and save up and then come to school. I like to study and I can't do as good a job of it as I'd like to when I have to work three or four hours every day to keep the wolf away.

I wouldn't particularly recommend to any other fellow that he attempt to put himself through without any help at all, but I've had to do it. I've learned to make the minutes and the pennies count. I've had to restrict my dates and, as a consequence, become very discriminating about girls and have a few girl friends who are really wonderful friends instead of a lot of flitting memories. I think I feel more responsible and independent than I might have if I'd gone through on someone else's money.

I've been entirely self-supporting all four years. I certainly wouldn't wish it on any other girl. Perhaps it has been the main factor, though, in making me work out a mode of living that seems to me much more economical of time and energy than I would have been able to achieve otherwise. I've had very thorough training in the value of money, you can believe.

Three students in this college made these remarks:

No, self-support has been detrimental to me. All it means is working to get enough money to live another week. What I really want to do is to be an artist.

I've had to be entirely self-supporting since I was a freshman in high school. I think it's been a detrimental influence.

Working my first two years to be entirely self-supporting was very bad for me, I think. It hurt me and bothered me and made me unhappy. There isn't any room in life for rest and fun when one has to work so hard. It made life absolutely unendurable.

One man was not entirely convinced of the unmitigated value of self-support, and said that he certainly had come to realize the value of money because he'd had to earn practically every penny he had, but that having to be self-supporting made him very resentful at times. Experiences he had encountered because he had to work made him wonder whether colleges weren't set up for the wealthy. He felt that his experiences had given him an exaggerated and undesirable idea of the value of money and social position.

Another man in the same institution said flatly that he thought self-support had been a bad factor in his college experience—it had distracted him and annoyed him and worn him out and he hated it and everything it entailed.

A general conclusion that these young people drew from their experiences in earning money is that self-support in quantities up to one-half of an individual's entire support teaches some valuable lessons to those who are strong enough emotionally, physically, and academically to undertake this responsibility in addition to their other college work.

Any young person facing the question of having to support himself, either wholly or partially, if he is to enter or to continue in college needs to consider what the experience of having to work will do to his self-respect. In some colleges, students who work are largely those who do so from deadly necessity, and they may be snubbed by others more fortunate. In other colleges working is socially acceptable and students are eager to work because "everyone does it" and because they recognize the value of working. In still other colleges, work experiences are a part of the curriculum and are expected of every student.

A student who must contribute to his own support in college might well evaluate this factor as he makes his choice of a college. It is much easier to find work in some communities than in others. As students make plans for self-support, they need to ask themselves whether they are strong enough, physically and academically, to carry this additional responsibility. If they are not, the experience may be detrimental, for they may be risking experiences of failure in too many areas. They need to watch themselves carefully so that, if they are strong, this strength is not exhausted in the course of their college years. If self-support is considered only as an added burden which may endanger an individual's total college adjustment, then he will wish to weigh carefully the relative values of college and self-support.

THE CHURCH

What do college students consider valuable in their church experiences? Is there something in this area that is not to be missed if one wishes to get the most out of college? The following testimony suggests many kinds of influences from church contacts.

The rector of the Community Church is a wonderful man with a real social conscience. I attend quite regularly and know that the church has influenced me.

Church attendance has influenced me in a general sort of way. It keeps me in touch with religious thought. I've been visiting around at various churches. At present I'm very much interested in some of the activities at the Reverend ———'s church. I have ushered in chapel much of the time.

I go almost every Sunday to hear the same minister. Most people would call him an agnostic or even an atheist. But to my mind he has his own religion which is a growing and dynamic one. He has an experimental attitude with regard to religion. He's intelligent and not merely emotional about it. It's quite inspiring to me to follow him from Sunday to Sunday.

I've joined the church recently. The assistant pastor is a graduate of this college. He kept after me until he got me to take a Sunday School class. He really is the man who got me into college and who got me my job in the bank so I could work my way through. But I don't think I am entirely confusing church with that man.

I've been connected with the Presbyterian Church all my life. The neighborhood where I live is extremely poor. The church community here at school comes from an entirely different kind of neighborhood, and I've met an entirely different class of people here. They've been nice to me and it's done me a lot of good. Perhaps the values which I have gotten out of church have been more social than religious but the church as an institution has been extremely important to me during these four years.

One of the deepest experiences I have had in college was a Christmas Eve mass at the Episcopal Church. I don't even belong to that church. I wouldn't mention church at all except for that one instance.

I belong to the Christian Science Church. We read the lessons every day, you know. The content of these lessons has helped me more than almost anything else when I've been going through college. When life gets almost too complicated, my Christian Science practitioner goes over things with me and advises and helps me organize my life a little better.

My church has influenced me during these years through the ideas I've gained from the rector in his sermons, from the experience of worship, through the beautiful music, and through young people's groups in which I've participated.

Dr. —— of the M. E. Church was the influence most responsible for a change from my precollege attitude to my present one.

My interest before college was entirely a denominational one, due to the influence of my mother; but now my interest in religion is quite nondenominational—it is much more religious.

The Presbyterian Church has had a stabilizing influence on me. I attend quite regularly. I also go to Dr. ———'s study group in the Methodist Church. I find that ritual itself has a deep and satisfying influence on me. It helps me sort of integrate myself.

I go to the Community Church most of the time—although I enjoy hearing Rabbi ——— sometimes. From both sources I have heard the gospel of social justice preached. Dr. ——— and Rabbi ——— both take such an active part in every social issue that it makes the church seem to me an institution of supreme importance.

I am always deeply influenced by church music—particularly by the emotional singing of the Jewish people; it seems to get somewhere. I also frequently drop in at the Catholic Cathedral to hear the organ. I am sure the deep, enriching experience that listening to religious music is for me deserves some cognizance.

I go regularly to Dr. ———'s church. I have come to know him personally. No one could touch the hem of that man's garment and not be deeply influenced thereby.

I was an atheist when I entered college. I got even more atheistic in my freshman year. In my sophomore year I began to change back again—perhaps because I went to the synagogue more. I began to ask my grandfather questions. I happened to pick up some books of religious stories which had always been available but just hadn't interested me before. I believe that religion really has meant something in my development during these four years.

I'm a Roman Catholic. I'm sure that my religion encourages me to exercise a valuable control of myself. Yes, it has helped even during these past four years.

I joined my mother's church when I was about fourteen. But I always have had doubts. My doubts have been more active ever since I took a course in Bible in college. But I've fought many things out with the minister and he has given me certain ideas in the religious realm that have been valuable. The best thing he ever did for me was to get me interested in Norman Thomas.

I'm an atheist—due to *This Believing World* and my study of the sciences.

Mother sees that I go to church regularly, but I've not been influenced any during the past few years—except to more or less dislike the whole business.

No, I haven't any religion at all. I've never even puzzled much over Deity, the way some students do.

I've been an officer in a young people's group. This has made me examine some of my religious beliefs more critically before passing them on to others.

Working in a boys' club in an Italian church has made church real to me. I've gotten a lot out of it during these years. I went to chapel during my freshman year quite a few times but I've not been since. At first I was quite interested in the talks about science versus religion. It was essential to my stage of thinking then. It doesn't seem important to me at all now. But I guess it served some purpose.

Church is just an awful hustle, bustle—like all the rest.

I have never had a church. I wish I did have a religious background.

I'm extremely skeptical about religion at present, due, I think, to modern psychology. I have entirely lost my old system of morality. I seem to find nothing in religion upon which to base my ideals of conduct now. But I still think that one has to have some sort of religion and morality in order to get along at all. Religion for me at the present time is simply aesthetic appreciation and social justice. But the churches I know anything about fail to satisfy even these wants.

One girl, a Catholic, said that church had certainly been important to her. She had been educated in a convent before she went to college. She said that the remarks of certain of the professors and some of their attitudes conflicted with her own. She found relief and renewed conviction in talking with her family and the priest. This student was one of the outstanding leaders on her campus, full of vivacity and enthusiasm on the surface, and full of struggle and conflicts beneath. Her church, she said, had been of inestimable value in encouraging her to champion her own convictions.

Individuals planning how to get the most out of college might consider the significance of this testimony. Some young people consider church a valuable part of their college experience because they are influenced by the music, the ritual, and the worship. Others find something of worth in their acceptance of a church and in regularity of attendance at church services. But the intellectual side of a church service seems to contribute most to young people's development, judging by the number of individuals who stated that ideas heard in sermons or acquired in study groups had influenced them. In addition, a few young people seem to find church a haven of quiet in a too-busy environment; for example, the cheerleader in one college said that he found chapel "kind of restful."

Other Experiences and Adjustments

The habit of budgeting one's time which most students cultivated in high school should not be discarded in college. A plan that was effective during high-school years, however, will probably be of little use in college, because so many elements in the immediate environment are changed. Even though perfecting a new plan may seem complicated, perseverance in working it out will be rewarded in the satisfactions accruing from accomplishing as much as possible, having experiences as varied as possible, and keeping a balance among varied interests.

Living by a time budget gives one the feeling of being in control of his life. It gives the calm and poise that one gains from the knowledge that one knows his goals and has a plan by means of which he is working toward them. Furthermore, we tend to grow the way we live.

A student who uses his time most effectively distributes his time in such a way that he leads a well-rounded life. The main items to be allowed for are the same in every time budget, but each student must use care in making his plan to suit his own way of living. The plan should be as flexible as possible to allow for taking advantage of unexpected opportunities for new experiences.

Time must, of course, be allowed for eating and for sufficient rest. The budget should allow for participation in extracurricular activities, for sufficient exercise, for meditation, for real recreation, for exchanging ideas with one's friends, and for cultural activities. Planning to spend a certain number of hours each day studying is important, but still more important is learning to finish one's work within the allotted time.

A student may discover, for example, that he is wasting time when he is supposedly studying, because he is merely reading and rereading material. In this situation, he needs to secure help on study techniques. The help available through excellent books and pamphlets might be supplemented by suggestions from professors based on research in methods of studying particular subject matter.

Studying under external conditions favorable to concentration will bring added accomplishment. Improving one's reading skills is a never-ending quest. Other helpful devices are skill in using aids to locating material, such as indexes and tables of contents, skill in taking notes effectively, and facility in collecting all needed materials in one place before one starts to study.

The college students who were interviewed considered of major importance the influences discussed in the preceding sections of this chapter. Their evaluation is probably tempered by the fact that making adjustments to other influences lacked novelty. While students are attempting to make the most of the particular resources offered them in the college environment, the new experiences of college life should not be allowed to retard development previously begun. One's life will not be well-rounded after college unless he continues through those four years to work out a satisfying adult relationship with his family, to develop his own personality toward his self-ideal, to use all his resources toward the achievement of happy relationships with his contemporaries, both men and women, to plan wisely for vocational activity, to try to understand and relate himself to his community, to build a life philosophy that will be effective in all situations.

LOOKING FORWARD

The student needs to try to picture himself as a member of society after the more or less sheltered years of college environment are over. He will want to make some worthy contribution to society. This need not be in the development of material resources. It may be in personal service, in contributing to the enjoyment of others, in widening the boundaries of knowledge, in improving the cultural level of the group, or in a creative accomplishment of such a nature as to contribute to the progress of a group.

It may be possible to set an example in his community by his appreciation of the finer things of life, by his utilization and further development of the cultural opportunities, and by the poise and beauty with which he lives his own life. Perhaps he can create beauty and harmony through his response to the atmosphere in his own home, through his social relationships, civilized attitudes, and sense of responsibility for the welfare of others and of the world.

He will want to have broad interests and a sympathetic understanding of the life and activities around him. He will want to be able intelligently to interpret current affairs.

In doing this he will find helpful his knowledge of the various phases of past civilizations which, in a measure, explain the present situation. He will want to continue his search for something higher, something that will enable him to carry on harmonious human relationships and to be of genuine service to others. Even a superficial study of society brings a realization that many changes are needed. The real test is not in recognizing situations where social changes are needed, but in organizing plans to improve these situations, in working in cooperation with others, and in giving wholehearted support to those plans of others that promise the greatest good for the greatest number.

One's personal efficiency in moving toward his goals, the amount of coordinated activity that he can direct toward the accomplishment of his ends is dependent, in part, on his health assets and status. He must know how his body works; he must know how to use it most efficiently, how to build it up to maximum efficiency. Good health means sufficient vitality and power to ensure excellent performance of tasks. Efficiency demands an honest evaluation of one's powers and weaknesses so that he can regulate his conduct in a manner most conducive to health. The latter includes an adjustment of one's emotional life to the tasks that must be performed, an avoidance of tensions and frustrations to the degree that one may know what can be accomplished and plan to keep within one's physical and emotional resources for its accomplishment, and the planning for a period of rest, recreation, or change of activity after one of expenditure of energy in work.

In addition to good physical equipment for carrying out one's plans, efficient habits of thinking are necessary. One needs the courage of his convictions, the persistence to see through to completion something in which he believes. He needs to follow his own best judgment in spite of his own fears or the selfishness of others. He will want to be able to discriminate between fact and opinion, to form habits of critical thinking, to apply principles to a specific situation and to reach a solution based on sound reasoning rather than on emotion. He will want to refrain from yielding to blind prejudice, and to display a genuine respect for opinions, customs, and beliefs different from his own.

Looking forward to carrying out the goals he has set for himself after college, the student will want to plan his entire educational program in such a way that it will truly serve his needs and advance him toward his goals of personal and social development. He will make periodic and honest inventories of his abilities, aptitudes, interests, ambitions, and desires. He will be conscious at all times of his needs, his uncertainties, his limitations, and his frailties. To get the most out of his education he must know what he wants, be critical of what he gets, be quick in his appraisal of each situation and appreciative of its place in his development.

CHAPTER VIII

WHAT CAN WE BELIEVE?

Many philosophers have pointed out that man is inherently a value-searching animal and a value-creating craftsman; that the most distinctive characteristic of man is his quest for values. People who begin early to search for the meaning and worth of life seem to gain a security and power that nothing else can give them.

When we begin to look for the meaning of life, the search may at first seem to be futile. Some of us may come to feel as Vera Brittain did when, in her *Testament of Youth*, she described herself as

. . . condemned to live to the end of my days in a world without confidence and security, a world in which every dear human relationship would be fearfully cherished under the shadow of apprehension; in which love would seem perpetually threatened by death, and happiness appear a house without duration, built upon shifting sands of chaos.[1]

Or perhaps Santayana's statement in *Reason in Common Sense* may more nearly catch the mood of the moment:

That life is worth living is the most necessary of assumptions and, were it not assumed, the most impossible of conclusions.[2]

It is true that life in terms of things may have disillusioned many of us. But life in terms of opportunity for growth and understanding may still hold hope. For example, if there are shorter hours of work, there may be

[1] BRITTAIN, VERA, *Testament of Youth*, pp. 469–470, The Macmillan Company, New York, 1933.

[2] SANTAYANA, GEORGE, *Life of Reason*, Vol. I, Reason in Common Sense, p. 252, Charles Scribners Sons, New York, 1911.

more leisure hours to be used for interesting and worth-while activities. The tension under which we live needs a balance which can come from security in friendships and from goals we think worth striving toward. The bewilderment which is all too common today bespeaks a vital need for an interpretation that will make life endurable and even interesting for us in the face of conditions that seem to hold nothing but frustration.

Every person always has problems of some sort. Since each of us is inclined to consider his own problems unique, it is reassuring to find that other people are facing the same problems, that they too are seeking for solutions and are trying to find a meaning in life.

SEEKING A PURPOSE IN LIFE

"Life has meaning," the poet Browning once said. "To find its meaning is my meat and drink."

We need points of reference against which to try our own ideas and ideals. We need an intellectual framework within which to do our thinking, an emotional standard by which to determine our loyalties. Then each of us can stop and say, "This is my bias; this is the reason I believe as I do now." Thus we learn to synthesize as well as to analyze, to build up as well as take to pieces, to have convictions as well as to be tolerant of others' ideas.

How are we to achieve these points of reference? We learn progressively and gradually to utilize our experiences in building our personalities. This is the process of becoming a "self." It is also the process of formulating ideals, for effort and reflection are equally important in building ideals that will function in our lives.

A person reaches early maturity with habits and ways of thinking that include certain definite ideas of what things are right and what are wrong. He broadens this group of ideas by attempting to find more things that are right and more things that are wrong as well as more reasons as to why these things are right or wrong.

Studies have revealed that many intelligent young people believe that nothing is, after all, absolutely right or absolutely wrong, but that everything is relative. Everything is better than some things and worse than some others. Everything arranges itself on a scale, shifting according to reevaluation of standards that also are relatively and tentatively held. In other words, one of the developments that seems psychologically to belong to the years between sixteen and twenty-four is an increased sensitivity to values.

Young people in their late teens and early twenties declare that, up until approximately early adolescence, they were ruled more or less by such external authority as parents, teachers, and the gang. These they gradually discard as absolute authorities. Some young people are less mature, however, than others of the same chronological ages. Theoretically, they may recognize that one value is superior to another as judged by certain standards which they themselves have evolved and which they consider valid, yet they are not sufficiently concerned about which value they choose—better or best seems to make little difference to them. They may even be satisfied to "sit on the fence," to have no strong convictions.

A person cannot be considered mature until he has, somehow, learned to develop an internal authority that gives him a sense of personal responsibility for making choices in the light of the best he knows. The discarding of external authority must be followed by an individual's assumption of responsibility for his own life. Gradually one's attitudes, reactions, and values tend to become habitual, through repetition, and to form a part of his total make-up or personality.

There is no satisfactory substitute for an individual's own intelligent activity. He cannot escape participation to some degree in life's affairs. As he becomes a part of life, he creates his ideals, for only as an individual functions in life's relationships can he evolve resources upon which his life can depend, far-reaching purposes that are of vital significance to him, meanings that he can live by because he has tested them and found them good. Thus an individual develops a program of action that he feels is "right" for him. He has ceased to regard "right" as given or fixed. It is being created as he creates himself and his environment, as he makes one choice in preference to another. Only as a moral law grows out of a person's own experience is it effective in the control of his conduct.

Maturity cannot be thought of as a definite point to be reached, as though it were the end of a journey. It is a goal toward which we are always striving. Perfection is not

. . . a final goal, but the ever-enduring process of perfecting, maturing, refining, is the aim in living—the bad man is the man who, no matter how good he has been, is beginning to deteriorate, to grow less good. The good man is the man who, no matter how morally unworthy he *has* been, is moving to become better. Such a conception makes one severe in judging himself and humane in judging others.[1]

This conception does not mean that we disregard past experience, the past experience of others as well as of ourselves. To read Plato, Socrates, the Bible, as well as the thoughts of many other great minds, brings the realization that, though certain experiences may seem unique in each person's life, all down through the ages far greater minds have been grappling with the same perplexing problems which each of us faces anew.

Past experience—others and our own—can and should enter into our present experience to remake it. Moreover, to the extent that we can bring into harmony the best of the experience of others and our own experience, we become free. Freedom we interpret, not as doing what we want, but as choosing to do whatever we will assume the consequences for doing. The following quotation illustrates this statement:

[1] DEWEY, JOHN, *Reconstruction in Philosophy*, pp. 176–177, Henry Holt and Company, Inc., New York, 1920.

A physician or engineer is free in his thoughts and his actions to the degree to which he knows what he deals with. Perhaps we find here the key to any freedom.[1]

André Malraux, in *Man's Fate*,[2] puts into words this desire of young people to find something vital in life. A young boy, about to die, was reviewing his life and found it good:

He had fought for what in his time was charged with the deepest meaning and the greatest hope. He was dying among those with whom he would have wanted to live; he was dying, like each of these men, because he had given a meaning to his life.

Young people's devotion to Fascist governments has shown us that they would rather worship false gods than none at all. A young person wishes to see himself, with his capacities, needs, interests, ambitions, and difficulties, related to contemporary and future needs of society. As he wholeheartedly accepts the social need, as he sees the relation between social conditions and the needs and difficulties of individuals, as he accepts his personal capacity to help change conditions, he develops a basis for considering himself a sharer in the making of a better world, one that is more concerned about the good life for all people. As he develops a critical social-mindedness, then loses himself in working for the good life for everyone, he finds the meaning and fulfillment of his own life. He knows that he is useful, that he is needed by society.

When a person has found a meaning in life, his perspective is broadened. Each action that he contemplates, each desire that he wishes to fulfill, each interest that he wishes to develop is appraised in relationship to its effect on his chosen purpose. Long-range planning is possible because significance is lent to the immediate present by bringing it into relationship with what is considered most valuable in

[1] DEWEY, JOHN, *Human Nature and Conduct*, p. 303, Henry Holt and Company, Inc., New York, 1922.

[2] Random House, Inc., New York, 1934 (translated by Haakon M. Chevalier), p. 323.

life. Conflicting desires and emotions are unified as they find their relationship to those interests, purposes, and desires that are the center of life.

As each of us finds a satisfactory center for life, we develop a basis for confidence in ourselves and in life. We are conscious of what we are working for; we know what we want life to be and what we want out of life. We are able to face and to admit unashamed what we have not yet attained. Then, because we have found peace within ourselves, we gain strength to live with uncertainty all about us.

CHOOSING WORTH-WHILE GOALS

Most people have unrealized potentialities within themselves, but too often they lack something solid and assured in which to believe. Without the secure basis a body of beliefs would afford them, they shift and dally and are not ready for opportunities that come.

A measure of that lack is the sense of unimportance and triviality that many young people say their daily lives hold for them. It is an inescapable fact that each of us must choose some values by which to sight if our lives are to lose their confusion and boredom, if we are to go forward.

However, the mere knowledge that some ideal is desirable does not guarantee that a person will strive toward that goal in his behavior. In the past, homes, schools, churches, and other institutions have operated on the basis that, once young people have been taught what is "right," they are likely to do "right." But it has been found[1] that there is not necessarily a relationship between ideals and habits. Moral and religious ideals cannot be effectively transmitted to or imposed upon one person by another, upon young people by adults. If ideals are to function in our lives, they must be the outgrowth of our own experience.

[1] Notably by H. Hartshorne and M. A. May in *Studies in Deceit* (The Macmillan Company, New York, 1928); and by H. Hartshorne, M. A. May, and F. K. Shuttleworth in *Studies in the Organization of Character* (The Macmillan Company, New York, 1930).

We must choose between making an effort to have things different and yielding to fatalism about things as they are. We must, however, guard against maintaining impossible ideals.   Unrealizable goals are also a basis for fatalism.   If a person feels, "I'm not equal to keeping on trying," or "It's so bad I cannot do anything about it," he will sit, defeated without having fought.   To see only the distant is to be ineffective in the process of effective change; it is to substitute daydreams for effort.   To see only the immediate is to be caught in unproductive detail.   The distant goal should be related to more immediate steps for achievement. Ideals must be incentives for effort, not excuses for evasion of effort.   Ideals can be our greatest assets, since the tension between the real which we re ognize and the ideal toward which we are striving can furnish the energy for our growth.

We need to keep in mind our goals and begin now—not next week or next year—to work step by step toward those goals.   We must begin with ourselves as we are; we cannot hope to accomplish anything by attempting suddenly and dramatically to change ourselves or a situation.   We take ourselves and our difficulties with us always unless we attempt, in the light of a goal, to change as we travel toward that goal.   William James speaks of the "expulsive power of new affection."   When a person wants something better or wants to be different from his present self, he changes the old ways.   But he needs to be definite about the manner in which he can become different.   He needs to discover, specifically, a preferable substitute for each thing he has done or is doing now.

Nor can we rely unthinkingly upon principles as points of reference.   They too must be modified in the light of experience.   · We need to be willing to recognize new truths, to admit that "truth is one species of good.   The true is the name of whatever proves to be good in the way of belief."[1]   We need to be alert enough to see that much of

[1] JAMES, WILLIAM, *Pragmatism*, p. 45. Longman's Green & Company, New York, 1908.

what passes for thinking is really the blind following of habits and the rearrangement of prejudices. If we would build convictions of our own, we cannot believe one thing or be prejudiced against something else just because of a precedent for the conviction or belief. We must be willing to say, in effect: I will build on the best I know, but I will trust intelligence still further. To the best that intelligence can discover, I will give my allegiance. I will not hold stubbornly to the old or even to the accepted beliefs merely because they are old and accepted.

In striving to carry out such a program, we need to pay due respect to the past as a basis for formulating the future. The best critic of something is often the person who is most appreciative of it. There must be some good in the things that have come to us from the past or they would not have endured so long.

There have been periods when individuals believed that there was unchanging moral laws to which universal and consistent obedience could be demanded. Out of this conviction arose the belief that anyone who slavishly followed laws in ethics and religion would develop "character," because right was right and was always the same. An individual was believed to be born depraved, selfish, antisocial, predatory. He could be "saved" only by divine transformation, it was believed. The purpose of education and of religion was to redirect the antisocial instincts and to encourage unselfish ones. Only to the degree that this was possible was nurture important.

Education and science have discovered new facts. The belief is now strong that situations are never the same— nor are individuals. Both are changed in the process of any experience. Impulses, once called inborn, have been proved to be learned or unlearned by experience. Human beings are born neither good nor bad; but they do have, in their original equipment, the capacity for developing either kind of behavior. We create ourselves; we become what we are in the process of sharing, of living, of experiencing, of pur-

somewhere. These factors differ in the degree of security that they represent to each person and in the degree of control that we have over them. What we can control, however, is our reaction toward them, the way in which we allow each to affect our estimate of ourselves. We should, from time to time, reappraise our abilities, limitations, and potentialities, as well as recognize the effective and ineffective ways with which we are attempting to solve everyday problems.

Learning to Work and to Play

Carlyle once said that genius is an infinite capacity for hard work. Many of us do not realize the truth of this statement. Too often we do our work halfheartedly; we find it too difficult actually to "cross the effort threshold." We still need to learn that we must spare neither pain nor trouble to arrive at an end. We must give ourselves over totally to what we are doing, apply all our faculties, our attention, and our action to the responsibility directly before us. Until we have learned how to become absolutely engrossed by the moment's thought and action, we cannot expect real accomplishment.

We need always to be learning how to play better as well as how to work better. There is a place for real play in every life. It releases tensions, develops new skills and interests, and keeps our minds flexible. No matter how brilliant or successful we may be, we become uninteresting to others if we can talk of nothing but our work, do nothing except work at a desk, at a machine, in a laboratory, or in a library.

In order to be happy in our social relationships, we need to know how to dance, to be proficient in active sports, and to play games. We must know something about books, plays, music, and art. We must plan our lives so as to include time for these activities. Play will toughen us to meet defeat, teach us to be generous to others as they meet defeat, and keep us from being too egotistical in victory.

Physicians and psychologists are pointing out how important it is for everyone to learn and practice alternation: the harder we play the more effectively we can work and vice versa. The old saying that all work and no play makes Jack a dull boy is being backed up by scientific knowledge of the way the human body works. Alternation is probably fully as important for rich and rewarding living as is moderation.

LEARNING TO THINK

We need to learn how to think. If we would make sound judgments, we must be honest; we must weigh facts scientifically. The habit of evaluating situations and of making decisions on the basis of our evaluations is far superior to that of drifting or of depending on outside authority for our decisions. If we use the former method, our conclusions are not based on imitation of other people, on outside authority, or on self-centeredness. We are protected against subjectivity, fuzzy thinking, and indifference. We have learned how to look at facts separately and in relation to one another, to regard no decision as final, to wait for verification of our conclusions, to suspend our judgments and to amend them in the light of new knowledge.

As we develop habits of thinking, we learn also to sense the relevance of specific facts and isolated actions to wider issues. We are able to recognize relationships between problems. For example, when we are on parties where there is drinking, we consider in our actions the fact that other people are trusting themselves to us as we drive them home. We learn to judge the complexities of a problem. We see the possibilities inherent in a person or situation, but we are not naive about the difficulties that must be met before a goal is achieved. We realize that the enthusiasm of people who have suddenly become aware of a problem is valuable, but we do not assume that the problem is as simple as the first conception would seem to indicate.

For example, one cannot solve the problem of race relations merely by bringing together people of different races and by hoping that, through such contact alone, they will learn to appreciate one another. Nor can a would-be economic savior remake an entire social system by giving people over sixty money to spend.

As we learn to rely less docilely on external authority, as we become more determined to reexamine old values and seek out new ones, and as we adapt our behavior in the light of new values and truths, we are developing a really effective ability to think.

Learning to Make Choices and to Accept Responsibility

We need to learn to make choices and to take responsibility for our own behavior. We need to become individuals in our own right, not onlookers in this life. There are too many wallflowers already. As day by day we are making choices, we need to ask ourselves, "Where are they leading us?" Often a person must choose between building the life that is most satisfying at the moment, making the choice that is the line of least resistance, and forcing his life into those channels that will offer, eventually, the major amount of satisfaction, although at present there may be accompanying disadvantages. It has been stated, "There is no tomorrow. When it dawns, it is today. We are determined by the way we face today." What are we making of our lives? We cannot blind ourselves to the inevitable consequences of today's choices.

As we learn to face each situation squarely, to understand it, to make a decision about it, and to be willing to take the consequences of the decision, we qualify ourselves to meet the uncertainty that faces us in the world of today.

Learning from Experience

We should be trying to develop the ability to learn from our experiences. All that we have lived through—the pleasant, happy experiences as well as the bitter, disillusioning ones—become a part of us.

Santayana says that "wisdom comes by disillusionment." It may be true. Certainly the mature person is one who will learn how to profit from bitter experience, who will accept necessary suffering and loneliness. The psychologist Kunkel believes that "only he who has been so alone that he could count on no sort of immediate answer to his need can realize how inexhaustibly life can speak through him."[1] Individuals must accept "the infinal purposiveness of life."[2]

It is possible, as the story *Of Human Bondage* by Somerset Maugham shows us, for a person to draw weakness instead of strength from his experiences. For example, we can either get hurt at what people tell us about ourselves or we can learn from their criticism. We can either inflict on other people our despair of ourselves or we can use our pains and sorrows, our disappointments and frustrations, to understand the struggles of others, to see the beauty in the lives of others, and to help others when we can.

We have a right to make mistakes and to feel low sometimes if we learn from the experience. But we must be willing to admit our mistakes and to suffer without whining. We can learn to face our failures without feeling inadequate or guilty or attempting to shift the blame for them. Even if we are sure that someone else was at fault, or even caused us to fail, it is always possible completely to forgive and forget—to close the incident.

The ability to learn from experience involves a recognition of the gradualness of growth. A person who is growing is able to admit sometimes that he doesn't know; to allow himself to be disagreed with gracefully; is able to disagree with others without excess emotion; is tolerant because he knows that other persons with whom he may disagree may sincerely think they are right.

We must develop the ability to wait for what we want. We must try to control our enthusiasms. Without enthu-

---

[1] ELLIOTT, H. S., and G. ELLIOTT, *Solving Personal Problems*, pp. 299, Henry Holt and Company, Inc., New York, 1936.
[2] *Ibid.*, p. 300.

siasm, we can do little, but we dare not be carried away by our enthusiasm into using poor judgment. Since we cannot be two, three, or four persons at once, we must learn to do one thing at a time satisfactorily.

We need to learn to face and accept our own and others' limitations. Only as we are patient with ourselves can we be patient with others. Are we willing to learn, and to be humble in our search for and acquisition of knowledge? Emerson said, "Do you know the secret of the true scholar? In every man there is something wherein I may learn of him, and in that I am his pupil." One test of ourselves is for other people to be able to acquire from us a feeling of their own worth because they have seen their value to someone else.

Appreciating Beauty

No life can be complete that does not develop a growing sense of the beautiful. We should cultivate our sensitivity to beauty as it is manifested in nature, in literature, in music, in art, and in its highest development, in human personality. It is not difficult consciously to expose ourselves to those influences by which we wish our lives to be molded.

We do not know as much about the acquisition of a deep appreciation of beauty as we do about the acquisition of skills, but the experience of many shows that the seeker after beauty is the finder, and that without this appreciation, material satisfactions are dull. Appreciation of beauty in life cannot be lost like money nor is it dependent on money.

Beauty resides in all forms of life and in all modes of living. It is present for us to see and recognize if we will consciously expose ourselves to it. We can take advantage of resources around us in our homes, our schools, and our communities. We can seek the aid of individuals more sensitive than ourselves to arouse and direct our appreciations, to help us to choose among aesthetic values and to help us understand how our choices are influencing our growing personalities.

Learning to Balance Keeping, Giving, and Taking

Learning how to balance keeping, giving, and taking so that life is truly rich and satisfying is a lifelong quest. We all know people who devote themselves to conserving their energies, keeping their time for their own use, saving their money, protecting their health, keeping their love for themselves. We can watch their energies dwindle, their time mean less and less, their money lose its worth, their health need more and more care. We know that they have not found the balance, because life for them usually becomes lonely and boring.

We also know the kind of person who pours out so profligately his physical energies, his time, his money, and his affection that he has no reserves to spend for special occasions, no life of his own to develop. After a short and cometlike career which consists of nothing but special occasions, there is likely to come a time when nothing any longer seems like a special occasion. When he does begin to see that some occasions are more important than others, he may have nothing left in the way of physical energy, time, money, or affection to spend. This sort of person has not struck a balance either.

There is also the kind of person who in his twenties or even at an older age keeps on taking from others as he did when he was a child. He continues to take his allowance as a matter of course. He takes without even expressing gratitude all the protection, self-denial, and consideration that a parent, a wife or husband, a sister or brother, or a friend is capable of giving. Such a person constitutes a millstone around the neck of at least one other person, and sometimes manages to attach his or her load to the lives of many others.

It is important to know how to keep, how to give, and how to take. But overpractice of any one throws life out of proportion. Each of us probably needs a little more emphasis at one time on one and then again on another. For some who naturally tend to conserve, cultivation of the practice of wholehearted giving can contribute much to their lives. There are some people, on the other hand, who enjoy being generous so much that they deny others the joy of giving to them. It is in the wise practice of balanced keeping, giving, and taking that art in living is manifested.

SOCIAL GOALS

Life insistently demands that we become thoroughly interested in the outside world so that our attention and energies are centered there, not on ourselves. One should not, at adulthood, have "the raving, hungry look of an egotist who expects to be noticed," as someone has expressed it.

We should work for the power to say "no" to our selfish demands, the power to refrain from actions that will tend to injure others, the power of guidance over our fears, angers, resentments, and loves. We should be attempting to develop the ability imaginatively to place ourselves in the lives of other people. In other words, we should desire the kind of sensitiveness to and awareness of personality that will make it impossible for us to use people as we would things, especially impossible to use them to our own advantage.

We need to see our accomplishments in terms of their value to someone else, rather than in terms of their competition with someone else. As we learn to do the former, we realize that there is no real inharmony between the welfare of the individual and that of society; they are inextricably bound together. In fact, the individual and society are merely aspects of the same reality.

Psychologists have called integration the process by which our individual and our social selves act together harmoniously. An absorbing interest in people and in human experience develops in us a virile personality to which everything is an adventure, a test of strength. However, this kind of behavior does not come to any individual for the asking. Its development will be a lifelong process of which emotional strains, tensions, and contradictory behavior inevitably will be a part. The development of certain habits, however, facilitates the process of integration. Habits determine, to a very large extent, what an individual is and does.

In recent books a number of interesting facts are pointed out which, summarized, indicate the critical need for a much higher level of human relations than the world has ever known or practiced. Some of these facts are:

1. Communication and transportation have cut down the barrier of distance. Columbus spent 37 days crossing the Atlantic. Now regular clipper service spans the same distance in less than the same number of hours. Messages are flashed back and forth between New York and London in one sixty-second of a second.

2. We live now at the peak of an unprecedented increase in the world's population. There are twice as many people in the world as there were just a century ago.

3. These two developments have led to a terrific multiplication and acceleration of human contacts.

4. The development of technology, specialization, and division of labor has led to a state of interdependence that is unique in the history of the world.

5. The advance that has taken place in civilization during the past 150 years has been largely materialistic in nature. Since the world has been made over in terms of machines, man has been able to command great material forces never before dreamed of. He has been tempted to dream of himself as the master of infinite power and has even deceived himself into believing that by completely mastering materials he can command happiness.

6. Phenomenal developments have been made in science and technology during the past century and a half, but progress in other important areas of human relationships such as law, religion, government, and language has lagged.

7. Our culture tends at present to accept material values as of paramount importance and to see human values as dependent on and therefore subsidiary to material values.

We are now beginning to fear that our command over physical forces is greater than we know wisely how to use. Unless our best minds turn soon from contemplation of materials to the cultivation of human relations and to invention in the realm of social organization, our civilization may disintegrate and pass away, some thinkers state.

A personal goal well worth striving for is the consistently better practice of human relations. This goal brings happiness for the person who becomes an artist in this field, and increases the happiness of those with whom the artist comes in contact. To strive toward this goal is perhaps the surest way of making one's best contribution to a world distorted out of all semblance of order and good will.

To become a competent artist in human relations, one must study and practice unceasingly. It is necessary to understand what the people in our homes, our communities, our country, and in other countries are doing and thinking— and why they think and act as they do. It would be well for each of us to ask himself recurrently: Of how much of the world am I aware? Am I building satisfactory relationships with others? Do I know how to make these relationships endure and even improve? Do I have an increasingly better understanding of people who seem to me "different"? Am I concerned about those less fortunate than myself? Am I sufficiently generous in my attitude toward those who seem more fortunate?

As we become mature, there should come a better understanding of others, a quickening of our responsibility for others, with a corresponding decline in our selfish sense of our own importance. We discover as we mature that any personal philosophy must include a social outlook, and that our maximum personal development cannot be realized unless it is accompanied by a maximum contribution to society.

Two alternatives are facing each of us today: to amass money and power for personal use, or to contribute our intelligence, strength, and good will to building a world that can offer security and peace for all. Of course, there are people whose lives are primarily influenced by their desire for material things. But there are other ways of looking at life. Let us consider two of them. We might look at the world and mankind as great and glorious phenomena that exist somehow apart and outside of ourselves, that are worthy, nevertheless, of personal sacrifice on our part. Or we might take a more practical point of view and recognize that we are a part of society. We can gain personal security and achieve our personal life goals only as we achieve them in society. Therefore, we must harmonize our purposes with those of humanity.

As we look out at a changing and distraught world, we realize the extent to which our own future is bound up with its future. The words "personal" and "social" have an interpenetrating relationship. The command, "Get thee to a nunnery," Hamlet's recipe for escape from the world, sounds hollow in our age because there is no escape from the world; whatever happens in the world will eventually happen to us. If unemployment continues, we shall inevitably be affected. As our government takes one significant step after another, many phases of our lives will be different.

A comprehensive outlook on life must include a concern for and a program for doing something in society. We must learn what we can from the past. But we must realize also that something has happened to the beliefs, attitudes, and doctrines that our elders took for granted. Youth has discovered that there is no security in doctrines. Knowledge has been and will again be assailed by further knowledge. The history of the world shows that this is inevitable. Tennyson warned us long ago, "The old order changeth, yielding place to new . . . lest one good custom should corrupt the world." We must find methods for attacking problems, methods of study. We must keep eternally at this thing called "truth." The search for it is an unending task which must be taken up anew by this generation.

With whatever knowledge we can gain from the past, we must find our place in the immediate relevant situation. After assimilation of knowledge, there should come transformation of that knowledge into action. When we discover a wrong, we should do something to right that wrong, rather than merely becoming bitter because it exists. Too often we are tempted to "rant" about the social order, race relations, the unequal distribution of wealth. Yet we do nothing when we are asked to join a committee that is interested in better housing in a community, or in housing for Negro students on a campus; we neglect to exercise our right to vote; we show no interest in a campaign begun by a group of churches to maintain a community recreation hall or in an adult school for the use of young people of the community.

We shall find the meaning in our own lives when we see the world as it is and do something to make it different, when we show our social viewpoints in our actions. If we want the opportunity to live reasonably secure and full lives, to contribute whatever capacities we have to society, and to receive the benefits of the contributions of others, then we must find our places in that society.

We must begin wherever we are, begin by living out in our daily relationships what we believe. We may make mistakes. We may choose the wrong group with which to align ourselves. We may choose the wrong methods by which to convince people of the need of the thing for which we stand. But we learn by experience. We must do something, take some part in the world in which we live.

We cannot excuse ourselves by talking glibly about the "choices" facing our country. Those choices are being made daily by men and women like ourselves. Either we do nothing in helping to make decisions, or we do our part as thoughtful and informed citizens in situations such as the following: our campus sends a petition to Congress about unemployment insurance or Federal aid to education; our doctor advocates in his medical association a more just distribution of the burden of illness; our City Council votes, in response to community pressure, to expand the community's public health and recreation facilities; our union joins in a lobby organized in the state legislature for more adequate wage and hour legislation; the League of Women Voters works for the abolition of child labor; the students in an economics class bring to the mayor recommendations on housing which they have made as the result of a community survey which they conducted. What interest and support have we given in instances similar to these?

If we believe in a happy home life, in abolishing poverty and exploitation, in more adequate economic security for everyone, we must attest to this farsightedness and social-mindedness by social action.

We all cannot be the kind of people who have the initiative and courage that displays itself in vigorous action. But we all can learn the fine art of thinking; we all can be sensitive to life situations. We can be certain that we are trying to learn all that it is possible to know about this mysterious transaction of living, that we are seeing things straight, are not confining ourselves to small fanaticisms or minor hatreds, are not avoiding conclusions that disturb our complacency. We can be proponents of honest-mindedness, of thoughtful criticism. We can express carefully thought-out opinions in the community forums and discussion groups which are annually becoming more numerous throughout this country. Thus we can help shape the values that will direct the new society.

We cannot ignore fundamental questions. We are living in an age in which we must take the long view, in which we must see ourselves as a part of a world civilization. Each of us must do this in whatever way he can. The person who wishes to do good work at some time or other in the future can learn how only by working in the present. We are no good anywhere unless we are attempting to see where we are, where we have been, and where we are going. Such a program should challenge anyone who wishes to relate his life to the life of mankind and to the eternal effort of human beings to find their places in the world.

Spiritual Goals

For many, a secular interpretation of life, no matter how fine its humanistic motives may be, is inadequate. Always, as far back as we know, most individuals have struggled to understand intangibles. They have felt these intangibles to be of such permanent value that they, in a sense, transcended men themselves and their transient concerns. Out of a recognition of the permanence and the universality of these principles, men have come to have reverence for them.

Some part of every man struggles to understand and find concord with this part of life. People differ widely in their need for recourse to abstractions and spiritual things. Many find a comforting solidarity in material and temporal things and cling to them with all their might. Characteristically, during early adulthood, "nostalgia for the cosmic" does not loom large.

In times of great crisis, however, many people find material things much too uncertain to serve as the value bases on which to build their lives. Property, material belongings, prestige, governments, human ties are much too casually swept out of existence. Abstract virtues such as courage, loyalty, freedom, sacrifice seem to some individuals to transcend them. But, above and beyond even these virtues, people search for other transcendent principles of life. The Bible is a record of this great search in an older time. All religion is devoted to it.

All of us, to a greater or lesser degree, tend in our experience to continue this search. We would do well to use all the accumulated wisdom which we can find to guide us. But for each who undertakes it, his own personal quest is a new and eternally worth-while experience which can add meaning to life as can nothing else.

Striving to Reach Our Goals

Maturity is not lightly won. It is not given us as our diplomas are when we are graduated from some school. It is not absorbed from others nor gained by reading books. It is not achieved once and for all. It does not automatically continue to develop as does our physical growth. If at any time during the life of a person he rests on maturity won at an earlier age, he has already lost ground. We have probably during the past generation had a philosophy that was a little too sweet and easy to serve the present generation usefully. Many of us need to seek out and learn for ourselves truths that are found over and over in the great philosophies of other periods. If life is too easy for us, if we have too few adjustments to make or too few difficulties to overcome, we may not develop a strength equal to that of others whom we admire—people who, as they grew up, have had to meet and overcome obstacles.

But few of us actually need fear that life will not offer us plenty of opportunity to stand up to difficulties. In the story *The Yearling*, Jody has his first bitter taste of deprivation, his first hard wrenching from the joys of his early boyhood, when his father has to kill his yearling deer, his only real companion. Jody at first responds by refusing to face the situation. He hates his father and runs away. He is lost, almost starves, but, in the process, realizes that he must go home. His father is ill; his place is with him; there he is needed.

As Jody and his father talk together, Jody begins to recognize this experience he has been through as, in a very real sense, his coming of age. His father says to him:

"I'm goin' to talk to you, man to man. You figgered I went back on you. Now there's a thing ever' man has got to know. Mebbe you know it a'ready. 'Twa'n't only me. 'Twa'n't only your yearlin' deer havin' to be destroyed. Boy, life goes back on you."

Jody looked at his father. He nodded.

Penny said, "You've seed how things goes in the world o' men. You've knowed men to be low-down and mean. You've messed around with ol' Starvation. Ever' man wants life to be a fine thing, and a easy. 'Tis fine, boy, powerful fine, but tain't easy. Life knocks a man down and he gits up and it knocks him down agin. I've been uneasy all my life."

His hands worked at the folds of the quilt.

"I've wanted life to be easy for you. Easier'n 'twas for me. A man's heart aches seein' his young uns face the world. Knowin' they got to git their guts tore out, the way his was tore. I wanted to spare you, long as I could. I wanted you to frolic with your yearlin'. I knowed the lonesomeness he eased for you. But ever' man's lonesome. What's he to do then? What's he to do when he gets knocked down? Why take it for his share and go on."

Jody said, "I'm 'shamed I runned off."[1]

[1] RAWLINGS, MARJORIE KINNAN, *The Yearling*, pp. 426–427, Charles Scribner's Sons, New York, 1938.

BIBLIOGRAPHY

Understanding Ourselves

ADLER, ALFRED; *What Life Should Mean to You*, Little, Brown & Company, Boston, 1931.

———: *Understanding Human Nature*, Greenberg, Publisher, Inc., New York, 1927.

BURNHAM, W. H.: *The Normal Mind*, D. Appleton-Century Company, Inc., New York, 1924.

———: *The Wholesome Personality*, D. Appleton-Century Company, Inc., New York, 1935.

CARREL, ALEXIS: *Man, the Unknown*, Harper & Brothers, New York, 1935.

DEWEY, JOHN: *How We Think*, D. C. Heath & Company, Boston, 1933.

ELLIOTT, GRACE LOUCKS, and HARRISON ELLIOTT: *Solving Personal Problems*, Henry Holt and Company, Inc., New York, 1936.

FEDDER, RUTH: *A Girl Grows Up*, McGraw-Hill Book Company, Inc., New York, 1939.

FREUD, SIGMUND: *Basic Writings of Sigmund Freud*, Modern Library, Inc., New York, 1938.

JUNG, C. G.: *Modern Man in Search of a Soul*, Harcourt, Brace and Company, Inc., New York, 1933.

KELIHER, ALICE V.: *Life and Growth*, D. Appleton-Century Company, Inc., New York, 1938.

KUNKEL, FRITZ: *God Helps Those—*, Ives Washburn, Inc., New York, 1931.

———: *Let's Be Normal*, Ives Washburn, Inc., New York, 1939.

MENNINGER, KARL A.: *The Human Mind*, Alfred A. Knopf, Inc., New York, 1930.

MORGAN, JOHN J. B.: *Keeping a Sound Mind*, The Macmillan Company, New York, 1934.

OVERSTREET, HARRY: *About Ourselves*, W. W. Norton & Company, Inc., New York, 1927.

PLANT, JAMES S.: *Personality and the Cultural Pattern*, The Commonwealth Fund, New York, 1937.

SCHWESINGER, GLADYS: *Heredity and Environment*, The Macmillan Company, New York, 1933.

SHAFFER, L. S.: *The Psychology of Adjustment*, Houghton Mifflin Company, Boston, 1936.

WALLIN, J. E.: *Personality Maladjustments and Mental Hygiene*, McGraw-Hill Book Company, Inc., New York, 1935.

Understanding Our Society

BEARD, C. A., and MARY: *The Rise of American Civilization*, The Macmillan Company, New York, 1930.

BELL, HOWARD M.: *Youth Tell Their Story*, American Council on Education, Washington, D. C., 1938.

CHAMBERS, M. M.: *The Community and Its Young People*, American Council on Education, Washington, D. C., 1940.

—— and HOWARD M. BELL: *How to Make a Community Youth Survey*, American Council on Education, Washington, D. C., 1939.

DEWEY, JOHN: *Human Nature and Conduct*, Henry Holt and Company, Inc., New York, 1922.

EDWARDS, NEWTON: *Equal Educational Opportunity for Youth*, American Council on Education, Washington, D. C., 1939.

ELLWOOD, CHARLES A.: *A History of Social Philosophy*, Prentice-Hall, Inc., New York, 1938.

KILPATRICK, WILLIAM H.: *Education for a Changing Civilization*, The Macmillan Company, New York, 1936.

KURTZ, RUSSELL H. (ed.): *Social Work Year Book* (Part I: An Authoritative Record of Organized Activities; Part II: A Directory of 1,023 National and State Agencies in Social Work and Related Fields) Russell Sage Foundation, New York, 1941.

LIPPMANN, WALTER: *Public Opinion*, Harcourt, Brace and Company, Inc., New York, 1922.

LYND, ROBERT, and HELEN MERRELL LYND: *Middletown*, Harcourt, Brace and Company, Inc., New York, 1929.

——: *Middletown in Transition*, Harcourt, Brace and Company, Inc., New York, 1937.

MEAD, MARGARET: *Coming of Age in Samoa*, William Morrow & Co., Inc., New York, 1928.

PRESCOTT, DANIEL A.: *Emotion and the Educative Process*, American Council on Education, Washington, D. C., 1938.

RAINEY, HOMER P., and others: *How Fare American Youth?* D. Appleton-Century Company, Inc., New York, 1937.

Recent Social Trends in the United States, McGraw-Hill Book Company, Inc., New York, 1933.

REID, IRA: *In a Minor Key: Negro Youth in Story and Fact*, American Council on Education, Washington, D. C., 1940.

SUMNER, WILLIAM GRAHAM: *Folkways*, Ginn and Company, Boston, 1906.

THRASHER, FREDERICK N.: *The Gang*, University of Chicago Press, Chicago, 1927.

VAN WATERS, MIRIAM: *Youth in Conflict*, Republic Publishing Co., New York, 1925.

WEMBRIDGE, ELEANOR: *Other People's Daughters*, Houghton Mifflin Company, Boston, 1926.

ZORBAUGH, HARVEY W.: *Gold Coast and Slum*, University of Chicago Press, Chicago, 1929.

Personal and Social Adjustment

BREEN, M. J.: *Party Book*, A. S. Barnes & Company, New York, 1939.

CRAIG, ALICE EVELYN: *The Speech Arts*, The Macmillan Company, New York, 1937.

ELDRIDGE, ELIZABETH: *Co-Ediquette*, E. P. Dutton & Company, Inc., New York, 1936.

GOODRICH, L. B.: *Effective Social Activities*, American Book Company, New York, 1940.

———: *Living With Others*, American Book Company, New York, 1939.

LLOYD-JONES, ESTHER: *Social Competence and College Students*, American Council on Education, Washington, D. C., 1940.

MACGIBBON, ELIZABETH G.: *Manners in Business*, The Macmillan Company, New York, 1936.

MARSH, HATTIE MARIE: *Building Your Personality*, Prentice-Hall, Inc., New York, 1940.

PHILLIPS, MARY C.: *Skin Deep*, Garden City Publishing Company, Inc., New York, 1937.

POST, EMILY: *Etiquette*, Funk & Wagnalls Company, New York, 1937.

STEVENS, WILLIAM O.: *The Correct Thing* (for men), Dodd, Mead & Company, Inc., New York, 1936.

STRATTON, DOROTHY, and HELEN SCHLEMAN: *Your Best Foot Forward*, Whittlesey House, McGraw-Hill Book Company, Inc., New York, 1940.

Family Relationships

CUNNINGHAM, BESS V.: *Family Behavior: A Study of Human Relations*, W. B. Saunders Company, Philadelphia, 1936.

DENNIS, LEMO, and M. H. STEELE (eds.): *Pictures of Family Life*, Home Economics Association, Washington, D. C., 1935.

ELLENWOOD, JAMES LEE: *There's No Place Like Home*, Charles Scribner's Sons, New York, 1938.

FLUGEL, J. S.: *The Psychoanalytic Study of the Family*, The International Psychoanalytical Press, 1921.

GOODSELL, WILLYSTINE: *Problems of the Family*, D. Appleton-Century Company, Inc., New York, 1936.

HART, HORNELL, and ELLA HART: *Personality and the Family*, D. C. Heath & Company, Boston, 1935.

STERN, BERNHARD J.: *The Family, Past and Present*, D. Appleton-Century Company, Inc., New York, 1938.

TAYLOR, KATHARINE WHITESIDE: *Do Adolescents Need Parents?* D. Appleton-Century Company, Inc., New York, 1938.

WALLER, WILLARD: *The Family: A Dynamic Interpretation*, The Cordon Company, New York, 1938.

WUNSCH, W. R.: *Thicker Than Water*, D. Appleton-Century Company, Inc., New York, 1939.

Men-Women Relationships

BURGESS, ERNEST W., and LEONARD S. COTTRELL, JR.: *Predicting Success or Failure in Marriage*, Prentice-Hall, Inc., New York, 1939.

BUTTERFIELD, OLIVER: *Love Problems of Adolescence*, Teachers College, Columbia University, New York, 1939.

ELLIOTT, GRACE LOUCKS, and HARRY BONE: *Sex Life of Youth*, Association Press, New York, 1929.

ELLIS, HAVELOCK: *Little Essays on Love and Virtue*, George H. Doran Company, New York, 1922.

FOLSOM, J. K.: *Plan for Marriage*, Harper & Brothers, New York, 1938.

GROVES, ERNEST R., and GLADYS H. GROVES: *Wholesome Marriage*, Houghton Mifflin Company, Boston, 1927.

HIMES, NORMAN E.: *Your Marriage*, Farrar & Rinehart, Inc., New York, 1940.

LEVY, JOHN, and RUTH MUNROE: *The Happy Family*, Alfred A. Knopf, Inc., New York, 1938.

NELSON, JANET FOWLER: *Marriages Are Not Made in Heaven*, The Woman's Press, New York, 1939.

TERMAN, L. M.: *Psychological Factors in Marital Happiness*, McGraw-Hill Book Company, Inc., New York, 1938.

STRAIN, FRANCES BRUCE: *Love on the Threshold*, D. Appleton-Century Company, Inc., New York, 1939.

Vocations

ALSOP, GULIELMA, and MARY F. McBRIDE: *She's Off to Work*, Vanguard Press, Inc., New York, 1941.

BABSON, ROGER: *Finding a Job*, Fleming H. Revell Company, New York, 1934.

BELL, HOWARD M.: *Matching Youth and Jobs*, American Council on Education, Washington, D. C., 1940.

BENNETT, G. VERNON, and GEORGIA SACHS: *Exploring the World of Work*, Society for Occupational Research, Los Angeles, 1937.

BINGHAM, WALTER: *Aptitudes and Aptitude Testing*, Harper & Brothers, New York, 1937.

BROPHY, LOIRE: *If Women Must Work*, D. Appleton-Century Company, Inc., New York, 1936.

CHAPMAN, PAUL W.: *Occupational Guidance*, Turner E. Smith and Co., Atlanta, Ga., 1937.

CRAWFORD, ALBERT B., and STUART H. CLEMENT: *The Choice of an Occupation*, Yale University Press, New Haven, 1932.

CRAWFORD, GEORGE W.: *The Talladega Manual of Vocational Guidance*, Talladega College, Talladega, Ala., 1937.

LEUCK, MIRIAM: *Fields of Work for Women*, D. Appleton-Century Company, Inc., New York, 1932.

PARKER, W. E.: *Books about Jobs*, American Library Association, Chicago, 1935.

ROSENGARTEN, WILLIAM: *Choosing Your Life Work*, McGraw-Hill Book Company, Inc., New York, 1936.

SHALLCROSS, RUTH: "Should Married Women Work?" *Public Affairs Pamphlet* 49, Public Affairs Committee, Inc., New York, 1940.

White House Conference Report on Vocational Guidance, Century Company, New York, 1932.

WILLIAMSON, E. G.: *Students and Occupations*, Henry Holt and Company, Inc., New York, 1937.

College

ALSOP, GULIELMA, and MARY F. McBRIDE: *She's Off to College*, Vanguard Press, Inc., New York, 1940.

American Council on Education, *American Universities and Colleges*, American Council on Education, Washington, D. C., 1940.

BENNETT, MARGARET: *College and Life*, McGraw-Hill Book Company, Inc., New York, 1941.

BOOK, WILLIAM F.: *How to Succeed in College*, Warwick and Co., Baltimore, 1927.

DAVIS, WAYNE: *How to Choose a Junior College*, Harper & Brothers, New York, 1939.

EELS, WALTER C. (Comp.): *Directory of Junior Colleges*, American Association of Junior Colleges, Washington, D. C., 1940.

HALLE, RITA S.: *Which College?* The Macmillan Company, New York, 1934.

HAMBIDGE, GOVE: *New Aims in Education*, McGraw-Hill Book Company, Inc., New York, 1940.

HAND, HAROLD C.: *Campus Activities*, McGraw-Hill Book Company, Inc., New York, 1938.

LOVEJOY, C. E.: *So You're Going to College,* Simon & Schuster, Inc., New York, 1940.

McCAUL, MARGARET: *Guidance for College Students,* International Textbook Company, Scranton, Pa., 1939.

McCONN, MAX: *Planning for College,* Frederick A. Stokes Company, New York, 1937.

U. S. Office of Education, "College Projects for Aiding Students," *Bulletin* 9, Government Printing Office, Washington, D. C., 1938.

Study and Reading Techniques

ADLER, MORTIMER: *How to Read a Book,* Simon & Schuster, Inc., New York, 1940.

BIRD, CHARLES: *Effective Study Habits,* Century Company, New York, 1931.

FAY, LUCY E., and ANNE T. EATON: *Instruction in the Use of Books and Libraries,* The F. W. Faxon Co., Boston, 1928.

GATES, ARTHUR I.: *The Improvement of Reading,* The Macmillan Company, New York, 1935.

JONES, E. S.: *Improvement of Study Habits,* Foster and Stewart, Buffalo, 1939.

WRENN, C. G.: *Practical Study Aids,* Stanford University Press, Stanford University, Calif., 1931.

———— and L. COLE: *How to Read Rapidly and Well,* Stanford University Press, Stanford University, Calif., 1935.

———— and R. B. McKEOWN: *Study-habits Inventory,* Stanford University Press, Stanford University, Calif., 1934.

Health

CRISP, K. B.: *Be Healthy,* J. B. Lippincott Company, Philadelphia, 1938.

DIEHL, HAROLD S.: *Textbook of Healthful Living,* McGraw-Hill Book Company, Inc., New York, 1939.

———— and CHARLES SHEPARD: *The Health of College Students,* American Council on Education, Washington, D. C., 1939.

FISHER, IRVING: *How to Live,* Funk & Wagnalls Company, New York, 1939.

Philosophy, Religion, Music, Drama, Poetry, and Art

AUBREY, EDWIN EVART: *Man's Search for Himself,* Cokesbury Press, Nashville, Tenn., 1940.

AUSLANDER, JOSEPH, and F. E. HILL (eds.): *The Winged Horse Anthology,* Doubleday, Doran & Company, Inc., New York, 1929.

BAUER, MARION, and ETHEL PEISER: *How Music Grew,* G. P. Putnam's Sons, New York, 1927.

BOAS, RALPH P., and EDWIN E. SMITH: *Enjoyment of Literature*, Harcourt, Brace and Company, New York, 1934.

BROWNE, LEWIS: *This Believing World*, The Macmillan Company, New York, 1926.

CABOT, RICHARD: *The Meaning of Right and Wrong*, The Macmillan Company, New York, 1933.

CALKINS, EARNEST ELMO: *The Care and Feeding of Hobby Horses*, The Leisure League of America, New York, 1934.

CLARK, BARRETT: *Study of the Modern Drama*, D. Appleton-Century Company, Inc., New York, 1928.

CRAVEN, THOMAS: *Modern Art*, Simon & Schuster, Inc., New York, 1934.

DURANT, WILL: *The Story of Philosophy*, Simon & Schuster, Inc., New York, 1926.

EINSTEIN, ALBERT, JOHN DEWEY, JAMES JEANS, and others: *Living Philosophies*, Simon & Schuster, Inc., New York, 1931.

ERSKINE, JOHN: *The Delight of Great Books*, Bobbs-Merrill Company, Indianapolis, 1928.

FADIMAN, CLIFTON (ed): *I Believe: The Personal Philosophies of Certain Eminent Men and Women of Our Time*, Simon & Schuster, Inc., New York, 1939.

GARDNER, HELEN: *Art through the Ages*, Harcourt, Brace and Company, Inc., New York, 1932.

GREENBIE, MARJORIE: *The Arts of Leisure*, Whittlesey House, McGraw-Hill Book Company, Inc., New York, 1935.

HARLOW, S. RALPH: *Honest Answers to Honest Questions*, Cokesbury Press, Nashville, Tenn., 1940.

Hazen Books on Religion, The Edward W. Hazen Foundation, Haddam, Conn.

HUGHES, GLENN: *The Story of the Theater*, Samuel French, Inc., New York, 1938.

LIN YUTANG: *The Importance of Living*, Reynal & Hitchcock, Inc., New York, 1937.

LIPPMANN, WALTER: *A Preface to Morals*, The Macmillan Company, New York, 1929.

MACY, JOHN: *The Story of the World's Great Literature*, Garden City Publishing Company, Inc., New York, 1925.

MAY, ROLLO: *The Springs of Creative Living*, Cokesbury Press, Nashville, Tenn., 1940.

MOORE, DOUGLAS S.: *Listening to Music*, W. W. Norton & Company, Inc., New York, 1937.

NEILSON, WILLIAM ALLAN (ed.): *Roads to Knowledge*, W. W. Norton & Company, Inc., New York, 1937.

O'CONNELL, CHARLES: *Victor Book of the Symphony*, Simon & Schuster, Inc., New York, 1935.

THOMPSON, OSCAR: *How to Understand Music*, Dial Press Inc., New York, 1935.

VAN LOON, HENDRIK WILLEM: *The Arts*, Simon & Schuster, Inc., New York, 1937.

Magazine Articles

ADAMIC, LOUIS: "30 Million Young Americans," *Harper's*, November, 1934.

ELLIS, HAVELOCK: "Marriages Are Not Made in Heaven," *Esquire*, November, 1936.

NEWTON, FRANCES: "The Revolt of the Free," *Mademoiselle*, August, 1939.

ROOSEVELT, ELEANOR: "I Was a Homely Girl," *Ladies' Home Journal*, November, 1935.

Magazines and Pamphlets

Careers, The Institute for Research, Chicago.

Occupational Index, New York University, New York.

Occupations, The Vocational Guidance Magazine, National Vocational Guidance Association, Inc., New York.

Success, Vocational Information Series, Morgan Dillon & Co., Chicago, 1937.

www.ingramcontent.com/pod-product-compliance
Lightning Source LLC
Chambersburg PA
CBHW031148270326
41931CB00006B/192